Talking Machine West

Talking Machine West

A History and Catalogue of Tin Pan Alley's Western Recordings, 1902–1918

MICHAEL A. AMUNDSON

UNIVERSITY OF OKLAHOMA PRESS : NORMAN

LIBRARY OF CONGRESS CATALOGING-IN-PUBLICATION DATA

Name: Amundson, Michael A., 1965– author.

Title: Talking machine west : a history and catalogue of Tin Pan
　　Alley's western recordings, 1902–1918 /
　　Michael A. Amundson.

Description: Norman, OK : University of Oklahoma Press, [2017] |
　　Includes bibliographical references and index.

Identifiers: LCCN 2016033167 | ISBN 978-0-8061-5604-0
　　(hardcover : alk. paper)

Subjects: LCSH: Popular music—United States—1901–1910
　　—History and criticism. | Popular music—United
　　States—1911–1920—History and criticism. | West (U.S.)—
　　Songs and music—History and criticism. | Indians of North
　　America—Songs and music—History and criticism. |
　　Cowboys—Songs and music—History and criticism. | Sound
　　recordings—United States—History. | Popular music—
　　United States—1901–1910—Discography. | Popular music—
　　United States—1911–1920—Discography.

Classification: LCC ML3477 .A49 2017 |
　　DDC 781.640973/09041—dc23

LC record available at https://lccn.loc.gov/2016033167

Talking Machine West: A History and Catalogue of Tin Pan Alley's Western Recordings, 1902–1918 is Volume 2 in the American Popular Music Series.

1 2 3 4 5 6 7 8 9 10

Contents

Acknowledgments

ALTHOUGH I BEGAN COLLECTING EDISON CYLINDERS back in the 1980s, this book began just a few years ago when my colleague Leisl Carr Childers at Northern Arizona University (NAU) asked me to give a presentation about phonographs to one of her classes. In preparing for that, I discovered the many cowboys songs available on cylinder, and the project took on a life of its own. Thanks Leisl. Thanks as well to Chuck Rankin at the University of Oklahoma Press for listening to my pitch about a book on talking machine cowboys and Indians when it existed only as a PowerPoint presentation, for his support in getting me a contract with the Press, and then especially for his editorial skills in helping me to rethink this project into one that appeals to both academic and public audiences. This book would never have happened without his support.

I also owed a debt of thanks to NAU colleagues Linda Sargent Wood, Eric Meeks, and Leilah Danielson, who read parts of this work and helped me work my way through some difficult stretches. Thanks Linda for the "writer's lunches," Eric for wanting to be my coauthor and helping me work through issues of race and identity in *Santiago Flynn,* and Leilah and her mother, Susan Danielson, for their help with *I'm a Yiddish Cowboy.* And a special thanks to NAU digital access archivist Todd Welch, who spent a long Saturday with me scanning all of my sheet music. It's great to have colleagues who are both scholars and friends.

Thanks as well to several institutions that provided assistance along the way. First, thanks to the NAU Scholarship and Creative Activity (SCA) Grants Program, which awarded me a SCA grant in 2015 that provided summer funding to work on this project. Thanks as well to Baylor University, Indiana University, and the University of Oregon, for permission to reprint sheet music covers for songs that I did not own, and to the University of California, Santa Barbara (UCSB), for making available on the Internet so many of the recordings found in this book. UCSB's *Cylinder Audio Archive* and its *Discography of American Historical Recordings*, along with the Library of Congress's *National Jukebox*, are treasure troves of period music history, and these collections inspired my own collecting and helped me to write this book. Likewise, Bill Edwards's "Perfesser Bill" website is *the* place to learn about sheet music of this period, and the Billy Murray website provides loads of information about the most popular ragtime singer. I also appreciate my many classroom audiences at Idaho State University, Colorado Mesa University, and especially NAU who have let me lug in the old phonographs and then marveled with me at their songs. The same goes to the local Flagstaff Westerners and the folks who came to hear me speak about this project at Riordan Mansion State Park. These kinds of public presentations helped me to hone what I was doing here.

There are several people in the antique phonograph world who also deserve thanks. First off, thank you to John Lewis of Albuquerque and his business, John Lewis' Mechanical Antiques, for repairing my Edison and for his love of old phonographs. Knowing a good mechanic is especially helpful when it comes to playing a 110-year-old machine. Second, thanks to all of my eBay friends who have sold me cylinders, one-sided 78s, needles, books, advertisements, and other phonograph memorabilia, especially Bart of Chicago, who not only sold me a five-foot-long phonograph horn but took the time to build a custom shipping crate and then send it to me via Greyhound bus lines. Thanks also to Tim Gracyk for his research.

My parents, Arlen and Joan Amundson of Loveland, Colorado, my sister, Kathryn of Denver, as well as my in-laws, Britt and Mary DeMuth of Flagstaff, have listened to me talk about these old songs for a long time. Thanks also to my wife's grandparents, Don and Barbara DeMuth of Cornville, Arizona, and her aunt and uncle Lynn DeMuth and Duke Mertz for their interest in my project. It's finally done, Duke! My border collie Tessa, though not usually as interested as Nipper—the dog Victor Records used—sometimes showed interest in the music I was playing but, more important, reminded me that a walk in the forest was just what I needed.

Finally, thanks the most to my wife, Lauren, for not getting mad when I told her about my late night eBay purchases, especially the $750 gigantic cylinder horn and the $237 for the cylinder of *Ragtime Cow Boy Joe,* and for enduring my hours of playing cylinders and 78s in the house. Even more thanks for her patience after I digitized all of them and played them in the car on long road trips. The fact that she, an aficionado of live concerts from the likes of the Moody Blues and the Dave Matthews Band, now knows the tunes and words to most of my ancient cylinders is testament to her patience. I also thank her for her archival skills and enthusiastic efforts to help me obtain the proper record sleeves and acid-free boxes to best preserve my collection. This book is for Lauren.

{ Talking Machine West }

Cranking Up My Talking Machines

While a master's student in the American Studies program at the University of Wyoming in 1989, I wandered into a downtown Laramie antiques store and found a 1906 Edison Home cylinder phonograph. Just looking at the thing was amazing. Made of beautiful oak, the phonograph was about the size of a small sewing machine, complete with a wooden cover, a hand crank on the side, and a small reproduction brass horn. The talking machine included a couple of cylinders, and when the sales lady cranked it up and played it I was hooked. It sounded tinny but delightful. Recall that 1989 was about the time that most of us were first buying CDs and were amazed by the lack of scratches and utmost clarity provided by digital stereo music. The Edison, on the other hand, was scratchy, mono, and played hard-to-find cylinders. I was mesmerized. I soon discovered that the machine's cost of $700 was much beyond my teaching assistant salary, but I also learned that I could pay a hundred bucks down and a hundred a month till it was paid off. I jumped at the offer, soon found a place for it in my dorm room, and began playing the strange whistling, yodeling, and xylophone songs for my friends.

Over the next two decades, I took that phonograph with me as I pursued a Ph.D. in the history of the American West at the University of Nebraska and then to my first job at Idaho State University, where I taught classes on the West, modern U.S. history, and Idaho and the Northwest. One day, while I was playing it for a class, the mainspring broke. I soon found a repair shop

My 1906 Edison Home Phonograph
with reproduction witches hat horn.
Author's collection.

(*Above*) **A sample of cylinder storage boxes.** (*Right*) **My 1906 Edison Home Phonograph with original morning glory horn.** (*Below*) **My 1906 Edison Home Phonograph showing the cover sitting atop the cylinder storage cabinet.** Author's collection.

just outside Salt Lake City and had it fixed for about $150. When I returned to pick it up, the shop's owner informed me that my Edison actually had a mechanism that could be enabled to play both the original two-minute cylinders I had been playing as well as later four-minute ones—if I had another "reproducer," the small mechanism that held the needle to the cylinder and projected the sound outward through the horn. And sure enough, he had not only the appropriate reproducer for about a hundred bucks but also some of the newer four-minute cylinders. He also had for sale an original large Home phonograph horn and support crane (a steel rod that projected out from the base of the phonograph to hold the horn in place) for another $250. The horn was about two and a half feet long and not quite two feet wide at the opening. I walked out of that shop much poorer but in possession of a "new" music system that allowed me to play both two-and four-minute songs loudly.

After landing a tenure track job at Northern Arizona University in the fall of 1997 teaching the modern United States, the Southwest, and the West, I moved to Flagstaff and brought my growing collection with me. On a chance excursion to nearby Prescott, I found a phonograph collector who sold me many more cylinders and an original circa 1910 oak cylinder cabinet that contains four pull-out shelves, each fitted with thirty pegs to hold the cylinders in place. Over the next fifteen years, I collected

The cylinder storage cabinet open to show the pull-out drawers with pegs to hold cylinder records. The morning glory horn sits in the background. Author's collection.

World War I songs such as *It's a Long Way to Berlin but We'll Get There,* sappy ballads like *The Longest Way Home,* and comedic acts like *The Two Poets.*[1] EBay provided much more access to cylinders than I ever could get going to antique shops, and Amazon had many books on their history. I delighted in hauling the heavy player into my classes and often found students fascinated by its beautiful craftsmanship and strange sounds. When approached by a colleague to present the phonograph to a class of teachers, I tried unsuccessfully to win some more World War I songs on eBay. Then, while examining a list of available songs that I probably could afford, I was intrigued to find some very early cowboy and Indian songs such as *Ida-Ho* and *Red Wing.* After easily winning these auctions, I specifically began searching for prewar western-themed records and was amazed to find how many there were and how inexpensive. I also discovered Internet resources such as the *National Jukebox* at the Library of Congress and the University of California–Santa Barbara's cylinder archives.[2] Both of

(*Left*) My 1913 Victor Victrola VV-VI with record and (*above*) with cabinet doors open for maximum volume. Author's collection.

1. I italicize all song titles in this book.

2. The *National Jukebox* website at the Library of Congress can be found at www.loc.gov/jukebox/. The *UCSB Cylinder Audio Archive* is found at http://cylinders.library.ucsb.edu, and UCSB's *Discography of American Historical Records* can be found at http://adp.library.ucsb.edu.

these resources provided access to company catalogues to search for titles and digitized recordings I could play on the computer. After learning that some songs were recorded only on flat records not playable on my Edison, I purchased a 1913 Victor Victrola in nearby Cottonwood, Arizona, and then began buying discs. Over the next two years, I compiled a wish list of songs and then went to work on eBay and other Internet sites looking for them.

While searching for the records, I discovered several sheet music repositories, such as that at Indiana University, which hold digital copies of the original scores of the same songs.[3] Even better, this music contained beautiful cover pages, highlighting scenes from the songs. Drawn by eastern artists who worked for the sheet music companies, these images proved to be a seemingly unknown collection of early twentieth-century western art.[4] After finding these also available on eBay, I added sheet music to my searches and began purchasing the music that accompanied my growing collection of cylinders and discs. Within a couple of years, I had compiled a list of more than fifty western songs, then found and purchased the recordings as well as most of the original scores. In doing so, I uncovered a slice of the western historical soundscape that mostly seemed to have been missed by historians of the American West.[5]

Listening to these century-old cylinders and discs on a period talking machine requires a delicate process. My 1906 Edison Home Phonograph looks like a small wooden

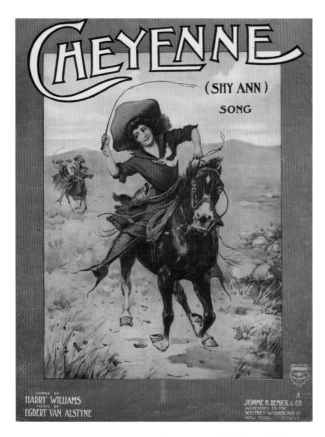

Cheyenne, words by Harry Williams, music by Egbert Van Alstyne (Detroit: Jerome H. Remick, 1906). Sheet music from author's collection.

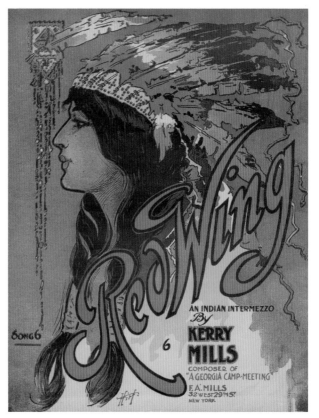

Red Wing, by Kerry Mills (New York: F. A. Mills, 1907). Sheet music from author's collection.

---

3. Indiana University's sheet music archives, *IN Harmony*, is available at http://webapp1.dlib.indiana.edu/inharmony/welcome.do.

4. Online sources such as Bill Edwards's website on ragtime music history contain wonderful information on the sheet music as well as its artwork and artists. See RagPiano, www.perfessorbill.com.

5. Note that this project focuses on recordings made for mass audiences, not ethnographic field recordings made by those studying Native Americans.

My 1906 Edison Home Phonograph with opera house model horn playing for a class at Northern Arizona University. This horn is 57 inches tall and 26 inches wide at the bell. Author's collection.

suitcase. Constructed of quarter-sawn oak and steel, it sits on a small cabinet that holds 120 cylinders. To begin, I remove the curved wooden cover and attach one of my playing horns, either the small reproduction horn that is about a foot long and six inches in diameter at the end; the Home Phonograph horn, a three-foot-long, black, tin megaphone with a twenty-five-inch diameter flower-shaped opening; or my newly acquired opera house model, a giant steel and copper "witches hat" horn that is just under five feet long and twenty-eight inches wide at the end. The small horn simply sits on the machine and moves along as the record plays. The larger horns connect to the phonograph with a piece of soft rubber hose and then are secured to a reproduction horn crane, a type of tripod with a question-mark-shaped bend at the top that loops around the horn and then suspends it by a small chain at the top. This allows the larger horns to pivot as they play.

The part with the rubber hose connects to a small metal tube coming off the reproducer, the heart of the phonograph where sound is produced. The reproducer, or speaker, is a small object about the size and shape of a cookie and contains a needle that rides in the groove of the record and transfers the hills and bumps inside the groove to a membrane that vibrates and reproduces the original sound recorded on the cylinder. The small tube connects this piece to the horn that amplifies the vibrations as music, much like a brass instrument such as a trumpet amplifies the buzzing of one's lip as music. Because the reproducer must travel the four inches of groove on the record, the horn pivots on its chain as the speaker travels the cylinder.

The Victor Victrola functions in much the same way, but instead of playing cylinders it plays discs, sort of like an old record player. Like the cylinder player, it is also made of quarter-sawn oak and is the size of a small square suitcase with a crank on its right side. It has no lid, so the turntable can be clearly seen, as can two small doors at the front of the cabinet under the turntable. Behind these doors is the internal horn; by opening and closing the doors, basic volume control is achieved. The reproducer works the same, but one must replace the small steel needle each time it is used to prevent damage to the record. The needles also can be used to control volume, with thinner ones producing softer tones and thicker versions playing louder. The records are thick shellac rather than thin vinyl and contain only one three-minute song per side. And many of them have only one side. Playing the Victor is easy. One places a record on the turntable, inserts a new needle, winds the crank, and releases the brake to start the record spinning; once it reaches playing speed, you simply set the needle on the outside of the record and open the doors and listen.

The Edison is more complicated. To prepare the cylinder talking machine, I carefully place my left hand down on the phonograph to hold it in place, then grasp the handle on the side with my right hand and start to crank it in a small circle. I feel the tension in the spring tighten as I complete about ten revolutions and stop. I then unlock and open the gate, a small metal hinge that allows me access to the mandrel, a shiny metal tube where the cylinder will go.

To listen to a song, I find the cylinder and take its box—picture a small shipping tube for posters rather than a square box—and remove its round lid. The cylinders themselves are a hard black wax. They are 4.5 inches long and 2.25 inches in diameter. Think of a soda can lacking end caps. The recording lies in one long groove that circumnavigates the tube. The song's title, performer, and record number are stamped on the narrow rim of one end. To retrieve the record, I hold my pointer finger and middle finger tightly together and place them into the box, then flex them outward to grab the cylinder's inner walls, and pull the record out, careful not to touch the grooves. I gently place it on the mandrel, slide it up till it's tight, and then close and lock the gate. I flip a switch to start the cylinder spinning like a wood lathe at the rate of 160 revolutions per minute. I then carefully lower the needle—which is connected to the reproducer and the big horn—to the left side of the cylinder and hear the whoosh, whoosh, whoosh of the unrecorded wax grinding before the song. As the sound begins, I find the matching sheet music from my collection, carefully remove the score from its archival sleeve, and gaze at the full-color cover art.

Very quickly a voice shouts out at me straight from the past announcing the song's title and artist before the music begins. It might be 1904 with "*Navajo*, sung by Harry Tally, Columbia Records," and the music starts. I hear the distinct beat of a tom-tom and the words "Out in the sand hills of New Mexico. . . ." Or it might be 1906 with "*Cheyenne*, sung by Billy Murray," and then the words "Way out in old Wyoming long ago. . . ." As I listen, my mind takes in both the quaintness of the process I just completed and the strange words and music coming from the horn. I gaze back at the song lyrics and the cover art. It's a nostalgic trip to another place and time in American history. And if I truly listen closely, I quickly realize that there is much more here than quaint old songs about the American West.

CHAPTER 1

The Phonograph and the West, 1877–1902

*A*lthough most people associate early western music with the singing cowboys Roy Rogers or Gene Autry, a western music craze featuring songs about cowboys, cowgirls, and Indians swept the United States about the time that Roy and Gene were born, the first decade and a half of the twentieth century. In the midst of what one historian has described as an era of "postfrontier anxiety," Americans listened to these first cowboy and Indian songs on wind-up talking machines such as the Edison cylinder phonograph or the Victor Company's Victrola or played the colorful sheet music on parlor pianos.[1] And in a generation before radio, these colorful fantasies of western life capitalized on a popular culture fascination with the West that was flourishing at the time in the Wild West exhibitions of Buffalo Bill, the fiction of Owen Wister's novel *The Virginian*, and Edwin S. Porter's film *The Great Train Robbery*. Like that era's heritage tourism that embraced cutting-edge railroad technology to explore Fred Harvey's anti-modern Southwest, talking machine western music used state-of-the-art recording technology and modern sheet music publishing to produce nostalgic songs about the American West. And though it illuminates the West's influence on the national culture, it is important to remember that this was not a home-grown vision but one imagined by easterners.[2]

This book brings together, for the first time, the varieties of cowboy, cowgirl, and Indian music recorded and sold for mass consumption between 1902 and 1918. Along the way, it examines cowboy and cowgirl songs, tunes written about western Native Americans, and commemorative recordings that recall the passing of the frontier and the presumed passing of the Indian. It also presents the era's sheet music of the same songs and its colorful artwork and scoring. To understand how all of this came together, two different histories—one of early twentieth-century recorded music, one of the fascination with the American frontier—need to be addressed. Let's start with the music.

The history of recorded popular music begins with Thomas Edison. Edison had been striving for years to improve the telegraph, which had been in wide use for a generation, and Alexander Graham Bell's telephone, which had been invented in 1876 but was too expensive for any but the wealthy. In the summer of 1877, Edison was working on a mechanism that transcribed the dots and dashes of Morse code onto paper tape and noticed that as the tape ran through the machine at a high speed the indentations gave off a sound. If he could replace these noises with the human voice, he realized, he might be able to record messages that could then be played at central telephone stations, in essence creating a voice

---

1. David M. Wrobel, *The End of American Exceptionalism: Frontier Anxiety from the Old West to the New Deal* (Lawrence: University Press of Kansas, 1993), 69–142.

2. Leah Dilworth, *Imaging Indians of the Southwest: Persistent Visions of a Primitive Past* (Washington, D.C.: Smithsonian Institution Scholarly Press, 1997).

telegram. Edison then brought these ideas together in a crude sketch of a crank-operated cylinder phonograph and gave it to his mechanic, John Kruesi, to construct. In less than two days, Kruesi gave the finished product back to the inventor, who wrapped a small sheet of tin foil around the cylinder and shouted into the horn the nursery rhyme "Mary Had a Little Lamb." As he did so, a small needle attached to a diaphragm at the end of the horn converted the sound of his voice into physical bumps and spaces on the soft metal sheet. Edison then returned the needle to the starting point, cranked the cylinder, and heard his machine play back his voice. As he later admitted, "I was never so taken aback in my life."[3]

Although Edison was credited with the phonograph's invention and given a patent in early 1878, ideas about reproducing sounds had existed as early as 1856, and the Frenchman Charles Cros published similar ideas about a recording disc in 1877. In fact, as phonograph historian Roland Gelatt so eloquently states it, Cros was the first to "conceive the phonograph" but Edison the first to "achieve it."

Edison soon exploited the novelty of his invention. In January 1878 he formed the Edison Speaking Phonograph company to manufacture and exhibit the new device. The inventor received $10,000 in cash and a 20 percent royalty in exchange for the phonographs' manufacturing and sales rights. Exhibitions featured a variety of recorded foreign-language speakers and animals prodded to make sounds; audiences were amazed when the phonograph always clearly replicated the unusual words or noises. Musicians recorded songs and then heard them played back at different speeds. Some exhibitors earned as much as $1,800 per week. In June 1878, Edison penned an article for the *North American Review* that outlined ten uses of the phonograph: dictation, phonographic books, teaching elocution, music reproduction, recording family voices for posterity, music boxes and toys, audible clocks, language preservation, educational purposes, and as a telephone accessory.

But it was not to be. Within a year, the novelty of the phonograph had worn off. The tin foil recordings proved to be difficult to handle and easily destroyed. In July 1878, Edison traveled to Wyoming to observe a solar eclipse and his attention turned to perfecting the electric lamp. By the time he returned to his invention a decade later, the phonograph field had changed dramatically.

In Edison's absence, both Alexander Graham Bell and Emile Berliner contributed to the evolution of recorded sound. After receiving the $10,000 Volta Prize from France for his invention of the telephone, Bell used the money to work on advancing electrical and acoustic research. Partnering with his cousin Chichester Bell, a chemical engineer, and Charles Sumner Tainter, a scientist and instrument maker, Bell introduced the use of sturdier wax cylinders to the phonograph to replace the delicate tin foil and also improved the needle for better recording and playback. In May 1886, Bell received a patent for his new machine, which he called a "graphophone."[4]

The story of German immigrant Emile Berliner's contribution to early recorded sound is also important. Adapting the theories of Charles Cros about using a revolving disc rather than a cylinder, in the mid-1880s Berliner began experimenting in his home laboratory using a hard rubber material for the discs. Unlike the cylinder machines that recorded vertically as the tube spun—what enthusiasts call "hill and vale" recording—Berliner's hand-cranked machine cut a lateral groove into the disc as it spun around a spindle. This produced a louder recording and, more important, one that could be easily reproduced through a mechanical etching process. After patenting his "gramophone" in 1897, Berliner partnered with machinist Eldridge R. Johnson to perfect a spring-motor-driven device that produced a more constant speed and therefore a better sound. After finally emerging victorious in 1901 from a series of patent infringement court cases, Johnson formed the Victor

3. This review of Edison's contribution is drawn from Neil Maken, *Hand-Cranked Phonographs: It All Started with Edison, an Introduction to Vintage Talking Machines, Records, and More* (Huntington Beach, Calif.: Promar, 1993); Roland Gelatt, *The Fabulous Phonograph: From Edison to Stereo* (New York: Appleton-Century, 1965), 17–29; and "Inventing Entertainment: The Early Motion Pictures and Sound Recordings of the Edison Companies," *Library of Congress*, http://memory.loc.gov/ammem/edhtml/edcyldr.html.

4. Gelatt, *Fabulous Phonograph*, 26–29; "Inventing Entertainment."

Talking Machine Company to produce and market the disc machines.[5]

The introduction of the new wax cylinders and discs in the late 1880s and early 1890s brought a decade of heated competition to the nascent recording industry. In addition to the debate over which format was better—cylinders or discs—or which company produced the best machine—Edison's phonograph, Bell and Tainter's graphophone, or Berliner-Johnson's gramophone—many of the industry's basics such as recording methods, power sources, and marketing strategies were still being tried and tested. Moreover, phonograph companies of the 1890s faced serious product limitations because records of this era were only two minutes long, provided poor sound quality, and were difficult to produce. Further, competing patent claims led to court cases and a short-lived phonograph monopoly. Most important, talking machines were priced beyond the means of most Americans, especially during the economic downturn of the mid-1890s. For example, Edison's cylinder player cost $190, when an average laborer worked 59 hours per week for an annual salary of just $411.[6] For this reason, Edison promoted his phonograph more for business as a dictation machine than for home entertainment. Indeed, the most noteworthy consumer products to emerge from this time were ill-fated talking dolls produced briefly by both Edison and Berliner and a form of an early jukebox through which patrons could hear a popular song in a public storefront machine for a nickel.[7]

By 1896, when the country was emerging from its financial troubles, the phonograph industry had figured things out and was on the cusp of two decades of expansion and a flourishing of music production. The Columbia Phonograph Company, as the sales agent for the American Graphophone Company, led the way with full-page ads in national magazines touting its machines costing as little as $10 or its larger, sturdier model, the Columbia Home Graphophone, selling for $25.

Edison's newly recreated National Phonograph Company manufactured and sold its own line of consumer models featuring a spring-driven motor. Its Edison Home Phonograph was an elegant machine selling for $40 in 1895, and its Standard model appeared the following year for half that.[8]

Recordings likewise had improved somewhat, with both cylinders and discs providing clearer reproduction with less surface noise. Reproduction capabilities also improved. Whereas discs could be stamped out from a master using molds, cylinders began the period using a basic "pantograph" mechanical means whereby one machine mechanically transferred its grooves onto another. Then, by 1902, Edison developed new technologies that created the "gold moulded" process. This new method used a harder black wax material that meant better sound and the ability to mass-produce songs through a master mold process. The variety of available music grew with these developments as all three companies, and several others, sold recordings of ballads, marches, talking records, comedy sketches, rags, and cakewalks.[9]

The center of the music scene at this time was the New York publishing center known as Tin Pan Alley. The term itself referred to the city's music publishing business from the 1880s to the 1920s. Centered on 28th Street between 5th Avenue and Broadway, this area had grown in importance after the Civil War along with the popularity of the piano. Seemingly ubiquitous in the Victorian parlor, the piano had become the foundation of music education in the country, with more than 500,000 youths studying the instrument by 1887. Sales skyrocketed during the next two decades, from 171,000 in 1900 to 261,000 just four years later, and to more than 364,000 by 1909. At the same time, music publishing, which had been scattered across the country, began to concentrate in New York City as musical talent focused in the Big Apple's many theaters and clubs. In an era before radio and movies, such sheet

5. Maken, *Hand-Cranked Phonographs*, 20–23; Oliver Read and Walter L. Welch, *From Tin Foil to Stereo: Evolution of the Phonograph* (Indianapolis: Howard W. Sams, 1976), 119–36.

6. "William McKinley: The American Franchise," *Miller Center, University of Virginia*, http://millercenter.org/president/mckinley/essays/biography/8.

7. Gelatt, *Fabulous Phonograph*, 46–82.

8. Sean Wilentz, *360 Sound: The Columbia Records Story* (San Francisco: Chronicle Books, 2012), 14–51.

9. Gelatt, *Fabulous Phonograph*, 17–29.

music represented a national culture. In 1881 the T. B. Harms company published its first score for this mass market, and within a decade every major music publisher had a presence in the area.[10]

For the most part, these companies focused on popular music, and the business became a cutthroat one that required market research and aggressive marketing techniques. Music publishers hired song composers who relinquished rights to their works. The companies then researched the markets to determine what style of music was popular and told the composers to write in that style. Once a song was completed, the publishing company tested it with performers and potential buyers to determine its viability. If a song was to be published, the company utilized in-house artists and the latest in color lithography to produce colorful title pages to attract attention. It also hired musicians, called "pluggers," to perform the songs in music stores across the country.[11] Efforts were also made to sell the music to professionals who used the songs in their acts and on stage. At this same time, vaudeville was replacing minstrel shows, and the new entertainment used more and more songs.

We call this popular music "ragtime"—a catchall phrase for a modern form of music with syncopation. But vaudeville also included cakewalks, two-steps, and trots, which were composed for dancing rather than listening. The era also produced comic songs, ethnic songs, minstrels, and the so-called coon songs, a racist and pejorative name for music that mocked African Americans. The most popular example of ragtime today is the music of piano composer Scott Joplin, whose instrumental song *The Entertainer* became a 1970s top hit for the movie *The Sting*. But rags, as they were known, were often sung and could play across the various genres, so all kinds of songs were described as ragtime. Often nostalgic, many of these rags used idealized

images of the past to reflect on the changing conditions of modern life.[12]

This nostalgia overlapped nicely with easterners' views of the American West. A look at the composers and title page artists of such songs suggests that few ever went west and therefore most likely created their songs and artwork from their own imaginings. Take, for example, one of the most enduring cowboy songs of this era, the 1912 hit *Ragtime Cow Boy Joe*. Although its toe-tapping lyrics describe the "roughest, toughest" cowboy who sings ragtime music to put his cattle to sleep every night, the real "Cow Boy Joe" was not a "high falutin', rootin' tootin', son-of-a-gun from Arizona" but the four-year-old nephew of Tin Pan Alley songwriter Maurice Abrahams, who liked to dress up in a cowboy hat and boots whenever he visited his Russian immigrant uncle in New York City.[13]

The title page artist for *Ragtime Cow Boy Joe*, Hungarian immigrant André De Takacs, was one of the most prodigious sheet music artists of the era and worked for many different Tin Pan Alley publishers between 1906 and his death at age thirty-nine in 1919. In addition to *Ragtime Cow Boy Joe*, which he designed in 1912 for the F. A. Mills Company, De Takacs also designed *My Pony Boy* for the Jerome H. Remick Publishing Company in 1909. Known for his use of strong bold colors, De Takacs must have imagined what these western figures should look like, since the little biographical information about him suggests that he never traveled west and lived entirely in either New York or New Jersey.[14]

Like the composers and cover illustrators, none of the recording artists who performed this era's western songs were authentic cowboys or Indians. In fact, no "country singer" emerged in the acoustic recording era until Dallas opera performer Vernon Dalhart recorded *The Prisoner's Song* for Victor Records in 1924. Even Denverite

10. This review of Tin Pan Alley and its music companies is drawn from Jeffrey A. Tucker, "The End of the U.S. Piano Industry," *Ludwig Von Mises Institute*, December 10, 2008, http://mises.org/daily/3253; "America's Music Publishing Industry: The Story of Tin Pan Alley," *The Parlor Songs Academy*, http://parlorsongs.com/insearch/tinpanalley/tinpanalley.php; and "U.S. Piano Sales History: Brand New Piano Sales Sold from 1900 to Present," *Bluebook of Pianos*, 2012, www.bluebookofpianos.com/uspiano.htm, along with specific sources cited below.

11. Bill Edwards, "An Essay on the Historic Role of Sheet Music Cover Art," *RagPiano*, www.perfessorbill.com/ragtime9.shtml.

12. David A. Jasen and Gene Jones, *That American Rag: The Story of Ragtime from Coast to Coast* (New York: Schirmer Books, 2000), xxi–xli.

13. Jim Bob Tinsley, *For a Cowboy Has to Sing* (Gainesville, Fla.: University of Central Florida Press, 1991), 23–24.

14. Bill Edwards, "André de Takacs," *RagPiano*, www.perfessorbill.com/artists/detakacs.shtml.

Jacques Urlus recording in Edison's New York studio in 1916. Image courtesy the U.S. Department of the Interior, National Park Service, Thomas Edison National Historical Park (29.430.6).

Billy Murray, the most popular singer of the ragtime era and the performer of many cowboy and Indian hits, was considered neither a western or country artist nor a singing cowboy. Instead, popular recording artists like Murray or Ada Jones were simply popular singers who happened to include songs about the West in their repertoire.[15] An overview of the recording industry as it existed will help to explain.[16]

In some ways, the new industry that emerged with the introduction of a master reproducible copy in 1902 resembled the music companies of Tin Pan Alley because it was centered in the East, with Victor and Columbia in New York and Edison at the inventor's lab in nearby New Jersey. This proximity also meant that the recording studios could respond quickly to public interest in popular songs put out by the publishing companies and

15. "The Official Website for Vernon Dalhart: A Tribute to the First Million Selling Country Artist!" www.vernondalhart.com.

16. Except where noted, the following overview of the recording industry is drawn from Tim Gracyk with Frank Hoffmann, *Popular American Recording Pioneers, 1895–1925* (New York: Haworth Press, 2000), 1–27.

market their records right along with the sheet music. The studios sometimes even used publisher's pluggers to teach recording artists songs, and in some cases they made records before the publisher released the music. Also, like the publishers, Victor, Columbia, and Edison all used in-house recording artists as well as singers contracted by individual song to make records. This assured the recording companies the continued use of talented recording artists in an era when performers needed special skills to transfer their music to record acoustically. This arrangement also provided companies the flexibility to take on hits as they became popular with other labels.

Despite these similarities, the actual recording studios and the processes they followed were significantly different from anything we might imagine today. In this acoustical era, there were no microphones. In their place, a large recording horn, sometimes several feet in diameter at the bell, carried the sounds of the performers down the tube, through a wall, and into a master talking machine located in the next room. To make the best recording, location next to the horn was most important, which led to a very crowded room, one that became hot and stuffy in the summer. It also meant that band members sometimes had to be placed on seats of various heights with their music dangling from overhead wires so that their instruments could play directly into the horn unimpeded by other musicians, music stands, or instruments. Some even resorted to specially made instruments like the Stroh violin, which was embedded with a diaphragm and a horn for better projection. Most important, this arrangement called for specialized sounds that best translated into music on cylinder and disc, accounting for the high number of banjo and xylophone recordings.

The limitations of the studio also called for a special kind of musical talent. Because there was no way to splice together different parts of a recording, takes had to be made of the whole song from beginning to end. This meant that performers had to have the ability literally to yell all day into the large horn in the stuffy, packed studio if repeated attempts were required. This demand precluded most of the Broadway stars of the time, who found the transition from theater and stage to studio and horn too wide a chasm to cross. Opera star Enrico Caruso, who had a "naturally warm, mellow voice that was powerful," was one of the few crossover stars of both stage and studio.[17] For the same reason, most of the early recording artists were men, simply because few female voices translated well. Indeed, those artists who could quickly learn new tunes and belt them out over and over were in great demand and made many, many recordings.

The person who accomplished these traits most successfully was Billy Murray. Possessed of "powerful lungs . . . excellent intonation, the ability to sing long phrases in rapid fire material without taking a breath, and an unerring sense for mastering the basics of a song prior to the first take," Murray was "arguably the most popular recording artist of the acoustic era," recording songs from the late 1890s to the mid 1940s. Writer Jim Walsh, who penned a long-running series of articles about acoustic era recordings in *Hobbies* magazine from 1942 to the mid-1980s, was a friend of Murray's who wrote that "everybody said Billy Murray's records were the only ones so clear you could catch every word on first hearing." Then, explaining why, Walsh suggested that "there was a certain ping to his voice . . . to make important words and phrases stand out."[18]

Murray used this unique sound to produce more than three thousand recordings. Indeed, the single-spaced discography in Murray's biography alone accounts for 152 pages. He recorded for Edison, Victor, Columbia, and numerous smaller labels. He sang solos and duets as well as in trios and quartets. He was as well known in his day as Charlie Chaplin and Babe Ruth. Some of his best-known hits were those written by George M. Cohan, including *Over There*, *You're a Grand Old Flag*, and

---

17. *Library of Congress, National Jukebox*, www.loc.gov/jukebox/, s.v. "Enrico Caruso."

18. Frank Hoffman, Dick Carty, and Quentin Riggs, *Billy Murray: The Phonograph Industry's First Great Recording Artist* (Lanham, Md.: Scarecrow Press, 1997), 6; Gracyk, *Popular American Recording Pioneers*, 233; Walsh quoted in Hoffman, Carty, and Riggs, *Billy Murray*, 50. Walsh's "'Cowboy Song' Recordings" in *Hobbies* is *the* place to begin research on the topic. The series ran in six parts during the bicentennial summer of 1976 from April to September.

Yankee Doodle Boy. Twenty-first-century listeners may also know his recordings of *Alexander's Ragtime Band, Casey Jones, It's a Long Way to Tipperary,* and *Meet Me in St. Louis, Louis.* Known in his day as a comedian, Murray did indeed record hundreds of comedic pieces in what his biographers describe as thirteen humor genres. But he also recorded ballads, ethnographic songs, patriotic ones, minstrel songs, and pop tunes.[19]

Most relevant here, Billy Murray also recorded some of the first, and most famous, cowboy and Indian songs about the American West, including many in this book. His cowboy hits include *Cheyenne, Ida-Ho, Denver Town, In the Land of the Buffalo,* and *San Antonio.* Some of his Indian songs are *Rainbow, Arrah Wanna, Red Wing, Oh That Navajo Rag,* and *Indianola.* Murray even had the background to be a western singer, having been raised in 1880s Denver, where he worked horses at the city's Overland Park racetrack. But to describe Murray as a cowboy singer or even a western singer would be incorrect because these types of songs were just one of the many that he recorded. Indeed, neither his biography nor any overview of early recording artists that includes Murray describes him this way. Instead, they point out that his Victor recording of *Cheyenne* in 1906 "was considered a technical marvel" for its realistic sound effects of horse hoofbeats and cowboy yells. But they also point out that Murray recorded "material from Broadway musicals, love songs and sentimental ballads, comic songs, vaudeville sketches, ethnic material, topical songs, and more faddish fare such as the jungle and cowboy songs then in vogue."[20]

To understand why cowboy songs were in vogue at this time, we need to understand some basic ideas about the history of the American West. The fact that the first recorded songs about the West appeared in 1902 is not a coincidence. That same year, Owen Wister's novel *The Virginian,* set in Wyoming, was taking the country by storm. Within three months of its May 30 appearance,

the book sold more than 100,000 copies, and it went through no fewer than sixteen printings before January. From the opening-page dedication to Wister's former Harvard classmate, former Dakota rancher, and sitting president, Theodore Roosevelt, the story of a soft-spoken southerner's life on the western range, his participation in the hanging of his friend-turned-cattle thief Steve, his ongoing trouble with the outlaw Trampas that ended with one of the first fictional shootouts, and most of all his romance with school teacher Molly Wood appealed to easterners and westerners alike. Indeed, this love story set out west became the basis for an expansion of western culture on the national scene, including plays based on the book and the first major cowboy song recorded four years later, *Cheyenne.*[21]

Although *The Virginian* stimulated fascination with the West, interest in the region had been building over the same quarter century in which recorded sound was working out its fits and starts. Since the end of the Sioux and Nez Perce wars in 1877, Americans were hard at work incorporating the region west of the Mississippi and its many peoples into the country's economy and culture. Over this quarter century, stories, events, and myths about sodbusters, homesteaders, railroad builders, miners, gunfighters, and the like filled dime novels and became the basis of popular plays and shows. At the same time, the forced confinement of the Native peoples of the West onto reservations, the assimilation efforts through revised land laws, cultural restrictions and boarding school education, and the tragic Ghost Dance movement placed Native Americans into this western story as well. An extensive recounting of this traditional western story line is not needed here; instead we look at six of the most important popularizers of the western myth that influenced early recordings: Buffalo Bill's Wild West show; anti-modern and primitivist western tourism; Frederick Jackson Turner and his frontier thesis; the cultural figure of Theodore Roosevelt as western rancher and hunter; the Indian craze of the turn of the century and its ties to the Jim Crow West;

19. Hoffman, Carty, and Riggs, *Billy Murray*, 3–11.
20. Ibid., 23–24, 51.
21. Darwin Payne, *Owen Wister: Chronicler of the West, Gentleman of the East* (Lincoln: University of Nebraska Press, 1985), 179–210.

and the publication and popularization of Wister's *Virginian*.[22]

The basic story of William F. "Buffalo Bill" Cody is known to most Americans. Born in 1846 in Iowa, Cody grew up mostly in antebellum Kansas. After his father's death in 1860, Cody served as a rider on the famous Pony Express. During the Civil War he worked as teamster for the Seventh Kansas Cavalry. After the war, Cody married, had four children, and worked a variety of frontier jobs. He served as a scout for the U.S. Army, worked as a buffalo hunter for the Kansas Pacific Railroad where he earned his nickname, and guided Russia's Grand Duke Alexi on a western hunt in 1872. After the Little Bighorn battle, Cody participated in a raid at Warbonnet Creek, where he supposedly scalped a Cheyenne warrior to avenge Custer's defeat.[23]

During this time, Cody also became a frontier celebrity. In 1869 dime novelist Ned Buntline published his first story, *Buffalo Bill, the King of the Border Men*, loosely based on Cody's life. Three years later Cody traveled to Chicago to play himself in a stage production of the story, and soon Buntline and Cody had created *Scouts of the Prairie*, which featured Buffalo Bill in the title role. In 1883, Cody expanded his depiction of the frontier with the creation of the first showing of what he called "Buffalo Bill's Wild West." Over the next three and a half decades, Cody reenacted his frontier exploits and provided enamored audiences in the United States, Canada, and Europe with glimpses of western life with trick shooters, Native American performers, cowboys, and other horsemen of the world. Along the way, Cody used profits from his shows to purchase a large ranch near North Platte, Nebraska, helped found and promote the Wyoming town that bears his name, and developed modern tourism in nearby Yellowstone National Park.

For later cowboy and Indian recordings, Buffalo Bill's Wild West served several important purposes. As a collection of decontextualized frontier tropes recontextualized into Cody's frontier vision, the Wild West shows provided a common link to the popular literary past of the frontier, going back to stage plays, dime novels, and even earlier paintings, tall tales, and George Catlin's collection of his own paintings and stories that he called the "Indian Gallery." Additionally, in an age before movies or radio allowed performers to convey their messages worldwide from a select number of locations, Buffalo Bill literally took his frontier to the people, casting it broadly across the United States and then Western Europe via several well-publicized trans-Atlantic trips. From his days on the stage to his death in 1917, Cody reconfigured his performance groups into five different touring organizations: Buffalo Bill's Combination acting troupe, 1872–86; Buffalo Bill's Wild West, 1884–1908; Buffalo Bill's Wild West and Pawnee Bill's Far East, 1909–13; Sells-Floto Circus and Buffalo Bill's Wild West, 1914–15; and Buffalo Bill and the 101 Ranch Combined, 1916.

Just how many places saw the Wild West becomes clear in a fascinating pamphlet created by Denver's Buffalo Bill Grave and Museum called "Did Buffalo Bill Visit Your Town?" According to this document, one or another form of Cody's circus reached what became all forty-eight states of the time plus the District of Columbia. They also traveled to three Canadian provinces and twelve European countries. The number of cities visited is staggering. For example, Cody traveled to thirty-six California cities, 123 in England, and fifty-eight

22. Any western history textbook will take a reader through the succession of these most popular western stories. Ray Allen Billington's *Westward Expansion* (6th ed., with Martin Ridge, Albuquerque: University of New Mexico Press, 2001) is the classic; Richard White's *"It's Your Misfortune and None of My Own"* (Norman: University of Oklahoma Press, 1991) takes a more recent New Western History approach. Excellent overviews of Native Americans and popular music are in Michael V. Pisani, *Imagining Native America in Music* (New Haven: Yale University Press, 2005); and Philip J. Deloria, *Indians in Unexpected Places* (Lawrence: University Press of Kansas, 2004), 183–223.

23. This overview of Cody and his exhibitions is drawn from Louis S. Warren, *Buffalo Bill's America: William Cody and the Wild West Show* (New York: Vintage, 2006); Robert W. Rydell and Robert Kroes, *Buffalo Bill in Bologna: The Americanization of the World* (Chicago: University of Chicago Press, 2005); Michael A. Amundson, *Passage to Wonderland: Rephotographing Joseph Stimson's Views of the Cody Road to Yellowstone National Park, 1903 & 2008* (Boulder: University Press of Colorado, 2013); William H. Goetzmann and William N. Goetzmann, *The West of the Imagination*, 2nd ed. (Norman: University of Oklahoma Press, 2009); and Paul Fees, "Wild West Shows: Buffalo Bill's Wild West," *Buffalo Bill Center of the West*, http://centerofthewest.org/learn/western-essays/wild-west-shows.

in Ohio, including nineteen show dates in Toledo alone between 1873 and 1916.[24] In 1899, at the height of the Wild West's popularity, the show logged more than 11,000 miles in two hundred days, giving 341 performances in 132 U.S. locations. Thus, Cody popularized the idea of the West to people all across North America and Europe. His version of the Wild West became *the* vision of the frontier for anyone who could see one of his performances or read about them on colorful posters.

Even more important than the number of visits was the fact that Cody assembled not just frontier acts such as trick shooting, bronco riding, and Native American performances but also a "Cowboy Band" that provided background music for all of his shows. Dressed in attire typical of working cowboys including blue jeans, long-sleeve shirts, and big hats, the Cowboy Band provided the audience with an aural representation of the West hardly like that associated with today's country or even cowboy music. Like many such music groups of this "golden age of bands," a sixteen-member band is shown in an 1887 photograph consisting of a "D-flat piccolo, an E-flat clarinet, three B-flat clarinets, three B-flat cornets . . . two trombones, a baritone, two E-flat alto horns, one tuba, a snare drummer, and a bass drummer." Nine years later, a twenty-one member band included "piccolo, four clarinets, three alto horns, five cornets, three trombones, a baritone, a B-flat bass tuba, an E-flat bass tuba, and two drums."[25]

According to music historian Michael L. Masterson, Cody had the band play both popular music of the day before the show and incidental music during the performance. He situated the musicians across from the performers' entrance, between the reserved seating and grandstand. Prior to the Wild West performance, the band played a concert that included marches, patriotic tunes, and popular arrangements including cakewalks, ragtime, and opera medleys. Masterson suggests that Wild West programs even included advertisements from

major music publishers and that the band performed popular ragtime songs from company catalogs. After playing the *Star Spangled Banner* to start the show, the Cowboy Band provided accompaniment for the Wild West acts and incidental music between them. In the tradition of circus bands, the group provided a sort of background musical score for the performance that "paced, animated, set appropriate moods, heightened audience's responses, and provided organized sounds to fill in the dead spots between acts."[26]

Music historians suggest that the ordered marches of brass bands were popular during this time because they represented nineteenth-century ideas of progress just as ragtime syncopation reflected the cultural diversity of an increasingly urban America. The Cowboy Band is important because it provided, like the Wild West exhibition itself, a popular version of the West. And this model of the region was not a home-grown one emanating from its peoples but a version created by eastern music publishers about the West. It remained for Cody and his show to provide the links that connected this staged West with the imagined one in the popular conscience.[27]

Buffalo Bill Cody is also significant because he presented these versions of the frontier using cutting-edge technology and organization. This mix of using the modern to sell visions of the anti-modern is a strong theme across American culture at this time, and Cody perfected it through his publicity agents, poster advertising, amalgamation of diverse ethnic performers, and show logistics. As Cody historian Paul Fees points out, Cody employed up to five hundred cast members at one time who all had to be fed three meals a day. In addition, the Wild West used its own train to carry hundreds of horses, two and a half dozen buffalo, grandstand seating for 20,000, and tents to cover the main stages. Further, Buffalo Bill hired advanced agents to secure performance locations and purchase

24. Buffalo Bill Museum and Grave, "Did Buffalo Bill Visit Your Town?" www.buffalobill.org/PDFs/Buffalo_Bill_Visits.pdf.

25. On Cody's Cowboy Band, see Michael L. Masterson, "Buffalo Bill's Famous Cowboy Band," *Buffalo Bill Center of the West*, http://centerofthewest.org/explore/buffalo-bill/research/buffalo-bill-band.

26. Ibid.

27. Juti A. Winchester, "All the West's a Stage: Buffalo Bill, Cody, Wyoming, and Western Heritage Presentation, 1846–1997" (Ph.D. diss., Northern Arizona University, 1999).

the tons of hay and food consumed by the show. The simple logistics of organizing and moving the entourage efficiently brought circus kingpin James A. Bailey, of the famed Barnum and Bailey Circus, to assist in 1895. That Cody could pull off the whole operation so quietly and efficiently is testament to his ability to utilize modern business practices to sell his anti-modern experience. Indeed, as historians Robert Rydell and Rob Kroes suggest, when Cody took the entourage to Prussia, army officers there were most impressed not with the anti-modern, frontier tropes Cody was selling on stage but with the modern, efficient organization that he used behind the scenes to move his army of performers. This tactic of using the modern to sell the anti-modern resonates throughout this book.[28]

The West's growing tourist industry, and especially Fred Harvey's Southwest, also capitalized on the modern/anti-modern relationship that brought the region into the national spotlight in turn-of-the-century America and served as a predecessor to the cowboy and Indian music craze. Indeed, in many ways western tourism and Buffalo Bill's Wild West were two sides of the same anti-modern coin. As Cody used modern business organization, emerging advertising, and cutting-edge transportation methods to take his assemblage of frontier icons all over America and Europe, western tourism utilized many of the same methods to bring travelers to a region increasingly being scripted for their pleasure. Both relied on the perception of authenticity: Cody wanted real Indians, cowboys, and sharpshooters for his shows; tourism functions by bringing people to visit real sites. Probably the major difference was one of class. Although Cody certainly played for kings and presidents, the majority of his shows across small-town America were aimed at the emerging middle class. With entrance fees at just 50 cents for anyone over nine years of age and just a quarter for those under that, Cody gave everyone an afternoon or evening of escape into the Wild West. Tourism, on the other hand, was much more expensive, requiring vacation time from work, train fare, hotels, and food costs, thus making it an elite endeavor. Nevertheless, the growth of modern tourism helped to bring the idea of the West to modern America.[29]

As historians have shown, although tourism to the American West began with a few elites in the antebellum period, the tourist industry developed in the post–Civil War years as easterners traveled West on the newly created transcontinental railroads. Destined for resorts like Colorado Springs, the new national parks such as Yellowstone and Yosemite, dude ranches in Wyoming, and Indian villages in the Southwest, tourists of this period were most likely wealthy elites seeking authentic experiences out west to help offset their supposedly inauthentic lives back home in eastern cities. Whether seeking heritage experiences that were cultural in nature or recreational ones that were more physical, turn-of-the-century tourists created a demand for a romanticized vision of the West that locals were happy to provide. In doing so, the western tourist industry commodified the experience of being out west and, right along with Cody, brought the region's icons—such as cowboys and Indians—into the national consciousness.

The Fred Harvey Company, which operated hotels, restaurants, and guide services from Chicago to Los Angeles for its partner, the Atchison, Topeka, and Santa Fe Railroad, is the best-known example. Starting from a series of lunch counters in the 1880s to provide high-quality food to railroad passengers, Fred Harvey grew into a modern tourist business that constructed elaborate hotels like the Alvarado in Albuquerque, La Fonda in Santa Fe, and Hopi House at the Grand Canyon to sell the local experience; created guide services that took travelers away from the tracks to primitive, exotic locales like Taos or the Hopi villages; and published multicolor guidebooks, picture calendars, postcards, and even playing cards that used modern illustrations to sell the anti-modern Southwest experience. Creating and performing what some historians call "staged authenticity," Fred Harvey helped bring western icons into the national discussion.[30]

28. See also T. Jackson Lears, *No Place of Grace: Antimodernism and the Transformation of American Culture, 1880–1920* (Chicago: University of Chicago Press, 1994).

29. The following exploration of tourism draws from Hal K. Rothman, *Devil's Bargains: Tourism in the Twentieth-Century American West* (Lawrence: University Press of Kansas, 2000); and Dilworth, *Imagining Indians.*

Harvey's treatment of southwestern Indians is indicative. The company disregarded the actual story of the conquest of Native Americans, their relocation onto reservations, and the forced assimilation that denied their language and customs in favor of off-reservation boarding schools where young people were stripped of their culture. Instead, the tourist trade focused on nostalgic, romanticized images of Native American artisans who produced handmade rugs and jewelry that seemed authentic in a time of increasing industrialization and the assembly-line manufacture of most consumer goods. Others sought out white reenactors like the Boy Scouts of America, who earned badges in Indian lore, or the Improved Order of Red Men lodge, where men "played Indian" to appropriate the version of Native American culture that best suited their own needs. As historian Leah Dilworth suggests, this primitivist version of the southwestern Indian became the one incorporated into the tourist trade.[31]

Other western tourism operators used modern transportation and cutting-edge advertising techniques to sell anti-modern, supposedly authentic western experiences in other regional settings. Along the Big Horns of northern Wyoming and elsewhere in the mountain West, ranchers such as Howard Eaton discovered that easterners would pay good money to come live in a cabin and play cowboy for a week at what came to be known as dude ranches. In national parks such as Yellowstone and Yosemite, travelers sought our remnants of the frontier to "get away from it all" and commune with nature.

As much as Cody and tourism sought to bring the West directly into the national culture, others such as historian Frederick Jackson Turner and President Theodore Roosevelt played more symbolic roles. Historians have most liked to focus on Turner's influence as the creator of the field of western studies with his famous 1893 address to the American Historical Association, "The Significance of the Frontier in American History." Responding to the prevalent "germ theory" that suggested that American culture was little more than the newest outgrowth of Europe, Turner's essay made a case for American exceptionalism by showing how western civilization continually encountered the savage frontier—that place with fewer than two people per square mile—and in so doing transformed Europeans into Americans. Often seen as an environmental determinist, Turner made a powerful case for an organic view of American history that highlighted the various stages of the frontier—explorer, trapper, cowboy, and farmer—as important symbols of American culture. Along the way, Turner suggested, this continual frontier experience created uniquely American traits such as democracy and innovation.[32]

Even more important, Turner noted, was the fact that by 1890 the frontier line—this crucible for American culture—had ceased to exist. Add to this the fact that America's population was shifting from rural to urban (1920 marks the turning point), and a nostalgia for all things rural contributed to this fascination with the West. Later historians would call this condition "postfrontier anxiety" and suggest that efforts to experience authentic remnants of the West, such as Cody's show or Fred Harvey's Southwest, were last-ditch attempts to hold onto the quintessential American experience. Whether or not one believes this, Turner's view that the frontier was both a place where American civilization overcame savagery and a process whereby Americans gained their essential cultural traits became the dominant view of American history not only in the jingoistic 1890s but for the next century. Like Buffalo Bill and tourism, Frederick Jackson Turner brought the West into the national spotlight and created a setting where cowboy and Indian music resonated with the American experience.

Just as Turner brought the idea of the West to the nation, President Theodore Roosevelt embodied a western spirit unmatched by any other leader before or since. Roosevelt's western connections are generally well known. Raised out of a sickly childhood through

30. See also Dean MacCannell, *The Tourist: A New Theory of the Leisure Class* (Berkeley: University of California Press, 1999).

31. See also Deloria, *Indian;* and Elizabeth Hutchinson, *The Indian Craze: Primitivism, Modernism, and Transculturation in American Art, 1890–1915* (Durham, N.C.: Duke University Press, 2009).

32. Wrobel, *End of American Exceptionalism.*

strenuous exercise, Roosevelt studied at Harvard and then, after losing his mother on the same day that his wife died during the birth of their daughter, went out west to the badlands of North Dakota to recover his body and spirit through cattle ranching. Emboldened by the frontier experience, Roosevelt returned to his native New York and worked as a progressive reformer, recreating the New York police department, and then serving as state legislator, New York governor, and assistant secretary to the navy. He also wrote a popular history, *The Winning of the West*, which, like Turner's essay, linked American exceptionalism to its frontier history. During the Spanish-American War, Roosevelt helped shape an assemblage of western cowboys and eastern college men into the famous Rough Riders, who gained national fame for their role in the taking of San Juan Hill. President William McKinley then used Roosevelt's popularity by placing him on the national ticket as his vice-president in 1900. After McKinley's assassination two years later, "that damned cowboy" became president.[33]

In the White House, Roosevelt became the national embodiment of the strenuous life and the western hero. His trust-busting and Square Deal efforts reflected an egalitarian, western attitude for fair play. Likewise, his unprecedented environmental efforts to set aside forests, national monuments, national parks, and reclamation lands all were important to the West. Indeed, his Newlands Reclamation Act has been called one of the most important pieces of legislation concerning the West ever signed into law. Just as important, Roosevelt had great popularity in the region and helped solidify his reputation as a true westerner during several visits to the region as president. One of my personal favorites is his 1903 trip to Laramie, Wyoming, where, after visiting with the locals, he rejected the short train trip to Cheyenne and instead mounted a borrowed horse and rode the sixty-five miles to the state capital. Such activities, along with his many legislative dealings, made Roosevelt the living embodiment of Turner's frontier just as the western recording craze began.[34]

At the same time that Roosevelt, Turner, Harvey, and Cody were commodifying the western experience, Americans across the country were doing the same to the region's original inhabitants. After centuries of battles over their homelands, culminating in the 1877 Plains Indian Wars and the 1880s Apache campaigns, Native Americans were imprisoned on reservations and forced into efforts to assimilate them into mainstream American life. From off-reservation boarding schools like Carlisle, where the motto was to "kill the Indian and save the man," to the culturally insensitive Dawes Act, which reduced tribal land holdings, to other efforts to ban religious practices and traditional songs, dances, and ceremonies, Native American life in this period faced a multiple-front cultural assault.[35]

At the same time, Native Americans suffered politically with the 1903 Supreme Court decision of *Lone Wolf v. Hitchcock*, in which the Court found that American Indians were dependent "wards of the nation" and that Congress had the unilateral power to break treaties signed on behalf of the government. Similar to the famous Dred Scott decision on the brink of the American Civil War that denied African Americans court standing, *Lone Wolf* further stacked the deck against Native Americans.

As these policies were being played out and Native Americans seemed no longer a threat, many white Americans began to romanticize Native American cultures as seemingly more authentic and real than increasingly modern America. Viewing Indian life through primitivist lenses, Americans began visiting tribal villages like those of the Hopi to touch the exotic within American life. This fascination with all things Indian belied official government policies of assimilation for tourist experiences that seemed to freeze Native Americans into imagined settings of place and time. Thus, at the same time that the West was becoming embodied in the American imagination, Native Americans in the West were systematically finding fewer and fewer opportunities in American culture

---

33. Edmund Morris, *The Rise of Theodore Roosevelt* (New York: Random House, 2001).

34. *WyoHistory.org*, www.wyohistory.org, s.v. "President Theodore Roosevelt's 1903 Visit to Wyoming" (Rebecca Hein).

35. On federal Indian policy of the time, see Frederick E. Hoxie, *A Final Promise: The Campaign to Assimilate the Indians, 1880–1920* (Lincoln: University of Nebraska Press, 1984).

as science, land policies, government programs, and schools transformed the national perspective on Native America from one of total assimilation into one of partial accommodation. For our purposes, this transformation meant that Native American life was often on center stage and fodder for song writers and composers who wanted to appropriate Native American stereotypes to assert American dominance.[36]

Native Americans were not alone in the search for equality in the Jim Crow West. As several historians have shown, the Progressive Era was a period of racial struggle, as a favored subset of white Americans used political, economic, and cultural power to assert their dominance over Native Americans, Mexicans, Irish, and other new immigrants. Just as in their use of Native Americans, this struggle meant that Tin Pan Alley songwriters made other peoples of color in the American West their targets for stereotypical racist songs.[37]

As much as Buffalo Bill Cody, western tourism, Frederick Jackson Turner, Theodore Roosevelt, and the Jim Crow West created the conditions for the nascent recording industry to appropriate the emerging images of cowboys and Indians to sell recordings, the publication of Owen Wister's novel *The Virginian* in 1902 served as the spark that ignited the hysteria. A native son of Philadelphia and Harvard classmate of Theodore Roosevelt, Wister had majored in music and after graduating in 1882 traveled to Paris to study composition. After a year there, he returned to America and began working in a bank. Wister suffered a health breakdown in 1885 and his doctor suggested that he go west to recover. He set out to visit family friends in Wyoming, from which began a lifetime love affair with the West. From the day that he set out from Philadelphia, Wister recorded his daily events and thoughts in a series of journals, which later were used in much of his published writing. After returning from Wyoming, Wister studied

law at Harvard, graduated in 1888, and then returned to Philadelphia, passed the state bar in 1890, and began practicing law. He also made annual summer sojourns to Wyoming and other parts of the region. Then, bored with law, in the summer of 1891 Wister decided that he would turn to writing about the West.[38]

Using his own Wyoming experiences, Wister wrote realistic stories about cowboys and their lives on the frontier that earned him the nickname "Kipling of the West." He published his first short stories, "Hank's Woman" and "How Lin McLean Went East," in *Harper's Magazine* in January 1892. The following year, he gave up the law practice when *Harper's* encouraged him to go back west and write stories about the region. By chance, he met the illustrator Frederic Remington in Yellowstone National Park and struck up a lifetime friendship. In 1895, Wister published his first collection of short stories, *Red Men and White*, and then used his annual sojourns west to collect new experiences that became the basis of more magazine articles, many of which were revised into collections of both fiction and nonfiction. In 1897, Wister published *Lin McLean*, a novel about a Wyoming cowpuncher, and three years later *The Jimmyjohn Boss and Other Stories*, a nonfiction collection. All of these stories were well received; some even described Wister as the new Bret Harte.

The publication of *The Virginian* in 1902 was something else altogether and catapulted Wister, cowboys, and the West into the national spotlight. Developing minor characters from *Lin McLean*, Wister's new novel focused on "the Virginian," a soft-spoken Wyoming wrangler, his pranks, his trials dealing with cattle rustlers and animal abusers, and, most of all, his long courtship with eastern schoolmarm Molly Stark Wood. From their initial chance meeting when the Virginian rescues the teacher from a broken-down stage stuck in the middle of a river to their honeymoon in the Tetons, the focus on the love story between the cowboy

36. Deloria, *Indians*, 183–223.

37. For example, see Linda Gordon, *The Great Arizona Orphan Abduction* (Cambridge: Harvard University Press, 2001); Eric V. Meeks, *Border Citizens: The Making of Indians, Mexicans, and Anglos in Arizona* (Austin: University of Texas Press, 2007); Katherine Benton-Cohen, *Borderline Americans: Racial Division and Labor War in the Arizona Borderlands* (Cambridge: Harvard University Press, 2011); and Douglas Flamming, *Bound for Freedom: Black Los Angeles in Jim Crow America* (Berkeley: University of California Press, 2005).

38. On Wister, see Fanny Kemble Wister, ed., *Owen Wister out West: His Journals and Letters* (Chicago: University of Chicago Press, 1958), 2–13; and Payne, *Owen Wister*.

and the teacher transformed Wister's novel from a western cowboy story into what the *Saturday Evening Post* called "pretty near . . . the American novel." Sales of the book soared, with more than 100,000 copies purchased within the first three months. By year's end, the novel had gone through no fewer than sixteen printings, and Wister was busy rewriting the novel into a play.

The fact that Wister dedicated *The Virginian* to Theodore Roosevelt was just one hint at the "perfect storm" of interest in all things West that Wister had created. Indeed, Wister biographer Darwin Payne wrote that the novel "create[d] a nearly insatiable appetite in the American public for cowboy heroes whose hearts were purer than gold, whose intentions for their women were beyond reproach, and whose quiet courage made them men to be feared by all."[39] With such sales, it is not hard to see how this "insatiable appetite" for cowboys had been created. Combining Wister's cowboy hero with Frederick Jackson Turner's frontier, Teddy Roosevelt, and Buffalo Bill's Wild West, the commodification of the Indian with the Jim Crow West, and Fred Harvey's Southwest, it is clear how the country's newest fad, the talking machine, picked up the country's fascination with cowboys and Indians and began producing and selling recordings set in the American West.

It is important to consider how we know that cowboy and Indian music actually was so popular. After all, radio did not come into play until 1920 and music charts not until 1940. Records of individual song sales do not exist. Overall record sales by company might be determined, but such broad strokes would not contain the details needed here. One comprehensive method is to employ collector Edward Foote Gardner's reconstructed top-twenty lists in his book *Popular Songs of the Twentieth Century*. Gardner first consulted popular music history books to create a list of every song mentioned between 1900 and 1929, corroborated these against weekly period trade papers such as

Variety, then examined the trade journal *Talking Machine World* to create spreadsheets showing when each song first was mentioned, the number of times it appeared, and when the song disappeared from popular coverage. Then, using these spreadsheets, he reconstructed top-twenty charts for each month of the year beginning January 1900.[40]

In addition to drawing from Gardner's top-twenty charts, I have conducted my own qualitative research to create a list of every cowboy or Indian song that I could find both in print and as a recording. Similar to Gardner's methods, I consulted period trade journals such as *Talking Machine World* and *Edison Phonograph Monthly*, both available through the online Internet Archive. These sources are, of course, industry booster magazines, and any data found in them must be qualified. Additionally, I consulted online searchable databases including the *Discography of American Historical Recordings* website and the *UCSB Cylinder Audio Archive* website, both housed at the Donald C. Davidson Library at the University of California–Santa Barbara.[41] I also traced stories about individual songs and recordings through searchable online digitized period newspapers.[42] Finally, through these sources I compiled my own lists of the number of times a song was recorded by different artists on the same label and by the same artists on different labels. In addition, I noted when songs were included in parodies, medleys, skits, and vaudeville-type recordings of jokes and music called at the time "minstrel recordings," suggesting an even greater popularity. Occasionally, I even found recordings not included in any of these sources for sale on sites such as eBay. All very subjective, my methods, combined with Gardner's lists, suggest that, between 1902 and 1918, cowboy and Indian recordings represented a small but popular segment of the early music industry.

To begin, let's start with my list of every song included in this book, starting in 1902 and continuing

39. Payne, *Owen Wister*, 199.

40. Edward F. Gardner, *Popular Songs of the Twentieth Century*, vol. 1: *Chart Detail and Encyclopedia, 1900–1949* (St. Paul, Minn.: Paragon House, 2000).

41. *Discography of American Historical Recordings*, http://adp.library.ucsb.edu, and *UCSB Cylinder Audio Archive*, http://cylinders.library.ucsb.edu. See also William Ruhlmann, *Breaking Records: 100 Years of Hits* (New York: Routledge, 2004), 1–18; and Gracyk, *Popular American Recording Pioneers*, 8–10.

42. For example, http://newspapers.com, http://news.google.com/newspapers, and http://chroniclingamerica.loc.gov.

to 1918. At almost sixty tunes, the annual list is rather extraordinary:

1902: *Custer's Last Charge, Indian War Dance*

1903: *Hiawatha; Anona; Hiawatha* (two-step)

1904: *Anona* (intermezzo)*; Navajo; Navajo* (two-step)*; Cumming's Indian Congress at Coney Island*

1905: *Lasca; Lewis and Clarke* [sic] *Centennial March; Feather Queen; Tammany; Sitting Bull*

1906: *Cheyenne; Iola, Silver Heels; Arrah Wanna; Ida-Ho*

1907: *Reed Bird; San Antonio; Broncho Buster; In the Land of the Buffalo; Broncho Bob and His Little Cheyenne; Pride of the Prairie*

1908: *When It's Moonlight on the Prairie; Rainbow; Red Wing; I'm a Yiddish Cowboy; Topeka; Rain-in-the-Face; Big Chief Smoke; Denver Town; Silver Heels* (intermezzo)*; Since Arrah Wanna Married Barney Carney; Santiago Flynn*

1909: *Blue Feather; My Rancho Maid; Wise Old Indian; My Prairie Song Bird; Lily of the Prairie; Little Arrow and Big Chief Greasepaint; My Pony Boy*

1910: *Silver Bell; Valley Flower; A Cowboy Romance; Ogalalla*

1911: *Red Wing*

1912: *Oh That Navajo Rag; From the Land of the Sky-Blue Water; Ragtime Cow Boy Joe; Silver Star*

1913: *At That Bully Wooly Wild West Show; In the Golden West; Snow Deer*

1914: *Navajo Indian Songs*

1915: none

1916: *Way Out Yonder in the Golden West*

1917: *Indianola*

1918: *Big Chief Killahun*

From this master list, a comparison with Gardner's book reveals that, of these fifty-nine songs, fifteen cowboy and Indian tunes at least appeared on one of his monthly top-twenty charts some time during their lifespan. This is what that list look likes:

1903: *Hiawatha; Anona*

1904: *Navajo*

1905: *Tammany; Silver Heels*

1906: *Silver Heels; Cheyenne; Iola; Arrah Wanna*

1907: *Arrah Wanna; Iola; San Antonio; Red Wing*

1908: *Red Wing; Rainbow*

1909: *My Pony Boy*

1910: *Silver Bell*

1911: *Silver Bell*

1912: *Ragtime Cow Boy Joe*

1913: *Ragtime Cow Boy Joe*

1918: *Indianola*

Of these fifteen, Gardner further suggests that eleven songs—*Navajo, Tammany, Silver Heels, Cheyenne, Arrah Wanna, Iola, San Antonio, Red Wing, Rainbow, Silver Bell,* and *Indianola*—cracked the top ten. Of these eleven, according to Gardner, only three made it to the number one spot on the charts: *Navajo* in March and April 1904; *Arrah Wanna* in January and February 1907; and *San Antonio* in May 1907. Examining the list another way, *Arrah Wanna* tops the longevity list, being on it for nine months; *Navajo* and *Cheyenne*, eight months; *Silver Bell* and *Red Wing*, seven months; *Tammany, My Pony Boy,* and *Ragtime Cow Boy Joe*, six months; and *Silver Heels*, five months.[43]

It is important to remember that these were not songs *of* the American West. Few songs of the region made it into the national culture until folklorist John Lomax published *Cowboy Songs and Other Western Ballads* in 1908. Instead, these songs and their colorful sheet music title pages are better categorized as songs *about* the American West, dreamed up by composers and artists living in New York City, working in Tin Pan Alley, and most likely never having set foot in the West. In that sense, these early recordings fit better into the mythic

43. Gardner, *Popular Songs*, 48–79.

West of the imagination than the authentic West. Indeed, the word used to describe those who appropriated Indian culture and then believed themselves to be speaking on Native Americans' behalf is "Indianists."[44] From trained ethnographers to politicians to hobbyists who donned Indian costumes in order to play Indian, Indianists believed that they truly represented Native American culture and that, as such cultures inevitably died out, they would remain to portray these "lost" peoples to the American public. Following in this vein, perhaps these songsters who wrote about cowboys are also better described as "cowboyists."[45]

Created out of the imaginations of Tin Pan Alley cowboyist composers living in New York or New Jersey, set to modern ragtime syncopation and then published with illustrations by immigrant artists who never traveled past the Ohio, these were the first recorded songs about the American West. Their history is complex and represents a coalescence of many things including the birth of a new communications industry, the growing popularity of the American West in the national consciousness, the turmoil of Jim Crow America, and the popularizing efforts of Buffalo Bill, Fred Harvey,

Frederick Jackson Turner, and Theodore Roosevelt. This spark first caught fire in 1902 with the overnight success of Owen Wister's *Virginian* and continued to Elliot S. Porter's 1905 movie *The Great Train Robbery*. And like culture today, success breeds imitation. The fact that this nostalgia for the Old West soon carried itself onto the cutting-edge communications system of ragtime and the talking machine should not surprise us, since Cody and Harvey had been capitalizing on the same relationship for more than two decades.

Author and legendary cowboy singer "Ranger Doug" Green of the cowboy group Riders in the Sky probably best summarizes this early period in his book *Singing in the Saddle: The History of the Singing Cowboy*. Although he notes that *My Pony Boy* became a "small sensation on Broadway" and that *Ragtime Cow Boy Joe* was a "hit," these songs were "neither ragtime nor cowboy." Nevertheless, Green suggests, they "still struck a national nerve, combining the thrill, danger, and nostalgia of the Old West with the exciting modern music that presaged the jazz age." Then, making a sly reference to the inauthentic nature of *all* cowboy music, Green writes, "It was a formula that would work again and again in the coming years."[46]

44. Pisani, *Imagining Native America*, 164–70.

45. Philip J. Deloria, *Playing Indian* (New Haven: Yale University Press, 1999), 183–223.

46. Douglas B. Green, *Singing in the Saddle: The History of the Singing Cowboy* (Nashville: Country Music Foundation Press and Vanderbilt University Press, 2002), 8.

CHAPTER 2
The Talking Machine West, 1902–1918

Between 1902 and 1918, a cowboy and Indian music craze played on hand-cranked talking machines swept through American popular culture. Much stronger than the "trickle" of "novelties" suggested by western music historians,[1] this furor produced almost sixty cowboy and Indian recordings, including cowboy poetry, western skits, cowboy tunes, love songs, Indian melodies, Wild West show ditties, cowgirl ballads, World War I Indian warrior anthems, and both cowboy and Indian ragtime dance tunes. At the same time, music companies printed elaborately illustrated scores of almost every song, providing a sort of cover art in an era when discs came in simple sleeves and cylinders in tubes. An estimated fifteen such songs made it into the top twenty, eleven into the top ten, and three reached number one, all back when Roy Rogers and Gene Autry were still in diapers.[2] This mostly unknown soundscape flourished two decades before radio became popular and suggests one way an imagined West affected American culture.

This early brand of western music not only reflected the nostalgic passing of the Indian and the frontier but also incorporated modern components in the rhythms of syncopated ragtime music and the racial attitudes of Jim Crow America. Hardly ditties about the Old West, recorded songs of this period depicted changing ideas about Indians and assimilation, cowboys and the frontier, the rise of the New Woman, ethnic and racial equality, and even the role of Native Americans in World War I. This chapter highlights the most important examples of these many themes and the places where significant shifts took place. The following catalogue offers lyrics, publication details, and documentation for the songs referred to here.

The earliest records about the West grew out of the anti-modern Indian craze that prompted fashionable Americans to decorate their modern homes with so-called Indian corners that featured Native textiles, pottery, and even clothing. Such decorations also often included Mission style furniture, whose simple lines, dark grains, and traditional joinery represented fine craftsmanship. Music also found its way into the American home during this period, first in the form of the piano and then, by the 1890s, the phonograph. Often located in Victorian parlors, these music makers also featured Craftsman styling while reproducing Indian songs that complemented their inclusion in the decor.[3]

The first Indian recordings, *Custer's Last Charge* and *Indian War Dance*, were instrumentals by popular

---

1. Green, *Singing in the Saddle*, 20.

2. See chapter 1 for an explanation of the popularity ratings cited in this chapter, which are based primarily on the reconstructions of Edward Foote Gardner in *Popular Songs of the Twentieth Century*, vol. 1.

3. Hutchinson, *Indian Craze*, 11–50; Dilworth, *Imagining Indian*, 1–20, 77–124; Rothman, *Devil's Bargains*, 50–80; Lears, *No Place of Grace*, 59–96; Thomas J. Schlereth, *Victorian America: Changes in Everyday Life, 1876–1915* (New York: Harper Perennial, 1992), 171, 191–93; William Howland Kenney, *Recorded Music in American Life: The Phonograph and Popular Memory, 1890–1945* (New York: Oxford University Press, 1999), 23–43.

bandleader John Philip Sousa in 1902–1904. The March King's band had been performing the former since at least 1895 in public concerts. He recorded the piece for Victor in January 1902 and again in August 1903. The music featured an instrumental orchestration with added gunshot sounds and horse's hoofbeats for effect.

The first Indian song with lyrics to become a hit was *Hiawatha*, recorded by both Victor and Edison in 1903. In fact, the new tune sparked an Indian love song fad that persisted for over a decade. Charlie Daniels, a Kansas City songwriter, wrote the piece under the pseudonym Niel Moret as a love song for his sweetheart then living in the small town of Hiawatha, Kansas. After the song sold more than a million copies of sheet music within a year, in 1903 lyricist James O'Dea added words to the tune that focused on the popular Longfellow poem "Hiawatha," essentially turning the original song about a Kansas town into an Indian love song. Apparently this struck a chord in the American public, and the song became even more popular as a ballad.

More than a dozen bands and artists recorded the song on multiple labels for both cylinder and disc. For Victor alone, six bands recorded either *Hiawatha* or *Hiawatha's Two-Step* in 1903. No doubt the most famous of these was the August recording by Sousa's band. Tenor Harry Macdonough sang the ballad with piano accompaniment that year for both Victor and Edison. Other than a reference to his "Indian bride," the song contains little to make it sound stereotypically Indian. The song's popularity even sparked a *Parody on Hiawatha* using the pun "higher water" instead of "Hiawatha" that same year for both disc and cylinder. All of these recordings made *Hiawatha* a major hit in the spring and summer of 1903. It first entered Gardner's top twenty as number ten in March 1903, rose to number two the next month, reached number one in May 1903, stayed in that spot through July, and remained in the top twenty until November.

Hiawatha's success produced immediate copycat songs with Indian themes, a pattern that became quite familiar during this time. The first of these, *Anona*, appeared in August 1903, just as *Hiawatha* began falling from the charts. Miss Mabel McKinley, daughter of Abner McKinley and niece of the president, wrote the

song under the pseudonym Vivian Grey. A soprano with an operatic voice, McKinley was an accomplished musician who often performed at the White House when her uncle was president. After his death, she performed in vaudeville and composed several western songs. *Anona* tells the story of another Indian maid—this one in the "western state of Arizona," even though at the time Arizona was still a territory.

At about the same time, a musical comedy called *Nancy Brown* swept across the country featuring an even edgier Indian love song titled *Navajo*. With words by Harry Williams and music by Egbert Van Alstyne, the song tells the story of the love between an African American man and a Navajo woman. Actress Marie Cahill made *Navajo* a hit on stage, and then Harry Macdonough, of *Hiawatha* fame, and Harry Tally, another well-liked singer, produced popular recordings. Over the next few years, the song transformed the genre, made the composers famous, opened up songs about the West to a national audience, and brought lyrics about racial stereotypes to the forefront of western music.

Navajo warrants further discussion for several reasons. *Hiawatha* and *Anona*, sentimental love songs of a passing people, had been imagined accounts of the noble savage. Although *Navajo* still told a fictional tale, its inclusion of a real western tribe brought a certain air of authenticity to this music that fed its popularity. This interest probably derived from the ascension of "that damned cowboy" Theodore Roosevelt to the presidency and the growing tourist market in the Southwest, well illustrated by the Fred Harvey Company enterprise of escorting visitors to the region and selling a primitivist relationship whereby tourists acquired authenticity by purchasing Navajo blankets and jewelry (see chapter 1). By creating a song that featured a real tribe of this reinvented Southwest, *Navajo* opened the door for more songs about the region.

More important, the lyrics imposed clear racial overtones for the Indian song market, creating another place to introduce racial stereotypes. The Supreme Court case *Plessy v. Ferguson*, which legalized segregation, had been handed down just seven years before *Navajo* debuted. Jim Crow was still working its way into American life, and so-called coon songs of the ragtime era, direct descendants of blackface and minstrel shows, were the embodiment of segregation in popular music. Indeed, the *Navajo* lyrics ask whether or not the Navajo maiden could have a "coon for a beau." Such language linked "second-class" African Americans to Native Americans, reaffirming Anglo-America by denigrating blacks and Indians.[4] Several period newspapers caught on to this when they described *Navajo* as an "Indian coon song."[5] If this was not clear enough to the listener, *Navajo* was the first Indian song to introduce skin color as a descriptor when it described the Navajo maiden as being of a "copper shade" and described her African American lover as a "colored man." It then hit both gender and racial stereotypes when it suggested that an African American would provide her with feathers if there were chickens near so that she would have "lots to wear" including laces, blankets, and jewels.

Navajo's success on the stage led Victor, Edison, and Columbia to all make several versions of the song as recordings. Victor and Edison capitalized on Harry Macdonough's familiarity with Indian songs by having him record it on disc and cylinder. Columbia used Harry Tally for its version. Tally, a tenor from Memphis, Tennessee, had been part of a popular vaudeville quartet before making records. He covered all types of music and worked almost exclusively for Columbia. Additional versions included orchestrations, banjo solos and duets, and a trombone solo, and the song appeared in medley recordings. With the combination of the stage performances and the many recordings, *Navajo* landed in the top twenty for eight straight months from January to August 1904, topping out as number one from March to April, and became the first hit about a specific Indian group from the American West.

Navajo served as a catalyst for new trends in early western recordings by showing other composers that songs about ethnicity and race in the West could make money. Its success also stimulated composers Williams

and Van Alstyne to do more work, most notably 1906's *Cheyenne*, which jump-started the cowboy music craze. *Navajo*'s success also encouraged other composers to create Indian love songs of their own, fortifying that market for another decade. These three themes—ethnic and racial stereotypes, cowboys and cowgirls, and Indian love songs—became the three dominant forms of western music during the talking machine era and were repeated in a variety of formats over the next decade and a half. An overview of each focus provides a glimpse into the proliferation of western themes during the talking machine era.

Historians have long argued that in the period between the Civil War and the Great War many Americans worried about a perceived breakdown in racial and ethnic boundaries that accompanied the end of slavery and Reconstruction, the massive immigration of peoples from southern and eastern Europe and Asia, the end of the frontier, and U.S. expansion into the Pacific. In place of the racial lines that defined antebellum America, it increasingly seemed that these definitions were up for grabs. Many European Americans worried that their traditional "white," Anglo-Saxon, Protestant country was being threatened from without and from within. In reaction, politicians tried to clarify the situation by excluding Chinese immigrants, denying Native Americans citizenship while forcibly assimilating them and their children, limiting African Americans to second-class status, levying taxes on "foreign" miners, and passing anti-miscegenation laws that prohibited different forms of interracial marriage. This period has come to be called the Jim Crow era for the efforts to reassert white dominance.[6]

It is important to note that white and whiteness here are social constructs that do not refer simply to skin color but to the concept of white privilege. Historically, this idea was bounded by a changing invisible barrier that privileged some peoples based on their values,

---

4. C. Vann Woodward, *The Strange Career of Jim Crow*, 2nd ed. (London: Oxford University Press, 1969); Meeks, *Border Citizens*; Gordon, *Great Arizona Orphan Abduction*; Robert C. Toll, *Blacking Up: The Minstrel Show in Nineteenth-Century America* (London: Oxford University Press, 1974).

5. "Portable Dressing Room," *Fort Wayne (Ind.) Journal-Gazette*, January 21, 1904, 3; "At the Theaters," *Minneapolis Journal*, January 15, 1904, 4.

6. Lauren L. Basson, *White Enough to be American? Race Mixing, Indigenous People, and the Boundaries of State and Nation* (Chapel Hill: University of North Carolina Press, 2008); Sucheng Chan, Douglas Henry Daniels, Mario T. Garcia, and Terry P. Wilson, eds., *Peoples of Color in the American West* (Lexington, Mass.: D.C. Heath, 1994); Flamming, *Bound for Glory*; Gordon, *Great Arizona Orphan Abduction*.

beliefs, habits, and attitudes. Thus, those considered white were advantaged, and their cultural practices were not questioned. But those not considered white at this time—including the Irish and many southern Europeans as well as African Americans and Native Americans—were found to be inferior and were subjected to racism.

At the same time that policy makers were working to diminish the power of the excluded ethnic groups, practices such as tourism created fantasies that boosted the cultures of some of these same peoples. For many white Americans who worried that modernity was undermining the country's authenticity, no better remedy existed than to experience the anti-modern in a controlled manner. Some have called this form of primitivism "imperialist nostalgia," a longing for something that you are working to destroy.[7]

Popular music reflected this complex mix of racial domination and curiosity. One of the most popular forms of music at this time was that referred to as the coon song. Derived from antebellum minstrel shows, these songs often featured white performers in blackface, mixing popular ragtime beats with grossly stereotypical portrayals of African Americans as foolish, lazy, and thieving. Along with African Americans, popular music also stereotyped Irish Americans, Jews, Native Americans, Asian Americans, and Mexicans.[8]

The American West served as a complex setting for these trends. As historians of the region have discussed, the West was one of the most ethnically and racially diverse areas of the United States. The region was home to hundreds of different Native American tribes, dozens of European ethnic groups, Africans and African Americans, Asians, Pacific Islanders, Central and South Americans, Canadians, and Mexicans who had immigrated to the region. It should come as no surprise that the meeting of cultures in the West was not well

represented in Tin Pan Alley tunes. Instead, as in the other western songs of the era, eastern songwriters and illustrators projected their own racial stereotypes onto western settings and the western peoples of which they were aware: Native Americans. Indeed, almost every song in this theme featured some kind of interracial love story with a Native American. From the African American/Native American focus of *Navajo* to the Irish/Native American love song *Arrah Wanna* to the Jewish/Indian courtship in *I'm a Yiddish Cowboy*, every one of these recordings reflected eastern concerns about white dominance and miscegenation by suggesting that it was acceptable for all of these other couplings to occur, so long as they did not involve white/Indian relationships. The lone exceptions were the cowboy/Indian romances *Ogalalla* and *Snow Deer*, which told the story of interracial love from an Indian point of view, and *Santiago Flynn*, which denigrated one minority, Mexicans, at the expense of another, the Irish.[9]

The result was a group of western songs that placed eastern racial overtones into music about the West. Indian love songs such as *Navajo* had made racist comments with lyrics describing an Indian maid with a "face of copper shade," but the next group of songs offered even more disparaging racist lyrics and illustrations. The fact that such love songs were also anti-Indian, anti-Irish, anti-Mexican, anti–African American, and anti-Semitic shows just how much these recordings were the product of the era of Jim Crow projected onto the passing frontier of the American West.

The first of these, *Arrah Wanna*, tells the story of Irishman Barney Carney's love for Indian maiden Arrah Wanna. Although this may seem like a strange combination, songs about the Irish at this time were as popular as songs about Indians, so it made sense that a composer brought the two genres together in what he

7. Lears, *No Place of Grace*; Dilworth, *Imagining Indians*.

8. Patricia R. Schroeder, "Passing for Black: Coon Songs and the Performance of Race," *Journal of American Culture* 33, no. 2 (June 2010): 139–53; Pamela Brown Lavitt, "First of the Red Hot Mamas: 'Coon Shouting' and the Jewish Ziegfeld Girl," *American Jewish History* 87, no. 4 (December 1999): 253–90; William H. A. Williams, *'Twas Only an Irishman's Dream* (Bloomington: Indiana University Press, 1996), 193; Mick Molony, "Irish-American Popular Music," in J. J. Lee and Marion R. Casey, eds., *Making the Irish American: History and Heritage of the Irish in the United States* (New York: New York University Press, 2006), 395; Pisani, *Imagining Native America*; Martin Nakata and Karl Neuenfeldt, "From 'Navajo' to 'Taba Naba': Unravelling the Travels and Metamorphosis of a popular Torres Strait Islander Song," in Fiona Magowan and Karl Neuenfeldt, eds., *Landscapes of Indigenous Performance: Music, Song, and Dance of the Torres Strait and Arnhem Land* (Canberra, Australia: Aboriginal Studies Press, 2005).

9. Duane A. Matz, "Images of Indians in American Popular Culture Since 1865" (Ph.D. diss., Illinois State University, 1988), 245–73.

called "An Irish Indian Matrimonial Venture." Indeed, something about the song resonated with the American public, and *Arrah Wanna* may have been one of the most popular Indian songs of the era. It broke into the top twenty in November 1906 and stayed there for the next eight months, hitting the top ten for six of those and climbing to number one in January and February 1907.

Like *Navajo*, the premise of *Arrah Wanna* is the courtship of a young Indian girl by a non-white suitor, thus asserting white dominance by suggesting the acceptability of interrelations between these two "lesser" peoples. Whereas *Navajo* uses a "colored man" to court the Indian maiden, in *Arrah Wanna* the Irishman serenades Arrah Wanna (Arrah was a popular stereotypical name for an Irish girl) outside her "tent" with his bagpipes. Of course there were Irish in the American West going back at least a century, most certainly Irish-Indian marriages, and dozens of popular songs about the Irish and Ireland during the Tin Pan Alley era. But as popular as they were, historian Mick Molony suggests that songs like *Arrah Wanna* "placed the Irish in incongruous situations with exotic 'others.'" This grouping meant that for many in Jim Crow America the Irish were less than white; "as mainstream as the Irish in America had become, they were still not members of the establishment." But as historian Linda Gordon and others suggest, this view of the Irish resided mostly in the metropolitan east, whereas many westerners considered them white.[10]

The lyrics to *Arrah Wanna* intermix stereotypical identities in the first verse, calling the Indian maid a "queen of fairies" and the Irish laddie a "buck." In the chorus, the Irishman promises to build her a "wigwam made of shamrocks green" that will "make those redmen smile." Then in the second verse, Arrah Wanna makes a plea for racial superiority, suggesting that before she will marry Barney "some great race must call you Big Chief," only to have the Irishman cleverly change the meaning by suggesting that his family were all great runners and "first in every race."

Arrah Wanna's tremendous success through much of 1907 led its composers to try something unusual in this era: a sequel. Some period writers had offered instrumental intermezzos to go with vocals, and others had used previous successes to reinvent new songs along similar lines. Recording companies had also capitalized on popular tunes by having different vocalists record them to keep the songs fresh. Still others had remixed the songs into instrumental medleys or as part of a minstrel recording. But a second Irish/Indian song in 1907, *Since Arrah Wanna Married Barney Carney*, was a rare sequel that followed up on the story told in *Arrah Wanna* with a update on the couple that suggests that Irish culture has taken over: the Indians now all have Irish names, they use only green feathers and have wigwams "full of Irish blarney," and their tom-toms all play the "Wearing of the Green."

Rather than sequels, most Tin Pan Alley hit songs bred imitation. In the wake of these Irish/Indian songs, in 1908 two more strange titles appeared promoting interethnic love stories, *Santiago Flynn* and *I'm a Yiddish Cowboy*. The first, *Santiago Flynn*, was a skit based on a song of the same name featuring Len Spencer and Ada Jones, a popular duo who recorded several vaudeville-type acts. Described as a "Spanish-Irish Episode," *Santiago Flynn* tells a story of the love between a supposedly Mexican man and an Irish woman.

Although it is not clear whether the song's opening line —"Way down by the Rio Grande"—is suggesting a setting of Mexico or Texas, it really does not matter from a historical perspective because both places experienced long histories of Irish immigration and settlement. Mexico had invited good Catholic immigrants to help settle its northern borders, and many Irish heeded this call. Irishmen were in Texas as early as the late eighteenth century. The 1850 census listed more than 1,400 Irish in Texas; a century later, more than a half a million Texans claimed Irish ancestry.[11]

Of course, *Santiago Flynn* is not an accurate historical reflection of Irish-Mexican relations but another

10. Williams, *'Twas Only an Irishman's Dream*, 193–94; Molony, "Irish-American Popular Music," 395; Gordon, *Great Arizona Orphan Abduction*; David M. Emmons, *The Butte Irish: Class and Ethnicity in an American Mining Town*, reprint ed. (Champaign-Urbana: University of Illinois Press, 1989).

11. *Handbook of Texas Online*, www.tshaonline.org/handbook, s.v. "Irish" (Phillip L. Fry).

assertion of white dominance through the comical interaction of two people considered less than white in the America of Tin Pan Alley. The song's plot focuses on the interaction between an Irish girl and a denied suitor she assumes is Spanish based on his clothing. When he actually turns out to be an Irishman, she relents and the girl lets him in, suggesting a proper intraethnic coupling and removing the fear of interethnic marriage.

Santiago Flynn represents the imagination of a New Yorker pondering the exotic Borderlands, illustrating the East Coast fascination with America's Orient on the border. It is scandalous, concerned about issues of miscegenation. At the same time, it is titillating, as if it is almost too good a scene not to watch these lesser peoples working through their squabble.

This theme became more complicated later that year when Edison issued Edward Meeker's recording of *I'm a Yiddish Cowboy*, the story of a Jewish cowboy in love with an Indian maiden, and then featured the song on the cover of its November 1908 newsletter. More than simply adding Jews to the list of Americans ridiculed in popular song, the tune reflected a sort of tongue-in-cheek nod to the western genre and the growing power of Jews in the leading sheet music companies and among composers. Indeed, there were 17,000 Jews in the United States prior to the Civil War; by 1900 the population had reached about one million, with half of them residing in New York City.[12] Indeed, so many Jews had replaced the original Germans and Irish involved in popular music, including at some of the bigger firms such as Jerome Remick, Leo Feist, and Harry Von Tilzer, that one writer suggests that "Tin Pan Alley was essentially a Jewish industry." This was not because the musicians had a "Jewish agenda" but simply because they were so numerous.[13]

Tin Pan Alley composers of this time were writing comic dialect songs that perpetuated offensive stereotypes for Hebrew impersonators who performed them on stage. Surviving sheet music songs include 1904's *Oi, Yoi, Yoi, Yoi (A Hebrew Love Song)*, *When Mose with His Nose Leads the Band* (1906), and *Under the Hebrew Moon* (1909). Regular performers sung some of these so-called Jewface songs for recording companies as well. Both Edison and Victor, for example, recorded Ada Jones and Len Spencer's *Becky and Izzy (A Yiddish Courtship)* in 1907.[14]

Jews had been in the American West in significant numbers since the California gold rush. One historian suggests that between 1850 and 1920 more than 300,000 immigrated to the region, first from Germany then from eastern Europe. And although many were pioneering merchants, Jews participated in all walks of life in the West, including being cowboys on the range. Whatever their pursuits, the lyrics and images played on the stereotypical assumption that American Jews were out of place anywhere but New York and that the power of the frontier would make them less Jewish and more American.[15]

The connection between the urban Yiddish stage and the western frontier began in 1895 with a play about two Jewish New York peddlers who meet in Kansas while trading with the local Indians. In 1907, Tin Pan Alley composers Will J. Harris and Harry I. Robinson wrote *Yonkle, the Cow Boy Jew*, and the following year Edgar Leslie, Al Piantodosi, and Halsey K. Mohr wrote the story of "Tough Guy Levi" in *I'm a Yiddish Cowboy*. One scholar believes the song might have been inspired by Jewish Buffalo Bill Wild West star William Levy "Buck" Taylor, the "King of the Cowboys."[16]

A key point in the song occurs when Tough Guy Levi, dressed in cowboy duds and wanting to marry an Indian maiden, sends for a rabbi and then sings his song in his "yiddish dialect." Historian Rachel Rubenstein suggests

12. Jonathan D. Sarna and Jonathan Golden, "The American Jewish Experience in the Twentieth Century: Antisemitism and Assimilation" *National Humanities Center*, http://nationalhumanitiescenter.org/tserve/twenty/tkeyinfo/jewishexp.htm.

13. Jonathan Karp, "Killing Tin Pan Alley: Bob Dylan and the (Jewish) America Experience," *Guilt and Pleasure* 6 (Fall 2007), www.guiltandpleasure.com/index.php?site=rebootgp&page=gp_article&id=62.

14. Jody Rosen, "'Cohen Owes Me Ninety-Seven Dollars': Images of Jews from the Jewish Sheet Music Trade," in Bruce Zuckerman, Josh Kun, and Lisa Ansell, eds., *The Song Is Not the Same: Jews and American Popular Music* (West Lafayette, Ind.: Purdue University Press, 2011), 9–28.

15. Ava F. Kahn, "Looking at America from the West to the East, 1850–1920," in Ava F. Kahn, ed., *Jewish Life in the American West: Perspectives on Migration, Settlement, and Community* (Berkeley, Calif.: Heyday Books, 2002), 13–14; Hasia R. Diner, "American West, New York Jewish," in Kahn, *Jewish Life*, 33–51.

16. Rachel Rubinstein, *Members of the Tribe: Native America in the Jewish Imagination* (Detroit: Wayne State University Press, 2010), 43–46.

that the song shows a "union of warring opposites—cowboy and Indian, mongrel immigrant with 'blue blood' native, the newest American with the oldest," and then summarizes historian Harley Erdman, who wrote that it was "as if in the meeting and mating of these two grotesque anomalies lay all the myriad possibilities of the nation."[17]

A few songs also focused on interracial relationships between Native American women and white cowboys. *Ogalalla*, recorded in 1910, took a different angle on interracial love and threats of miscegenation by suggesting that the Indians became upset about having a white man steal away an Indian girl. It did this using the racist broken English attributed to Native Americans. Set in Mexico on "the Indian reservation," the song tells the story of a cowboy from the North who rides down and steals away the "sweetest girl in all the dusky nation." He explains his love for her simply as "heap much lovee, you love me," and promises to make her "his squaw," much to the chagrin of the chief who gets sore and makes "much war." Three years later, *Snow Deer* would tell a similar story of a cowboy who steals his Indian sweetheart away from her tribe to his ranch.

Songs from this genre shock modern audiences. Far less subtle than *Hiawatha* in terms of racism, Indian songs such as *Navajo, Arrah Wanna, Santiago Flynn, I'm a Yiddish Cowboy, Since Arrah Wanna Married Barney Carney, Ogalalla*, and *Snow Deer* all surprise the modern listener by their overt discrimination. Moreover, their popularity indicates the strength of Jim Crow sentiments in American popular culture of this period. What they say about the West is less clear, other than the fact that the region continued to be an important setting for eastern projections of ethnicity.

The presence of cowboys in these songs reminds us that the image of the man on horseback was also prominent in the talking machine era. But these were not songs from the West penciled by cowpokes in the bunkhouse after a long day on the range but ones written by Tin Pan Alley

writers imagining the passing frontier. Indeed, between 1905 and 1916, seventeen songs featuring cowboys and cowgirls appeared on talking machine cylinders and discs: *Lasca, Cheyenne, Ida-Ho, San Antonio, In the Land of the Buffalo, Broncho Buster, Broncho Bob and His Little Cheyenne, When It's Moonlight on the Prairie, Pride of the Prairie, My Rancho Maid, Denver Town, My Pony Boy, A Cowboy Romance, Ragtime Cow Boy Joe, At That Bully Wooly Wild West Show, In the Golden West*, and *Way Out Yonder in the Golden West*. At the same time, music companies published sheet music illustrated with colorful cover art depicting the stories presented in each song.

The first cowboy record was not even a song but the recitation of the first cowboy poem, Edgar L. Davenport's "Lasca." British immigrant Frank Depresz composed the ode in 1882 after a three-year stay in Texas. A London literary magazine published it that fall, and within a few years American newspapers reprinted it.[18] The poem tells the story of a Mexican girl named Lasca and her cowboy sweetheart. Set during a cattle drive on the Rio Grande in Texas, its opening stanza befits any western story: "I want free life and I want free air, and I sigh after the canter of cattle." Caught in a stampede, the cowboy and his girl race ahead on a mustang, only to be caught by the herd. Desperate, he shoots his horse, hoping to use the carcass as a shield from the oncoming stampede, but finds that the steed's fall has also killed Lasca. The poem ends after the cowboy has buried his love, "in Texas, down by the Rio Grande."

Davenport recited an edited version of "Lasca" for a two-minute Edison cylinder in the summer of 1905 and for a Victor disc a year later. Along with his father and sister, he was part of a famous acting family and had a "powerful baritone that registered quite well with the acoustical [recording] process." He used that voice, recording twenty-one different pieces for Edison, Victor, and Columbia between 1905 and 1913.

The cowboy record craze began when Billy Murray made the Victor recording of *Cheyenne* in 1906, in Philadelphia. Murray was the most popular singer in the acoustic talking machine era, making thousands

---

17. Ibid., 45–46.
18. The earliest publication on Newspaper.com is "Lasca," *Newark (Ohio) Advocate*, January 29, 1883, 2.

of recordings including covers of the songs of George M. Cohan such as *Give My Regards to Broadway* and *Yankee Doodle Boy*. He had a unique tonal quality that reproduced well in the acoustic era, so that his records are very clear. As noted in chapter 1, Murray, the so-called Denver Nightingale, had been raised in Denver and supposedly was "well acquainted with both Indians and Cowboys."[19]

Written by the same composing team who had written *Navajo*, Harry Williams and Egbert Van Alstyne, *Cheyenne* began life on stage in the two-act music comedy *The Earl and the Girl* in 1905. It then ran concurrently in England and New York, with the American version starring comedian Eddie Foy.[20]

Although sometimes characterized as an Indian song or part of the Indian craze, *Cheyenne* did not include any reference to Cheyenne Indians but was instead a love story between a cowboy and a cowgirl known as Shy Ann.[21] In fact, the cowboy-cowgirl relationship story line clearly recounted a scene from Owen Wister's novel in which the Virginian rescues the schoolmarm. In the Tin Pan Alley version, the cowboy asks Shy Ann to "hop up on his pony" so he can take her to Old Cheyenne to get married. The Victor recording added to the story with western sound effects including whoops, yells, wind, gunshots, and horses. All of these efforts catapulted the song into the public eye. It made the top twenty in April 1906, cracked the top ten the following month, and then rose to number three in June that year. It remained in the top five throughout the summer and did not fade until November.

Cheyenne's success spurred the creation of similar songs almost immediately, including a *Cheyenne March and Two-Step* and *Cheyenne Medley*. In December 1906, Billy Murray even recorded a parody of the song inspired by Upton Sinclair's popular muckraking novel *The Jungle*

set in Chicago's meatpacking area. This time Murray told the tale of a sick horse bound for the slaughterhouse, thankfully sans sound effects.[22] A comparison of the choruses illustrates the point that sometimes imitation is not the sincerest form of flattery:

Original	*Parody*
Shy Ann, Shy Ann, hop on my pony,	Cheyenne, Cheyenne, you sick old pony
There's room here for two dear,	We'll take you, And bake you
But after the ceremony,	And make you into baloney
We'll both ride back home dear, as one,	And the folks who eat you won't know
On my pony from old Cheyenne.	You're that pony from old Cheyenne.

Cheyenne's popularity also prompted other Tin Pan Alley songwriters to produce copycat cowboy songs. In fact, just eight days after recording the parody, Murray recorded for Victor *Ida-Ho*, another love song about a cowboy and his cowgirl sweetheart. Unlike *Cheyenne*, *Ida-Ho* had no stage connection; it was written specifically for the recording industry. Nevertheless, the new song basically told the same story of a cowboy pursuing his cowgirl and once again played a pun with a western place name. Edison, which had never recorded *Cheyenne*, jumped into the cowboy craze by having Murray record a copy of *Ida-Ho*, accompanied by the Edison Male Quartet, for its cylinder business. Soon after, an instrumental two-step version appeared specifically for dancing.

An interesting comparison can be made between the sheet music covers of *Cheyenne* and *Ida-Ho*. Both feature images of the New Woman emerging in the early twentieth century. *Cheyenne* pictures a rough-and-tumble independent cowgirl, whip in hand, riding astride

---

19. Jim Walsh suggests that Victor catalogue editor Sam Rous had asked Murray if he had a nickname that could be published and Murray "facetiously replied that it might be appropriate to call him a 'Rocky Mountain Canary,'" the name given to mules who worked in western mines. Rous instead thought of Jenny Lind's nickname, the "Swedish Nightingale," and started referring to Murray as the "Denver Nightingale." See Walsh, "'Cowboy Song' Recordings," Part 2, *Hobbies*, May 1976, 35–36.

20. Armond Fields, *Eddie Foy: A Biography of the Early Popular Stage Comedian* (Jefferson, N.C.: 2009), 161–64; *Wikipedia*, s.v. "The Earl and the Girl."

21. The inside cover of the March 15, 1906, issue *Talking Machine World* ran an advertisement for the American Record Company's version of Cheyenne depicting a cowboy and an Indian maiden riding on a horse. See http://archive.org/details/talkingmachinewo2bill.

22. Billy Murray, *Cheyenne—Parody* (Victor Talking Machine, 1906), 78 disc #4974. *Library of Congress, National Jukebox*, www.loc.gov/jukebox/recordings/detail/id/6119/, s.v. "Cheyenne: Parody."

a galloping horse with several distant cowboys in hot pursuit. *Ida-Ho* depicts more of the athletic Gibson Girl image, with a cowgirl in long skirt, long-sleeve blouse, kerchief, and leather gauntlets waving a cowboy hat.[23] Of course, neither image really has anything to do with its associated song. In *Cheyenne*, Shy Ann rides up to the cowboy and they ride away together to get married. In *Ida-Ho*, Ida is described as "wild as any injun" and goes "dashing cross the plains," leaving her cowboy to beg for her not to run away. It is almost as if the two cover girls are reversed.

Period descriptions called *Ida-Ho* a "breezy catchy two step typifying the true life of the Western Cowboy" and indicated that the horse's hoofbeats and cowboy yells made it realistic. Likewise, *Edison Phonograph Monthly* described it as "the 'melodious cyclone' that is sweeping the country."[24] Despite these accolades, *Ida-Ho* did not break into the top twenty.

Although the West is usually imagined as the home of tough guys, nearly all the cowboy songs of the talking machine era also depicted tough, independent western women. Most western states and territories had passed women's suffrage by this time, and thousands of women had also taken advantage of the Homestead Act and other federal land programs to settle in the West. Thus, the cowgirls depicted here in lyrics and sheet music covers were more like the New Woman, the Gibson Girl, or the Virginian's love interest—the independent and resourceful Molly Stark Wood—than a submissive doting bride.[25]

Following *Cheyenne*'s success, songwriters Williams and Van Alstyne published another cowboy song, *San Antonio*, in 1907. This was also a cowboy love song, although this time one cowboy tells his forlorn friend about how his girl has "hopped up on a pony," then left him for another man. *Variety* magazine described the song as "absolutely the greatest of all cowboy songs. A hit the world over."[26]

Billy Murray made several recordings of *San Antonio* in 1907, all accompanied by orchestra. Victor recorded its version as a one-sided eight-inch disc. Edison released its two-minute cylinder version with the Edison Male Quartet as backup. The *Edison Phonograph Monthly* reported that the sheet music's popularity had continued to the recording industry when it said that the "new cowboy song . . . has rapidly achieved popularity from coast to coast. As a Record it is exceptionally entertaining and tuneful."[27]

San Antonio's popularity also derived from its inclusion in other formats including "minstrels" and instrumentals. The former were a type of entourage recording based on a segment of a minstrel or vaudeville show. These often included a small group of performers who sang a chorus of a new or popular song, told a few jokes, and then one member sang a verse and chorus of another song. Columbia, Busy Bee Records, and Victor all released versions of *San Antonio* as minstrel recordings.

Instrumental medleys also popularized such recordings. For these, a band played a medley of three to five tunes as an instrumental version. Columbia produced such a record in its July 1907 *San Antonio Medley*, followed by an Edison release the next month called the *Poor John Medley*, which included *San Antonio*. These instrumentals continued the cowboy music craze and elevated *San Antonio* into Gardner's reconstructed top twenty between March and October of 1907, including a month as the number one hit that May.

Victor's release of *Broncho Buster* by Harry Tally in October 1907 suggests that the genre was still hot. Although Tally had popularized *Navajo* three years earlier, this release was unusual in a couple of ways. First, with lyrics by ASCAP (American Society of Composers, Authors, and Publishers) charter member Edward Madden and music by his wife and singer Dorothy "Dolly" Jardon, *Broncho Buster* was the first cowboy song with music written by a woman. Second, unlike nearly

---

23. "The Gibson Girl's America: Drawings by Charles Dana Gibson," *Library of Congress, Exhibitions*, www.loc.gov/exhibits/gibson-girls-america.
24. Quoted in Walsh, "'Cowboy Song' Recordings, Part 4," *Hobbies*, July 1976, 36; *Edison Phonograph Monthly* 4, no. 12 (February 1907), 2, 11.
25. Stephen Tatum, "Pictures (Facing) Words," in Melody Graulich and Stephen Tatum, eds., *Reading the Virginian in the New West* (Lincoln: University of Nebraska Press, 2003), 1–38.
26. *Variety* 6, no. 3 (March 30, 1907): 20, quoted in Tinsley, *For a Cowboy*, 6.
27. *Edison Phonograph Monthly* 5, no. 1 (March 1907), 9.

every other western song of the era, it was written in a minor key, giving it a gloomier feeling. Third, its cover art looks like an illustration of Frederic Remington's famous "Broncho Buster" sculpture, and its very title suggests the popular image of a cowboy taming a wild horse. The lyrics, though, present a story of a cowgirl coercing her beau and a parson to marry them—at gunpoint! The New Woman of *Cheyenne* and *Ida-Ho* was one thing, but perhaps this level of female independence was simply too much for this time and explains why the song never cracked the top twenty.

In 1907, Harry Williams and Egbert Van Alstyne, who composed the hits *Navajo*, *Cheyenne*, and *San Antonio*, released their third cowboy song, *In the Land of the Buffalo*, with cover art that featured a lone cowboy on the plains silhouetted against a crescent moon. Its lyrics matched the scene with this beautiful description: "In the land of the buffalo, where the western breezes blow, where the goodnight kiss of sunshine, sets all the plains aglow." Billy Murray recorded the song for Edison in August and Victor in September 1907, but despite the cover art, notable phrasing, and Murray's popularity the song had mixed reviews. *Edison Phonograph Monthly* described it as a "fine, swinging cowboy song by the composers of the exceedingly popular 'San Antonio' . . . and sung in Mr. Murray's best style. It is certain to be very much liked. These cowboy songs strike a note of originality that is very refreshing." The Victor supplement, however, described it as a "semi-pathetic cowboy song which seems to possess all the elements of a popular success—some breezy Western humor, a touch of pathos and a pretty melody."[28] Perhaps because of this mixed description, the song never cracked the top twenty and marked the last cowboy tune by Williams and Van Alstyne.

Edison finally made its version of *Cheyenne* in the autumn of 1907 with the two-minute cylinder *Broncho Bob and His Little Cheyenne*, which featured the powerful baritone voice of Len Spencer and the singing of Ada Jones. Spencer wrote these so-called vaudeville specialties, and he and Jones recorded several of them between 1905 and 1910, with Jones concluding each bit singing a popular chorus. Available also as either a Columbia disc or cylinder or Victor ten-inch disc, *Broncho Bob* was never reproduced as sheet music. The recording basically tells the story of *Cheyenne*'s lyrics where a cowboy named Broncho Bob meets his sweetheart Shy Ann and convinces her to ride off with him to get married. At the end, Ada Jones sings the *Cheyenne* chorus up tempo. This was the first recording of a cowboy song by a woman. Full of sound effects, this recording marked Edison's only attempt to sell a *Cheyenne* version.[29]

The most popular early songs focused on places such as Cheyenne, San Antonio, and Idaho, but newer ones included lyrics about prairies and ponies. On one level this simply was easy wordplay because, for instance, "prairie" rhymed with "Mary" and "pony" with "Tony." On another level, though, this focus reflected the growth of twentieth-century farming in the American West. Passage of the Newlands Act in 1902 enabled federal water development, and the Enlarged Homestead Act of 1909, which doubled farm size, created a new land rush to the West. Contrary to popular belief, more homesteaders filed land claims after 1900 than before, many of them on the high prairies east of the Rockies on lands formerly used for grazing. The increased size of these new prairie farms required mechanization to be successful. At the same time, the introduction of the Model T in 1908 and the growing automobile craze, combined with the ever-growing railroad network, furthered fossil fuel use and displaced horses. One result of this transformation was a rise in western heritage tourism, especially dude ranches, where easterners could travel cross-country to ride horses and play cowboy for fun. Another was increased use of prairies and ponies in the era's newest cowboy songs.[30]

In 1908, Harry Breen and George Botsford capitalized

---

28. " The New Edison Gold Moulded Records Advance List for October 1907," *Edison Phonograph Monthly* 5, no. 6 (August 1907), 4; Victor quote from Walsh, "'Cowboy Song, Recordings, Part 4," *Hobbies*, July 1976, 35.

29. Gracyk, *Popular American Recording Pioneers*, 183–98, 314–19.

30. White, *"It's Your Misfortune,"* 435–39; Rothman, *Devil's Bargains*, 113–42; Peter J. Blodgett, ed., *Motoring West*, vol. 1: *Automobile Pioneers, 1900–1909* (Norman: University of Oklahoma Press, 2015).

on these trends with *Pride of the Prairie*, published by the Jerome H. Remick Company. Jim Walsh calls it "one of the best of all cowboy songs." Set on the "wild and wooly prairie" near Pueblo, Colorado, the lyrics retold the now familiar story of *Cheyenne* and other songs about a cowboy stealing his beautiful cowgirl love away by having her jump up on his horse. It was reported that the sheet music sold more than 300,000 copies, and Victor, its off-brand Zon-o-phone, Edison, and Columbia all made versions of it.[31]

According to Jim Walsh, Columbia "boldly proclaimed it to be the best cowboy song thus published." A company advertisement in *Talking Machine World* featured a cowboy on horseback and noted that *Pride of the Prairie* was one of the "the first records. . . that have waked up Broadway." It then described *Pride of the Prairie* as the "best song of the Western plains that has been produced" and that its "broad swing of 'cowboy' music" was "rapidly becoming the leading feature of the big music successes in New York."[32] Likewise, *Edison Phonograph Monthly* noted that the song was heard "in vaudeville, in illustrated songs at the moving picture shows; the bands took it up in the parks and passed it on to the orchestras on excursion boats. It is just the stripe of song that starts the gallery whistling."[33] Despite these many accolades, Gardner does not include the song on any list.

The final cowboy song of the decade, 1909's *My Pony Boy*, was probably the biggest western hit to emerge from the talking machine era. It has spanned generations and played on the widest variety of venues, including a 1908 Ziegfeld show, a 1931 Krazy Kat cartoon, a 1950s television commercial for juice concentrate, as a character name in the 1967 S. E. Hinton novel *The Outsiders*, and even rocker Bruce Springsteen's 1992 album *Human Touch*.

My Pony Boy tells the story of a handsome cowboy, Tony, who is loved by all the girls. A "fluffy ruffle girl," perhaps a tourist or a visitor to a dude ranch, visits from New York and falls in love with the cowboy hero, whose "heart was lassoed" until she wants to take him home and he refuses. The chorus line "marry me, carry me, right away with you," and the whole song, for that matter, clearly harkened back to *Cheyenne* and *The Virginian*.

Ziegfeld used *My Pony Boy* in a 1909 play, and it became an instant hit. Advertisements for the sheet music raved about the song. One suggested that it was "without doubt one of the greatest cowboy songs published. It is being sung, played, and whistled *everywhere throughout the East*.[34] Another called it the "most contagious song that ever happened" and that "you can't dodge it. My Pony Boy is in the air wherever you go." That newspaper stated that it made "everybody more cheerful and happy" and was a "romantic ballad of the plains" because it was "inspiring, full of 'dash' and 'go'" before finally concluding that the song should also appeal to piano players because it was "easy to play—easy to sing—hard to forget."[35]

My Pony Boy also became a hit record. In the fall of 1909, Columbia reported to *Talking Machine World* that the song was the "best selling record" for August.[36] Indeed, *My Pony Boy* and *San Antonio* were the only other cowboy songs of the talking machine era listed by Gardner as number one. Victor also capitalized on the song's popularity by adding it to a medley disc. Curiously, like *Cheyenne*, Edison never made a recording of *My Pony Boy*.

By late spring 1909 the cowboy song had again become entrenched in American culture, and *My Pony Boy* proved that by going back to the basic cowboy love song of *Cheyenne* and setting it to a catchy new tune one could again catch lightning in a bottle. In April that year, singers Billy Murray, Will Oakland, John H. Bieling, and W. F. Hooley joined together as a new combination called the Premier Quartet and chose for their first release a new cowboy love song, *Denver Town*, which became a minor hit that summer. Harry J. Breen and George Botsford, the same team who created *Pride of the Prairie*,

31. Walsh, "'Cowboy Song' Recordings, Part 5," *Hobbies*, August 1976, 35; *Variety* 13, no. 1 (December 12, 1908), 4.

32. Walsh, "'Cowboy Song' Recordings, Part 5," *Hobbies*, August 1976, 53; "Columbia Records," *Talking Machine World* 4, no. 3 (March 15, 1908), 39.

33. *Edison Phonograph Monthly* 6, no. 8 (August 1908), 16.

34. "New 'My Pony Boy' 'Giddy up—Giddy up—Whoa,'" *Indianapolis News*, April 20, 1909, 16, emphasis added; see also "Sheet Music, 9¢," *Brooklyn (N.Y.) Daily Eagle*, May 16, 1909, 5.

35. "My Pony Boy," *Harrisburg (Pa.) Telegram*, August 29, 1909, 3.

36. "Indianapolis Happenings," *Talking Machine World* 5, no. 8 (September 15, 1909), 18.

This Edison advertisement called "The Last Roundup" captures the popularity of the cowboy during the talking machine era. It appeared in the May 1909 issue of the trade magazine *Edison Phonograph Monthly.* Author's collection.

wrote the song. The lyrics retold *The Virginian* meeting tale as the story of a Colorado ranchman out riding who is passed by a beautiful girl who falls from her pony, is helped up by the cowboy, and then rides away, only to be caught by the fellow and made his bride. The writers also produced another tear-jerker of a line that shows up on André De Takacs's striking winter sheet music cover: "Tell your pony that your heart is lonely, he'll take you

flying into Denver town."

The May 1909 issue of *Edison Phonograph Monthly* confirmed that the cowboy music craze was in full swing. In a page headed "The Last Roundup," Edison used an image depicting three cowboys in full Wild West regalia listening to an Edison Home Phonograph with a crane and a large horn with a smattering of cylinder boxes nearby. It reminds one of a modern Docker's ad, with men sitting around being men. The text in the ad had nothing to do with cowboys or the West but simply used the ongoing popularity and iconography of cowboys to present an alternative to the growing competition from Victor and Columbia disc records.[37] It is fascinating to think that the company that invented recorded music turned to the nostalgic past of the Wild West to sell its modern machines.

Despite this ad, within two years the cowboy craze seemed to be winding down. It had been five years since *Cheyenne* and *San Antonio* first made it big and three since *My Pony Boy*'s popularity. In the meantime, America had become enmeshed in the ragtime boom, illustrated by the popular 1911 Irving Berlin tune *Alexander's Ragtime Band* as sung by Murray on Edison cylinders and Collins and Harlan on Victor. In fact, ragtime had been a popular form of music since Scott Joplin's 1899 hit *Maple Leaf Rag*, but the momentum was picking up as Berlin's tune spawned other rags such as *The Ragtime Goblin Man*, *In Ragtime Land*, *Ragtime Soldier Man*, *Ragtime in the Air*, and the most popular *Ragtime Violin* and *Ragging the Baby to Sleep*.[38] Perhaps the public simply was tiring of *The Virginian* love songs, or maybe the new rags just resonated better with them.

The differences between the two types of popular music could not have been more clear. The best-selling cowboy songs longed for a nostalgic, rural America where white cowboys on horses carried away their sweethearts. Ragtime, a predecessor to jazz, was urban, influenced by African American music, democratic, and innovative. Cowboy songs seemed to tell stories of the frontier past, whereas ragtime presented modern America. With ragtime's syncopation gaining popularity, what was needed was a song that grafted the cowboy's popularity onto a ragtime score.[39]

The 1912 hit song *Ragtime Cow Boy Joe* did just this and revived the talking machine era cowboy craze by appropriating a title and words that seemed to draw from both popular genres. Technically neither ragtime nor cowboy, the song came to be associated with each music type and, like *My Pony Boy*, has enjoyed tremendous success as a hit song for big bands, crooners, movie stars, and even the Chipmunks. The chorus has even been adopted by universities as their school fight song, most notably by my alma mater, the University of Wyoming. As a basketball player there in the mid-1980s, I learned the unusual phrases in the song, especially the one adapted for Wyoming, about the "high falutin', rootin'-tootin', son-of-a-gun from Old Wyoming, Ragtime Cowboy Joe." As incongruous as it may be, there's really nothing like hearing 15,000 people singing that at a basketball game to cheer on their team.

Three Tin Pan Alley songwriters, Grant Clarke, Lewis F. Muir, and Maurice Abrahams, penned the tune in 1912 after seeing Abrahams' four-year-old nephew Joseph all dressed up in a cowboy costume with boots and a big hat. As noted, the writers drew from both western and ragtime ideas in the song. The cowboy elements included the new state of Arizona, herding cattle and sheep, gunplay, and the popularity of dance halls. Ragtime influences included Joe's ability to sing "raggy music to the cattle," his horse's "syncopated gaited" pace as the cowboy "swings back and forward in the saddle," and the "funny meter to the roar" of his gun. There is also a line about Joe being a "ragtime bear" on the dance floor, most likely a reference to the Irving Berlin/George Botsford 1910 song *The Grizzly Bear*, which became a big dance hit after Fanny Brice performed it in the 1911 Ziegfeld Follies.[40]

Several artists recorded *Ragtime Cow Boy Joe* before the Great War, including "Ragtime" Bob Roberts, Edward Meeker, and baritone Ed Morton. An instrumental version also appeared in the 1913 medley *Here Comes My Daddy Now* played by the National Promenade Band.

---

37. "The Edison Phonograph," *Edison Phonograph Monthly* 7, no. 5 (May 1909), 10.

38. Charles Hamm, *Irving Berlin: Songs from the Melting Pot, the Formative Years, 1907–1914* (Cambridge: Oxford University Press, 1997), 102–36. Two stories on National Public Radio, one about Irving Berlin and another about *Alexander's Ragtime Band*, provide good context for the popularity of ragtime. For the Irving Berlin piece, see www.npr.org/artists/15744000/irving-berlin; for the song, see www.npr.org/2000/03/20/1071829/alexanders-ragtime-band. A search for "ragtime" at the *UCSB Cylinder Audio Archive*, http://cylinders.library.ucsb.edu, revealed 123 recordings.

39. Jasen and Jones, *That American Rag*, xxi–xxxix.

40. "Hello, Frisco! Ragtime Songs," *The Frederick Hodges Website*, www.frederickhodges.com/hellofriscolinernotes.html. Recall that Botsford wrote the music for *Pride of the Prairie*.

These efforts made the song a minor hit, reaching the charts between September 1912 and February 1913 after peaking at number eleven in October 1912. Ironically, the song became a bigger hit in England after Alf Gordon, a.k.a. "Arizona Jack," recorded a version for the British "Cinch" record label in spring 1913. Gordon, a comedian, baritone, and prolific recorder of songs, could be considered the British version of Billy Murray.

A few more nostalgic songs about the West appeared before 1917, but none of them were very popular. By the time the United States entered the Great War, the cowboy music craze had ended.

Although *Navajo* had opened the possibilities in 1904 of adding questions of race and region to recorded music about the American West, simpler Indian love songs that harkened back to the earlier hits *Hiawatha* and *Anona* remained mainstays through the first two decades of the century. Like the many cowboy songs, Indian love songs suggested a simpler, more primitivist West. Tin Pan Alley songwriters imagined the Indian as part of a passing tableau, with such music mere glances into a romanticized, idyllic past. These tunes reflected a continued fascination with Native America through a more subtle racism than the overt bigotry of *Navajo*. Since assimilation was the assumed fate of Native Americans, many considered such tunes authentic representations of Native cultures. And like the cowboy songs, they often conveyed messages of middle-class domesticity in which Indian maidens tended house for their warrior braves.[41]

With the exception of *Red Wing*, the songs have mostly been forgotten. Others from before World War I include *Feather Queen*, *Silver Heels*, *Iola*, *Reed Bird*, *Topeka*, *Rainbow*, *Blue Feather*, *Lily of the Prairie*, *My Prairie Song Bird*, *Silver Bell*, *Valley Flower*, *Silver Star*, and *Golden Deer*. Many were offered as both vocal songs and instrumental intermezzos. Like the cowboy

songs, composers sometimes wrote multiple pieces if a previous song succeeded. Sheet music illustrators also flourished, with *Reed Bird*, *Red Wing*, and *Blue Feather* providing some of the most popular images. The *Red Wing* cover, with its beautiful maiden wearing a rainbow-colored headdress, continues to this day to be sold as an art poster. These songs also found their way to some of the era's most productive and popular recording artists, including Billy Murray, Ada Jones, Harry Tally, Harry Macdonough, and Arthur Collins. All in all, the music and recordings showed that the Indian love song remained fertile ground for the early music industry.

Silver Heels, written by *Hiawatha* composer Neil Moret and lyricist James O'Dea, was just such an Indian love song. After Moret, a.k.a. Charlie Daniels, had achieved success with *Hiawatha*, the Jerome Remick music publishing house hired him as a publishing executive and encouraged him to find more such songs. The firm published *Navajo* in 1904, and then in 1905, caught up in the Indian craze themselves, Moret and O'Dea teamed again to write *Silver Heels*.

Although it lacks the interracial ambiguities of *Navajo*, the *Silver Heels* love story between an "Indian brave" and the "sweetest and the neatest little girl" clearly has overtones of assimilation and domesticity. During the chorus, for example, the young chief suggests that he will build Silver Heels "a big teepee" if she comes to cook his meals. Then, during the second verse, he suggests that the two of them will be "right at home" with a "hubby and chubby little papoose on her knee." The artificial Indian speech in lines such as "heap much kissing" suggests a derogatory attitude toward Native Americans rather than the admiration Moret purported at the time.[42]

Ironically, some in the period press praised *Silver Heels* for its authenticity. One California newspaper noted that its composition was "founded upon the Sioux style of chant" and that its "Indian aroma" was "pregnant

41. "Indian Maidens: Tin Pan Alley Sings Indian Love Songs," *Parlor Songs Academy*, http://parlorsongs.com/issues/2006–6/thismonth/feature.php. See also Deloria, *Playing Indian*; Pisani, *Imagining Native America*; Matz, "Images of Indians"; and Walsh, "Indian Songs on Edison Cylinders," Parts 1, 2, 3, *Hobbies*, April–June 1977.

42. Pisani, *Imagining Native America*, 248–54, discusses the significance of what he calls "fake Indian speech."

with all the glamor of the Wigwam—the fire dance, the holocaust, and the triumphal march of conquest."[43]

Like many of these Indian love songs, the fact that recording companies issued both instrumental and vocal versions of *Silver Heels* contributed to its success. Popular vocalist Harry Tally recorded it for Victor in 1906 and Columbia and Edison featured instrumental versions. The song made the top twenty between December 1905 and April 1906, peaking at number six in February 1906. That fall, *Edison Phonograph Monthly* listed the title among its "250 Good Selling Edison Records."[44]

Red Wing, though, is by far the most popular Indian love song ever. Its 1907 melody actually derived from composer Robert Schumann's "The Happy Farmer Returning from His Work" from his 1848 piece *Album for the Young*.[45] But there is more to the song than just this long history. Although *Red Wing* features a story of battle and loss, it does so in a major key, making the music light and seemingly happy. It also stays clear of references to skin color, making its message more palatable over time.

Red Wing also benefited from its popular composer and beautiful sheet music cover. Composer Frederick Allen "Kerry" Mills had trained with Florenz Ziegfeld Sr., the father of the famous showman, taught music, and became famous for two previous songs, his 1899 vaudeville cakewalk *At a Georgia Camp Meeting* and his 1904 song *Meet Me in St. Louis, Louis* about the World's Fair.[46] The sheet music cover by artist Joseph Hirt is easily the most beautiful created during this time with its colorful profile of an attractive Native American woman.

A catchy tune, an interesting composer story, and beautiful graphics helped *Red Wing* become a popular piece. In 1907–1908, Edison, Victor, and Columbia each produced an instrumental and a vocal version of *Red Wing*. Seven more recordings made over the next four years helped to land *Red Wing* in Gardner's top twenty

from November 1907 to May 1908, peaking at number three in March 1908.

A couple of other Indian love songs became big hits during their day but are today lost to history. One of these is the 1908 Percy Wenrich and Alfred Bryan song *Rainbow*. Billy Murray recorded it twice that year, once with the Hadyn Quartet and again with Ada Jones. Set not on the prairie but under a palm tree, *Rainbow* tells the typical tale of love between a chief and a "pretty maiden of a copper shade." Its lyrics, though, seem upbeat, especially the chorus, which ends with "In rain or sunshine, my Rainbow, Keep your love light aglow, I love you so, my sweet Rainbow." The combination of the many recordings as well as the star power of Murray and Jones made *Rainbow* successful, landing it in the top twenty for five months, from July to November 1908. *Edison Phonograph Monthly* raved about the tune, suggesting that the vocal was "sweeping the country," the song "destined to be as popular as 'Hiawatha,'" with the instrumental's popularity "none the less enduring."[47]

Percy Wenrich followed *Rainbow*'s success the next year with another hit, *Silver Bell*, which also made appeals to domesticity and assimilation. Although the song's lyrics contain few references to specific Indian items (e.g., "lonely little Indian maid" and "chieftain longing to woo" while "paddling his tiny canoe"), its sheet music cover was the first to show an Indian couple rather than just the girl.

For the recording, Edison featured the popular duet of Ada Jones and Billy Murray along with a novel technique that featured a bell solo with violin accompaniment between each chorus. Even better, Murray sang a few bars of *Home, Sweet Home* while Jones was singing the *Silver Bell* lyrics. This use of a countermelody clearly suggested the broader theme of domesticity in these Indian love songs and was popular as well. *Edison Phonograph Monthly* suggested that the song would "vie with the biggest sellers we have ever

43. "New Musical Composition," *Santa Cruz (Calif.) Sentinel*, December 20, 1905, 11; see also "New Musical Work by 'Hiawatha's' Author," *Washington Post*, September 24, 1905, 3; "A Musical Hit," *Minneapolis Journal*, November 26, 1905, 5.

44. "A Jobber's List of 250 Good Selling Edison Records," *Edison Phonograph Monthly* 4, no. 9 (November 1906), 20.

45. Guy Logsdon, *"The Whorehouse Bells Were Ringing" and Other Songs Cowboys Sing* (Champaign-Urbana: University of Illinois Press, 1995), 207–10.

46. Bill Edwards, "Frederick Allen 'Kerry' Mills," *RagPiano*, www.perfessorbill.com/comps/famills.shtml.

47. "Advance List of Edison Standard (Two Minute) and Edison Amberola (Four Minute) Records for February 1909," and "Selling the Goods," both in *Edison Phonograph Monthly* 6, no. 12 (December 1908), 17, 9.

cataloged," and the prediction came true.[48] Five different record companies made almost a dozen different versions of the song between 1910 and 1914, helping *Silver Bell* crack the top-twenty list from October 1910 to April 1911 and reach number six in January and February 1911.

Since *Hiawatha* had become a hit in 1903, Indian love songs remained a popular genre for early recorded music for more than a decade. Looking at them collectively, some broad themes emerge, including the music and internal rhyme schemes, lyrics that generalized all Native American life, a focus on assumed domestic practices and the presumption of assimilation, the generic cover art work, and the recording artists and their styles. At the same time, all of these songs suggest a stereotypical, racist attitude toward Native American life. With their references to skin color, assumptions about gender roles, and stereotypical cover art images, these so-called Indian love songs really had nothing to do with Native Americans or love; they were simply fantasy projections made by white Americans to assert their perceived dominance.

Every song thus far reviewed here that depicted Native Americans misrepresented them. From the noble savage tropes of the sweet Indian maiden and her brave warrior to the interethnic love stories between Irishmen and Indians to the romantic Red Men of *Hiawatha*, recording companies in the talking machine era stereotyped Native Americans as a dying people soon to be extinct or needing to be retrofitted into their secondary place in American culture. But that is not all. In so-called comic songs, recording companies expanded these stereotypes to include songs that portrayed Indians as dumb, drunken, and bloodthirsty. Other composers contributed to Indianist songs in which whites reinterpreted authentic Native American music or even cleansed it of its "savagery" for repackaging to white audiences. Much more than the romanticized fantasies of Indian love songs, the final collection to be reviewed not only intentionally misrepresented Indian life but did

so in an openly hostile way that probably best represents the cultural forces Native Americans faced in Jim Crow America.[49]

The comic song *Sitting Bull* first appeared in the 1905 stage musical *The Wizard of Oz* and basically ridiculed the name of the Hunkpapa Sioux holy man. Oz creator L. Frank Baum had collaborated with composer Paul Tietjens to turn the popular book into a musical play, which debuted in 1901 and was very different from the later 1939 movie. After several years of success, it was revived in 1904 with new songs and dances. More numbers were added the following year, including composer Vincent Bryan's song *Sitting Bull*.[50]

For the 1905 version of play, costar Fred Stone, who played the Scarecrow, added *Sitting Bull* to "The Dance of All Nations" number in which he sang the tune while dressed as an Indian chief surrounded "by a chorus of girls dressed as Mexicans, cowgirls, and squaws." Following this, Stone performed the "Green Corn Dance," a strenuous, "spineless, or loose-limbed dance" that became popular with the public and boosted the song with it. One newspaper described the piece as an "Indian war dance in which he [Stone] impersonates Sitting Bull with a scintillating background of pretty girls, garbed as cowboy and Indian squaws."[51] Bryan's lyrics poke fun at the name "Sitting Bull," connect scalping to barbering, suggest that the holy man hated the Indian police, and state that his portrait adorned the penny.

An interesting connection does exist between the actual Sitting Bull and *Wizard of Oz* creator L. Frank Baum. From January 1890 to March 1891, Baum lived in Aberdeen, South Dakota, where he published a small newspaper called the *Saturday Pioneer* and reported and editorialized on the Ghost Dance movement then occurring in western South Dakota. On December 20, 1890, Baum wrote an editorial after Sitting Bull's death that first reviewed the white man's conquest of the plains as justification for the Holy Man's attitude. He wrote,

48. "Edison Amberol Records for December, 1910," *Edison Phonograph Monthly* 8, no. 10 (October 1910), 16.

49. These stereotypes are discussed at *Authentichistory.com*, http://www.authentichistory.com/diversity/stereotyping.html. See also Matz, "Images of Indians," 245–73.

50. Mark Evan Swartz, *Oz before the Rainbow: L. Frank Baum's* The Wonderful Wizard of Oz *on Stage and Screen to 1939* (Baltimore: Johns Hopkins University Press, 2000); Robert M. Utley, *The Lance and the Shield: The Life and Times of Sitting Bull* (New York: Random House, 1994).

51. Swartz, *Oz before the Rainbow*, 144; "News of the Theater," *Scranton (Pa.) Republican*, May 6, 1906, 7.

"what wonder that a fiery rage still burned within his breast and that he should seek every opportunity of obtaining vengeance upon his natural enemies." Then, suggesting that with Sitting Bull's death the "proud spirit" of his brothers also died, Baum wrote that "the best safety of the frontier settlements will be secured by the total annihilation of the few remaining Indians" because "their glory has fled, their spirit broken, their manhood effaced; better that they die than live the miserable wretches that they are." After Wounded Knee, Baum further suggested that "having wronged them [Indians] for centuries we had better, in order to protect our civilization, follow it up by one more wrong and wipe these untamed and untamable creatures from the face of the earth."[52]

Only Columbia, Zon-o-phone, and the International Record Company made discs of *Sitting Bull*. For Columbia, Frank Williams recorded the disc for an April 1906 release, and Arthur Collins and Byron G. Harlan sang it for Zon-o-phone. Despite the popularity of the play and these recordings, the song does not make Gardner's charts.

Other comic recordings painted equally degrading and dehumanizing Indian images. Reflective of the stereotype one scholar labels the "Ignoble Indian" or "the Buffoon" is the Edison recording of Len Spencer and Ada Jones's 1909 comedy skit *Little Arrow and Big Chief Greasepaint*. This exceptionally racist record used grunts and the words "heap" and "squaw" as it tells the story of the courtship of Little Arrow played by Jones and Big Chief Greasepaint played by Spencer. Jokes suggest that the Big Chief wears feathers to keep his "wig" "wam" [warm] and that he fights the white man twice a day—at the Wild West show. At the end, Jones breaks into a song, this time declaring Little Arrow's love for her beau. Like other such acts, the recording does not appear in Gardner's charts.

Another type of Indian song reflected the changing view that many Americans had about assimilating Indian peoples. As historian Fred Hoxie has shown, by

1910 older views that Native peoples could be forcibly mainstreamed into American society had given way to a new reality in which assimilation "no longer meant full citizenship and equality." Instead, Indians would "remain on the periphery of American society, ruled by outsiders who promised to guide them toward 'civilization.'"[53] One such song was Harry Williams and Egbert Van Alstyne's 1912 ragtime song *Oh That Navajo Rag*. Williams and Van Alstyne had started both the Indian music craze with their 1904 hit *Navajo* and the cowboy music furor with the 1906 song *Cheyenne*. This new number brought their story full circle back to the Navajos of New Mexico.

The song's lyrics and sheet music are pure fantasy. The song tells the fictional story of Navajo chief Bounding Deer, a man who returns from an eastern college to his reservation in New Mexico, bringing with him civilization in the form of a ragtime dance to replace his traditional "old time prance." It further hints that more assimilation is needed because Indians are lazy, have lost their cunning, and so are no longer "in the running." It then suggests that perhaps the Indian should "massacre" some songs the white man wrote. The sheet music cover, although artistic, represented an appeal to the general public's stereotypical composite notion of what an Indian should look like rather than a exhibition of Navajo men's clothing. The long-sleeve buckskin tunic with blue breastplate and fringed leggings and moccasins fits more with Northern Plains tribes like the Lakota Sioux or Crows than the Navajos, who preferred velvet shirts and cloth headbands to the long-sleeve tunics and trailer warbonnet featured on the cover.[54]

Like *Ragtime Cow Boy Joe*, *Oh That Navajo Rag* appeared in 1912 and had some popularity on the vaudeville circuit because it seemed to represent the trendy ragtime sound. And although all three companies—Edison, Victor, and Columbia—made recordings of the song, including one by Billy Murray, it never broke into the top twenty.

---

52. *Saturday Pioneer* (Aberdeen, S.Dak.), December 20, 1890; *Aberdeen (S.Dak.) Saturday Pioneer*, January 3, 1891. These editorials can be seen at www2.warwick.ac.uk/fac/arts/english/currentstudents/undergraduate/modules/fulllist/second/en213/term1/l_frank_baum.pdf.

53. Hoxie, *Final Promise*, 239–44.

54. "Navajo Culture: Clothing," *Miss Navajo: A Documentary by Billy Luther*, www.pbs.org/independentlens/missnavajo/clothing.html; National Museum of the American Indian, "A Life in Beads: The Stories a Plains Dress Can Tell (Washington, D.C. NMAI Education Office, n.d), http://www.nmai.si.edu.

Such songs furthered the belief among many Americans that the nation's aboriginal peoples no longer threatened American security and were now destined to become extinct. This outlook created another desire to preserve the "essential Indian" for posterity while continuing to guide Native Americans toward civilization. Edward S. Curtis photographed this transformation in his catalogue of Indian images, and others such as George Bird Grinnell documented the "vanishing" Indian through interviews and fieldwork. Similarly, some Indianist composers and preservationists sought to record Native music before it "vanished," and others sought to discover the essence of the Indian "sound" and preserve it, free of its "savage" context.[55]

From the Land of Sky-Blue Water and *Navajo Indian Songs* are two such examples which, rather than simply springing from the imaginations of Tin Pan Alley songsters, were based on authentic Native American songs recorded by ethnographers on the reservations. Non-native composers then revised and elaborated on them, believing they could preserve the "Indianness" of the music to acculturate Indian schoolchildren. The fledgling recording industry also discovered that this form of Indian music was palatable to white audiences, who saw it to be, despite its air of authenticity, not much different from the canned Indian songs coming out of Tin Pan Alley. Indeed, one scholar suggests that as the original Native American songs were "transcribed, idealized, and harmonized, they seemed in the end to share much more in common with the imagery found in Tin Pan Alley numbers than with the performances as originally observed and recorded by the ethnologists."[56]

The Indianist movement in American music served as one source for this music. This group of nationalist composers believed that to find a truly original American sound classically trained musicians should look to authentic Native American music for inspiration, doing what one scholar calls "making Indian-themes

palatable to non-Indian ears."[57] One place they looked for such themes was in Alice Fletcher's pioneering ethnographic work among the Omahas of Nebraska in 1880, as recounted in the first book on Native American music, *Indian Story and Song: From North America*, published in 1900.[58]

In the summer 1909, Charles Wakefield Cadman, a music critic, conductor, and composer from Pittsburgh, followed in Fletcher's footsteps to the Omahas and Winnebagos of Nebraska, learning about Fletcher's work as well as collecting and recording tribal melodies for himself. He then reproduced several, in collaboration with local poet Nelle Richmond Eberhart, in a work that he titled *Four American Indian Songs, Op. 45*, which included *From the Land of the Sky-Blue Water*. Unlike Fletcher's book, Cadman's work was not an ethnographic study to preserve tribal sources but rather primary sources essentialized and then commodified for the market as new sheet music.[59]

Throughout the 1910s, Cadman toured the country with Creek-Cherokee singer Tsinina Redfeather Blackstone, performing Cadman's Indianist songs on stages decorated with Navajo rugs, baskets, and Alaskan totems to sold-out houses. Perhaps it was the popularity of these performances that inspired Victor and Columbia to produce multiple discs of *From the Land of Sky-Blue Water* between 1911 and 1918. Nevertheless, the song just cracked Gardner's top forty in August 1909, the same month that *My Pony Boy* became number one.

If *Land of Sky-Blue Water* represented the Indianist side of appropriation, Geoffrey O'Hara's 1914 Victor record *Navajo Indian Songs* represented the more complex preservationist/assimilationist view of the early twentieth century. Office of Indian Affairs (OIA) representatives worked feverishly to eradicate traditional songs and dances as antithetical to the assimilation of Native Americans into American culture. As a way to preserve such music as it was being silenced,

---

55. Timothy Egan, *Short Nights of the Shadow Catcher: The Epic Life and Immortal Photographs of Edward S. Curtis* (Boston: Mariner Books, 2013); Sherry L. Smith, *Reimagining Indians: Native Americans through Anglo Eyes, 1880–1940* (New York: Oxford University Press, 2000), 45–66.

56. John W. Troutman, *Indian Blues: American Indians and the Politics of Music, 1879–1934* (Norman: University of Oklahoma Press, 2009), 157.

57. Ibid.

58. Alice C. Fletcher, *Indian Story and Song: From North America* (Boston: Small, Maynard, 1900).

59. *Naxos*, www.naxos.com, s.v. "Charles Wakefield Cadman."

in 1913 the OIA hired O'Hara, a Tin Pan Alley composer and vaudeville singer, to travel out to Indian reservations to record Indian music and arrange it for use in the Indian schools. What prompted the government to hire O'Hara is unclear. Born in Canada in 1882, O'Hara had played piano and organ as a child and sang in the local Anglican church. After his father's death around 1900, he worked for a few years as a bookkeeper in a piano store and continued to sing tenor in church. In 1904 he toured the United States with a minstrel group that performed in blackface. Over the next decade he sang in vaudeville, taught some, and even recorded his first Edison cylinders as part of a quartet. Nothing in this past, though, seems to have prepared him for his new job to study Native American music and then preserve it on cylinder.[60]

O'Hara began his project in the spring of 1913 by recording Native Americans visiting the East. He began his work at Carlisle Indian School in Pennsylvania in April with Indians who had come to the school for commencement exercises.[61] He then returned to New York City and recorded visiting Blackfeet Indians from the vicinity of Montana's Glacier National Park who had been brought to the city by Louis W. Hill to promote the park at the Travel and Vacation Show held at the Grand Central Palace.[62] In an Oklahoma news article that featured a photograph of O'Hara and three Blackfeet, O'Hara worried that Native American music would soon fade away.[63] Soon after, the *Washington Herald* described O'Hara not simply as an unbiased recorder of Indian music but as the man "who is going to *teach* the Navajos music."[64]

O'Hara began this task when he traveled to Arizona in September 1913 to record the Navajos, one of the few Native groups actually increasing in population. He spent several weeks there working with "full blooded" Navajo interpreters and "medicine men" to learn their ways

before asking them to sing into his cylinder phonograph. According to one newspaper story, O'Hara explained that since there were more than 15,000 Navajo songs and each filled a four-minute cylinder, he tried to secure "the song I knew each medicine man was most perfect in." He then explained that he often had to pay each man, like photographers did their Navajo subjects, to entice them to sing into his phonograph. In the end, O'Hara found the Navajos to be "extraordinary musicians, from the standpoint of range, and lovers of music."[65]

Despite professing that he had only wanted to preserve Native American music, within a year O'Hara had recorded his own versions of Navajo songs for both Edison and Victor, adding the Blackfeet recording to the disc's other side. The Victor version, called *Navajo Indian Songs*, offered four pieces in which O'Hara introduces a song and describes its unique time signature and then sang the piece: "A Navajo Indian War Song," "A Navajo Indian Medicine Song," "A Navajo Dance Song Used for Social Diversions," and "Dance Song Showing Various Rhythms." In the Edison version, O'Hara notes that "at first hearing, they sound as if they were simply improvisations of a savage mind. But upon investigation, the student finds that they are composed along well-established rules and are bound in poetic figures of speech."

O'Hara added in his remarks that "in the performance of most of them, not the slightest error is tolerated." This last point is most important, because Navajo speakers today suggest that, although O'Hara may have used traditional music in his recordings, his words are nothing more than gibberish, with perhaps a few real Navajo phrases included, suggesting that O'Hara was not preserving Navajo culture but simply playing Indian.

This complicates O'Hara's legacy. Scholars have noted that Native Americans who performed in Buffalo

60. *Library and Archives Canada*, www.collectionscanada.gc.ca, s.v. "Geoffrey O'Hara."

61. "Indians Sing Their Ancient Tribal Songs," *Harrisburg (Pa.) Telegraph*, April 8, 1913, 9; Troutman, *Indian Blues*, 174–76.

62. Lacy Schutz, "The Blackfoot Indians in New York City: Historic Photos from the Museum of the City of New York," *Huffington Post*, www. huffingtonpost.com/lacy-schutz/the-blackfoot-indians-in-_b_847936.html.

63. Mary Boyle O'Reilly, "Blackfeet Braves Sing into Heap Big Horn and Now Lo's Songs Will Never Die," *Muskogee (Okla.) Times-Democrat*, April 9, 1913, 6. The *Roanoke-Beacon* included a cartoon image of an Indian singing into a phonograph with a white man holding the horn. See "'Canned' Indian Songs to Be Placed in Archives," *Roanoke-Beacon* (Plymouth, N.C.), May 9, 1913, 8; see also Smith, *Reimagining Indians*, 45–66.

64. "Doings of Society in and around Washington," *Washington Herald*, April 29, 1913, 8, emphasis added.

65. "Composer Cans Music of Indians," *Oakland (Calif.) Tribune*, September 6, 1914, 10.

Bill Cody's Wild West, so-called show Indians, used the performances as a means to make money in difficult times, to assert their tribal identity publicly, and to demonstrate their virtue and skill in music. O'Hara often paid his Navajo singers, and his uninterpreted recordings of the Blackfeet serve as ethnographic recordings of tribal identity. He also commented several times on the skills of Navajo singers. And even though O'Hara clearly played Indian, he also preserved melodies while not exposing what might be sensitive cultural materials. Though they are seemingly very different from all of the other Indian songs described here, *From the Land of Sky-Blue Water* and *Navajo Indian Songs* were both released by the same recording companies for popular audiences and should perhaps best be considered along with the rest of the Tin Pan Alley tunes.[66]

The final Indian songs reviewed here bring together several important themes including social assimilation and the Indian warrior stereotype. Created and recorded as the country began ramping up its Great War efforts, both *Indianola* and *Big Chief Killahun* can be viewed as patriotic Indianist songs that incorporated Native Americans into the national war effort.

The United States had been preparing for war since the sinking of RMS *Lusitania* in 1915. After Germany resumed unrestricted submarine warfare in the summer of 1917 and the U.S. government learned of the ill-fated Zimmerman telegram trying to ally Mexico with Germany, President Woodrow Wilson asked Congress for a war declaration, which it passed on April 6, 1917. The Selective Service draft soon followed. After that, it took more than a year for the first Americans to enter the Western Front, arriving at the rate of 10,000 a day in the summer of 1918.

American Indians numbered about 13,000 of those troops. Because most Native Americans were not yet citizens, only about half of this number were drafted. The rest volunteered. It is estimated that more than 90 percent of those at boarding schools entered the war.

Motivations for joining included a feeling of patriotism born out of the boarding school curriculum and its military-style training; a chance to fight for freedom as a common cause between Indians and the Allies; an opportunity to display loyalty to the United States; a chance to continue ancestral warrior cultures; and an opportunity to escape the poor economic conditions on the reservations. The Army did not segregate Native American men but had them fight side by side with white soldiers. A few Native American women also served in the war effort as nurses and entertainers for the troops. Regardless of their motives, Native Americans joined the war effort for a country with which some had been in open combat just four decades before and which, since that time, had been trying to assimilate them into American culture.[67]

The 1918 song *Indianola* capitalized on these feelings to use Indians to sell American intervention. S. R. Henry, the alias of Henry R. Stern, and D. Onivas, the alias of Domenico Savino, introduced the piece as a piano solo in 1917. Stern was a music composer in Tin Pan Alley who had helped write *When It's Moonlight on the Prairie* and later became a music publishing executive. Savino trained in Italy as a classical composer and then immigrated to the United States. After the song became popular, the partners first arranged it as an instrumental fox-trot and then had Frank H. Warren, a writer for the *New York World*, add lyrics.

Warren made the song "into an international hit"[68] by capitalizing on America's growing involvement in the Great War, anti-German sentiment, and the continued popularity of the stereotypes of the Big Chief, Indian love songs, and Indian warriors. From the very first derogatory words naming the Indian chief "Bugaboo," to using the agrammatical subject "Me" in the chorus, to repeatedly using "heap," "squaw," "war paint," and "war dance," to wanting to "tomahawk Kaiser Bill," *Indianola* walked a fine line of setting Native Americans apart from mainstream America while calling upon them

---

66. Warren, *Buffalo Bill's America*, 358–90; L. G. Moses, *Wild West Shows and the Images of Indians* (Albuquerque: University of New Mexico Press, 1999); Troutman, *Indian Blues*, 34–37.

67. Diane Camurat, "The American Indian in the Great War: Real and Imagined," http://net.lib.byu.edu/estu/wwi/comment/Cmrts/Cmrt6.html#81; Thomas Britten, *American Indians in World War I: At Home and at War* (Albuquerque: University of New Mexico Press, 1997).

68. "S. R. Henry's Phenomenal Record," *Music Trades* 57, no. 12 (March 22, 1919), 46.

to come do their "heap big bit" for "their" country. The remark about Kaiser Bill also allied Indians with many Americans swept up in the anti-German hysteria of the day.[69] As historian Frederick Hoxie suggests, such attitudes fit the new model of assimilation that suggested that Native Americans were not ready to be treated as equals but could, with guidance, move toward that goal.[70]

Victor, Edison, and Columbia each made both instrumental versions and vocals, featuring Billy Murray, of *Indianola* in 1918. Emerson, a new disc company begun in 1916, recorded its own version that featured a vocal by George Beaver, the alias of Irving Kaufman, another prolific vocalist. The song cracked the top twenty in February of 1918, peaked at number three in May, and remained popular until September.

A similar song, *Big Chief Killahun*, features a sheet music cover of a giant Indian crashing through No Man's Land with German soldiers in his hands. Its racier lyrics are exceedingly anti-German, with phrases that include "good bye fritzel, no more schnitzel" and "good bye vulture, no more culture, Big Chief Killahun." Unfortunately for its composers and vocalist, the record appeared just after the armistice.

The first era of talking machine cowboy and Indian songs came to a quick end after the war. The final Indian love song, *Snow Deer*, had been recorded five years earlier, and it had been two years since the last cowboy song, *Way Out Yonder in the Golden West*. In 1919 things began to change. That year, concert singer Bentley Ball recorded *The Dying Cowboy* and *Jesse James*, the first traditional cowboy song to originate out west rather than in Tin Pan Alley. Radio started the next year, Eubie Blake's *Shuffle Along* sparked the jazz craze in 1921, the first string bands made records in 1922, and the following year the Glenn and Shannon Quartets recorded another traditional cowboy song, *Whoopee Ti Yi Yo*. WLS radio from Chicago started broadcasting its *WLS Barn Dance* in 1924, and the following year Nashville's WSM began its *Grand Ole Opry*. Recording technology also improved in 1925 with the first electronic recording studios, which eliminated the need for Billy Murray's particular style of shouting into an acoustic horn. New artists such as Vernon Dalhart and Carl T. Sprague soon became famous as the first traditional cowboy artists.[71]

But prior to that, between 1902 and 1918, songs about the American West proliferated in American culture. During that time, companies produced more than fifty cowboy and Indian recordings, including cowboy poetry, western skits, cowboy songs, love songs, Indian songs, Wild West show songs, cowgirl songs, and both cowboy and Indian ragtime dance songs. In addition, sheet music companies simultaneously printed elaborately illustrated scores of almost every song, providing a sort of cover art in an era when discs came in simple sleeves and cylinders in tubes. Of these, fifteen cowboy and Indian songs made it to the top twenty, eleven made the top ten, and three songs reached number one. Hardly a trickle, songs about cowboys and Indians were abundant in the talking machine era and suggest the existence of a flourishing, but heretofore unknown, western audio culture during these years. And when listened to closely, these talking machine songs about the American West represent a nostalgia for the lost frontier, the passing of the Indian, and the complex race relations of Jim Crow America.

---

69. "War Hysteria and the Persecution of German-Americans," *Authentichistory*, www.authentichistory.com/1914–1920/2-homefront/4-hysteria.

70. Hoxie, *Final Promise*, 239–44.

71. Green, *Singing in the Saddle*, 20–31.

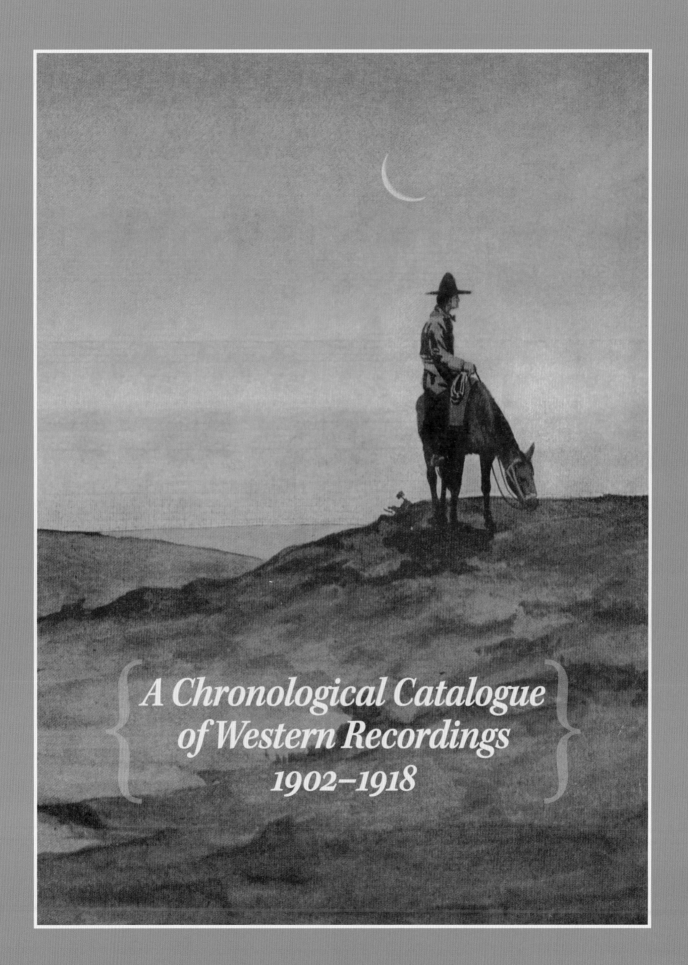

*A Chronological Catalogue
of Western Recordings
1902–1918*

*T*his catalogue features a chronological survey of western recordings. Entries provide the full lyrics of each song, its history, and when possible illustrations of the period sheet music covers. Information about the composer, lyricist, and sheet music illustrators is included when available. To ascertain the popularity of each song, I examined articles from period newspapers and trade journals such as *Talking Machine World* and *Edison Phonograph Monthly* as well as listings from Edward F. Gardner's reconstituted charts in his book *Popular Songs of the Twentieth Century*, vol. 1: *Chart Detail and Encyclopedia, 1900–1949*. Digitized recordings of each song are available online via the *UCSB Cylinder Audio Archive* (http://cylinders.library.ucsb.edu), the *Discography of American Historical Recordings* (http://adp.library.ucsb.edu), and the *Library of Congress National Jukebox* (http://www.loc.gov/jukebox).

Song List

1. *Custer's Last Charge,* **1902**
2. *Indian War Dance,* **1902**
3. *Hiawatha,* **1903**
4. *Anona,* **1903**
5. *Cumming's Indian Congress at Coney Island,* **1904**
6. *Navajo,* **1904**
7. *Tammany,* **1905**
8. *Lasca,* **1905**
9. *Sitting Bull,* **1905**
10. *Feather Queen,* **1905**
11. *Silver Heels,* **1905**
12. *Cheyenne,* **1906**
13. *Arrah Wanna,* **1906**
14. *Iola,* **1906**
15. *Ida-Ho,* **1907**
16. *Reed Bird,* **1907**
17. *San Antonio,* **1907**
18. *Red Wing,* **1907**
19. *Since Arrah Wanna Married Barney Carney,* **1907**
20. *In the Land of the Buffalo,* **1907**
21. *Broncho Buster,* **1907**
22. *Broncho Bob and His Little Cheyenne,* **1907**
23. *Rain-in-the-Face,* **1907**
24. *Santiago Flynn,* **1908**
25. *When It's Moonlight on the Prairie,* **1908**
26. *Topeka,* **1908**
27. *Big Chief Smoke,* **1908**
28. *Pride of the Prairie,* **1908**
29. *I'm a Yiddish Cowboy,* **1908**
30. *Rainbow,* **1908**
31. *Little Arrow and Big Chief Greasepaint,* **1909**
32. *Denver Town,* **1909**
33. *My Rancho Maid,* **1909**
34. *Blue Feather,* **1909**
35. *My Pony Boy,* **1909**
36. *Wise Old Indian,* **1909**
37. *Lily of the Prairie,* **1909**
38. *My Prairie Song Bird,* **1909**
39. *Ogalalla,* **1910**
40. *A Cowboy Romance,* **1910**
41. *Silver Bell,* **1910**
42. *Valley Flower,* **1910**
43. *From the Land of the Sky-Blue Water,* **1911**
44. *Silver Star,* **1912**
45. *Golden Deer,* **1912**
46. *Ragtime Cow Boy Joe,* **1912**
47. *Oh That Navajo Rag,* **1912**
48. *Snow Deer,* **1913**
49. *In the Golden West,* **1913**
50. *At That Bully Wooly Wild West Show,* **1914**
51. *Navajo Indian Songs,* **1914**
52. *Way Out Yonder in the Golden West,* **1916**
53. *Indianola,* **1917**
54. *Big Chief Killahun,* **1918**

Custer's Last Charge and Indian War Dance, 1902

John Philip Sousa made the first recordings with western themes with his one-sided Victor discs *Custer's Last Charge* and *Indian War Dance* in 1902. The March King's band had played the Custer song since 1895 in public concerts.[1] He recorded it for Victor in January 1902 and again in August 1903. The music features an instrumental orchestration, gunshots, and hoofbeats that accompany the following scenes: "Sioux Indians' war dance night before the battle; bugle calls in Custer's camp; approach of American cavalry; approach of the Indians; the battle, in which Custer is mortally wounded; dirge; Indians rejoicing after the battle; burial of Custer by General Bentline; finale."[2]

One of the earliest listings for *Custer's Last Charge* is a July 1903 Arizona newspaper story that mentions its inclusion as a "descriptive selection" in an "open air Victor concert" given at a local music store.[3]

Indian War Dance was also a popular selection for bands at this time and featured lots of yells and whoops over the music. Like *Custer's Last Charge*, Sousa had been performing this song since at least 1896 before recording it for Victor in 1900 and then again in 1902. Most interesting, a December 1905 issue of the Phoenix Indian School's paper, *The Native American*, noted that at a special evening demonstration of the school's new talking machine *Indian War Dance* was played on the machine and that it had a "warm spot in the hearts of the boys and girls and received its due acknowledgment from them."[4]

NOTES

1. "Sousa's Performance," *Atlanta (Ga.) Constitution*, December 5, 1895, 4.

2. This information is from a concert of the piece performed three decades later by a different band. Nevertheless, the description fits the recording; "Concert of Legion Post to Be Given Tonight," *Evening News* (Harrisburg, Pa.), November 14, 1932, 9.

3. "Concert," *Arizona Republican* (Phoenix, Ariz.), July 18, 1903, 3; *Discography of American Historical Recordings*, http://adp.library.ucsb.edu, s.v. "Custer's last charge."

4. *Native American* 6, no. 46 (December 23, 1905), 467. "GAR Memorial Day Literary and Musical Exercises at the Emporium," *San Francisco Call*, May 30, 1896, 7, is an early listing showing *Indian War Dance*. For the Victor recordings, see *Discography of American Historical Recordings*, http://adp.library.ucsb.edu, s.v. "Indian war dance."

Hiawatha, 1903

Hiawatha, words by James O'Dea, music by Neil Moret (Detroit: Whitney-Warner, 1903). Sheet music from author's collection.

Hiawatha (summer idyl), music by Neil Moret (Detroit: Whitney-Warner, 1902). Sheet music from author's collection.

Hiawatha was the first Indian love song to become a hit when both Victor and Edison recorded it in 1903. Its success created this genre and started a fad that persisted for over a decade. Kansas City songwriter Charlie Daniels wrote it as *In Hiawatha* under the name Niel Moret as a love song for his sweetheart, who lived in the small town of Hiawatha, Kansas. After the tune was sold in 1902 to the Whitney-Warner Publishing Company of Detroit for $10,000, the publisher shortened the title to simply *Hiawatha,* thus changing the tune's focus. Within a year, the sheet music sold more than a million copies.

In 1903 lyricist James O'Dea sharpened its Indian focus by adding words based on the popular Longfellow poem "Hiawatha." Dripping with sentimentality, the new love song to Minnehaha used an internal rhyme scheme and referenced a birch canoe. The revised ballad became even more popular.[1]

The Whitney-Warner Publishing Company that published *Hiawatha* was the predecessor of the Remick-Shapiro company that eventually became simply the Jerome H. Remick Company of New York, one of the largest publishers of cowboy and Indian music.[2] When it published *Hiawatha* in 1902, it did so as both an instrumental and a song with lyrics.[3] The lyrics are as follows:

> Oh the moon is all agleam on the stream
> Where I dream here of you my pretty Indian maid.
> While the rustling leaves are singing high above
> us overhead
> In the glory of the bright summer night
> In light of the shadows of the forest glade
> I am waiting here to kiss your lips so red.
>
> There's a flood of melodies on the breeze
> From the trees and of you they breathe so tenderly
> While the woodlands all around are resounding
> your name,
> Oh my all in life is you only you
> Fond and true and your own forevermore I'll be.
> Hear them the song I sing with lips aflame
>
> In the tresses of your hair, lies a snare and its there
> Where my heart a willing captive is.
> Oh my woodland queen I pray you'll hold it ever in
> your care
> In my little birch canoe love with you
> Just we two down the stream of life in wedded
> bliss
> I would drift sweetheart with you my lot to share.
> When the birds upon the wing in the spring
> Gaily sing of the green and golden summer time
> When the snows of early winter robe the
> woodlands in white,
> Then your Hiawatha free I will be
> And to thee ev'ry thought of mine will o'er incline.
> Heed then the vows I pledge to thee this night.
>
> *Refrain*
> I am your own your Hiawatha brave—my heart is
> yours you know
> Dear one I love you so
> Oh Minnehaha gentle maid decide—decide and
> you'll be,
> My Indian bride.

More than a dozen bands and artists recorded *Hiawatha* for both cylinder and disc. For Victor, six different bands, including Sousa's, recorded either the song or the instrumental in 1903. Jules Levy, a cornet soloist, also recorded it for Victor that year, as did banjo soloist Parke Hunter. Harry Macdonough sang the ballad with piano accompaniment twice that year for Victor discs and another time for Edison cylinders.[4] The Edison version features Macdonough rolling his *r*'s with great emotion through the first chorus and two versions of the refrain. There are no tom-toms or anything else to make it sound "Indian" other than the references to his "Indian bride."[5] The Edison Concert Band also recorded the song on cylinder, and the Columbia Orchestra recorded it for both disc and cylinder formats. Finally, comics Arthur Collins and Byron G. Harlan produced *A Parody on "Hiawatha"* using the pun "higher water" instead of "Hiawatha."[6]

These many recordings made *Hiawatha* a big hit in 1903. In his analysis of popular songs, Gardner lists the song as number ten in March 1903, raises it to number two in April, and then declares it number one in May 1903, where it remained through July. He lowers the song to number two in August, number four in September, and then down to eleven in October before dropping it from his list altogether the next month.[7]

The new trade journal *Edison Phonograph Monthly* also raved about the song's popularity. Its first issue, published in March 1903, already referred to the song as the "$10,000 composition" when it noted that the Edison Concert Band had produced a "charming air" that "must become very popular." Three months later, the *Monthly* noted that "Harry Macdonough sings the famous $10,000 song . . . [which] as an instrumental Record found a very large sale, and given now as a vocal solo, it cannot fail to be equally popular. It is probably one of the best advertised songs in the country."[8] By August that year, Macdonough's version was the best-selling recording thus far for 1903, and in October a letter from a Pennsylvanian noted that *Hiawatha* played 1,525 times on his coin-operated phonograph before the record wore out. That same month, an advertisement for the Edison phonograph in a Kentucky newspaper described the Edison as the "best imitation of the human voice known" and suggested that customers drop in to "hear it play *Hiawatha* as sung by Harry Macdonough."[9]

NOTES

1. "Composer of Hiawatha Played for Dance after Receiving $10,000 Check in St. Louis," *St. Louis Republic*, August 30, 1903, 31.

2. Al Kohn and Bob Kohn, *Kohn on Music Licensing*, 4th ed. (New York: Aspen, 2010), 75–78.

3. Neil Moret, *Hiawatha* (Detroit, Mich.: Whitney-Warner, 1902); Neil Moret and James O'Dea, *Hiawatha* (Detroit, Mich.: Whitney-Warner, 1903).

4. Phonograph historian Tim Gracyk notes that Macdonough was perhaps the "most popular ballad singer" and that his real name was John Macdonald. But recording company personnel did not feel that "John was romantic enough" so renamed him Harry Macdonald, only to have his first recording actually list his name as Harry Macdonough. The artist reportedly later explained in a letter to phonograph historian Jim Walsh, "I was completely indifferent to what they called me. I thought then that record-making was a sort of lowdown business, anyway." Gracyk, *Popular American Recording Pioneers*, 223–24.

5. Harry Macdonough, *Hiawatha* (New York: National Phonograph, 1903), cylinder #8425.

6. *Discography of American Historical Recordings*, http://adp.library.ucsb.edu, s.v. "A parody on 'Hiawatha.'"

7. Gardner, *Popular Songs*, 48–49.

8. "The March Records," *Edison Phonograph Monthly* 1, no. 1 (March 1903), 8; "The July Records," *Edison Phonograph Monthly* 1, no. 4 (June 1903), 5.

9. *Edison Phonograph Monthly* 1, no. 6 (August 1903), 7; "One Record Played 1525 Times," *Edison Phonograph Monthly* 1, no. 8 (October 1903), 7; "Do You Love Music," advertisement, *Maysville (Ky.) Evening Bulletin*, August 8, 1903, 3.

Anona, 1903

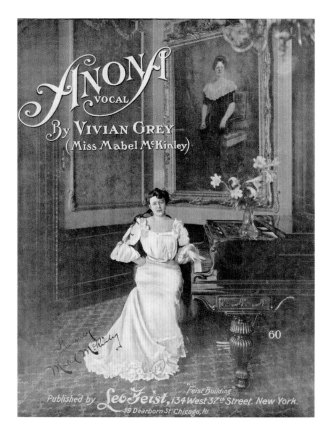

Anona, words and music by Vivian Grey [Miss Mabel McKinley] (New York: Leo Feist, 1903). Sheet music from author's collection.

Anona (intermezzo two-step), music by Vivian Grey [Miss Mabel McKinley] (New York: Leo Feist, 1903). Sheet music from author's collection.

Hiawatha's success produced immediate copycat songs with Indian themes. The first of these, *Anona*, appeared in August 1903, just as *Hiawatha*'s popularity began fading. Written by Miss Mabel McKinley, niece of President McKinley, under the pseudonym Vivian Grey, *Anona* tells the story of an Indian maid in Arizona. In fact, the song lists the title character's home as the "western state of Arizona," even though at the time Arizona was still a territory and did not become a state until 1912. Like *Hiawatha*, this song appeared both as an instrumental intermezzo and also as a vocal. The intermezzo sheet music cover features a beautiful Native American woman

with amulets around her neck and a single feather in her hair, gazing into the distance. The vocal, however, features a painting of Mabel McKinley in a long dress sitting at a grand piano in a fashionable parlor with a stamped signature, "Sincerely Mabel McKinley," just above the publisher, Leo Feist of New York and Chicago.[1]

Anona's popularity spread across the country even before a recording was made. An announcement for an August band concert in Humboldt, Kansas, that featured the song called it "the latest popular craze." An Ohio paper the next month said the two-step version was "so popular everywhere . . . [and was] almost as 'catchy' as *Hiawatha*."

New York ads called it "the newest music success" and noted that the song was "melodious, possessing rare and quaint tunefulness" and that Miss McKinley sang *Anona* at vaudeville houses all over the country.[2]

The song goes like this:

In the western state of Arizona, lived an Indian
    maid;
She was called the beautiful Anona so 'tis said.
Graceful as a fawn was she,
Just as sweet as she could be,
Eyes so bright, dark as night,
Had this pretty little Arizona Indian Maiden.
All the chiefs who knew her,
Came to woo her.
For her pined
To marry she declined,
At last she changed her mind,
But 'twas not a chief so grand,
who won her heart and hand,
But a warrior bold, who wooed her with a song.

When her father heard that his Anona, Loved this
    youthful brave
Straightaway he said he would disown her, things
    look grave.
She must marry "heap big chief,"
Sweet Anona hid her grief
Ran Away, so they say
And got married to the man she loved with out
    delaying.
There her father sought her, Never caught her,
Till one day
When two years passed away,
They both came back to stay,
Then the chief declared a truce, when they named
    their young papoose
After him and his grandchild would sing.

Refrain
My sweet Anona, in Arizona
There is no other maid I'd serenade
By campfires gleaming, of you I'm dreaming,
Anona, my sweet Indian maid.

All three major recording companies created versions of *Anona* in the fall of 1903. The Edison Grand Concert Band recorded it as an instrumental, and Henry Burr sang it for Columbia cylinders. Victor made numerous recordings of the song as both an instrumental and a vocal in 1903 and 1904. Vess Ossman registered the first disc as a banjo solo with piano accompaniment, and the Victor Orchestra produced a full instrumental version. Harry Macdonough, the artist who sang *Hiawatha*, recorded a solo version with piano accompaniment in November 1903, and Mina Hickman made a solo disc soon after. Arthur Pryor's Band made still another recording in December and Pryor's orchestra recorded a version as part of a medley the following year. The Columbia Band made its own disc version, and Henry Burr and Vess Ossman also created renderings for Columbia.[3]

These recordings made *Anona* a second Indian-themed hit. Gardner ranks the song on his top twenty from September 1903 to January 1904, peaking at number two in October 1903. The *Edison Phonograph Monthly* for August 1903 called it an "unsurpassed Record" and said that "without in any way comparing it to *Hiawatha*, it may be said that it fully equals it in sweetness, tenderness, and romance."[4]

In 1909, McKinley again recorded *Anona*, this time on Edison's new four-minute Amberol cylinder. The new cylinder provided 200 threads-per-inch (TPI), or double the 100 TPI of the Gold Moulded Cylinders in service since 1902. Although this innovation required retrofitting existing phonographs or purchasing a new model exclusively designed for them, it also doubled the length of recording time for Edison cylinders from two minutes to four. Because companies continued to produce the older two-minute cylinders as well, Edison placed a new marker, 4M, on the Amberols to indicate the longer play time. Although conceived as a way to compete better with discs by allowing more time for creative expression, one historian suggests that many earlier songs were simply given a "facelift—a new verse here, a verbal or non musical interlude there," to fill the longer-playing records.[5]

Edison Phonograph Monthly noted that the song had been McKinley's "first great success as a composer" and was often played in public band concerts. It concluded by suggesting that "the graceful way in which Miss McKinley sings the selection is delightful."[6] With this production, Edison also announced that it was withdrawing the Edison Concert Band version of *Anona* for sale to the public. Despite these pronouncements, the new versions of *Anona* did not make a splash or crack Gardner's charts.

NOTES

1. Vivian Grey [Miss Mabel McKinley], *Anona* (intermezzo two-step) (New York: Leo Feist, 1903); Vivian Grey, "Miss Mabel McKinley," *Anona* (New York: Leo Feist, 1903).
2. "Band Concert," *Humboldt (Kans.) Union*, August 8, 1903, 3; *Wilmington (Ohio) News Journal*, September 16, 1903, 5; "Anona," *New York Evening World*, October 6, 1903, 9.
3. Gathered through searches at *UCSB Cylinder Audio Archive*, http://cylinders.library.ucsb.edu, and *Discography of American Historical Recordings*, http://adp.library.ucsb.edu.
4. Gardner, *Popular Songs*, 49–50; "Comments on September Records," *Edison Phonograph Monthly* 1, no. 6 (August, 1903), 5.
5. "Edison Amberol Records (1908–1912)," *UCSB Cylinder Audio Archive*, http://cylinders.library.ucsb.edu/history-amberol.php.
6. "New Republican Song," *Harrisburg (Pa.) Telegraph*, September 11, 1908, 11; "Edison Amberol Records for June," *Edison Phonograph Monthly* 7, no. 4 (April 1909), 21, 23.

Cumming's Indian Congress at Coney Island, 1904

The success of *Hiawatha* and *Anona* provided an opportunity for a recording of actual Native Americans performing in a Wild West show. In an unusual recording made by Columbia sometime in 1904, would-be showman Frederick T. Cummins presented his "Indian Congress" as it performed for spectators at Coney Island. Labeled incorrectly as *Cumming's Indian Congress at Coney Island*, the recording featured the performance of real Indians.[1] The 1903 article "Stagenotes" noted that Cummins had been successful at the 1901 Pan-American Exposition held at Buffalo, New York, before bringing his entourage to Steeplechase Park at Coney Island. According to the newspaper, Cummins promised to

> bring the representative chiefs and warriors of its forty-two different savage tribes, with their bronchos, weapons, war paint, wives, papooses and typical village of fifty tepees, and a big contingent of aboriginal artisans, vaqueros, broncho busters, dead shots and frontier daredevils. The colonel took the snorting war horse for the far West yesterday to pilot his red brethren and their belongings to the holiday beach of the big salt water.[2]

Later that fall, the show performed at Madison Square Garden, and then in 1904 it traveled to the St. Louis World's Fair.[3]

My cylinder recording begins with the standard announcement of the recording's title and then mixes music and chanting with audio descriptions of the show. The full transcript is as follows:

Cummins Indian Congress, Columbia Records. Five Hundred Indians representing forty-two tribes, living in tepees, wigwams, adobe houses. Admission: Twenty Five Cents. [music, tom-tom, and chanting]

Introducing Colonel Frederick T. Cummins, otherwise known as Chief Lakota [trumpet fanfare and hoofbeats followed by cheers]

Congress of Indians, cowboys, and Mexican Vaqueroes, preceded by the Carlisle Indian Band. [music and cheers]

Princess Winona, Champion Rifle Shot of the World! [trumpet fanfare, hoofbeats, and gunshots followed by cheers]

Ground Indian sham battles concluding with the battle cry of "Victory!" [tom-tom, music, chanting, and cheers, then more music and cheers]

With its admission price of twenty-five cents and the appropriation of Native American names by Cummins, this recording represents a more cutting view of Native Americans as a passing race needing to be placed on display before they vanished.

NOTES

1. *Cumming's Indian Congress at Coney Island* (New York: Columbia Records, 1903), indestructible cylinder #32302; *Discography of American Historical Recordings*, http://adp.library.ucsb.edu, s.v. "Cumming's Indian Congress at Coney Island."
2. "Stagenotes," *Brooklyn Daily Eagle*, April 12, 1903, 41.
3. "Amusements: Hundreds of Wildest Indians Now at Madison Square Garden," *New York Evening World*, September 19, 1903, 9; "Cummins' Wild West Show," *The Pike Attractions*, http://atthefair.homestead.com/pkeatt/CumminsWildWestShow.html.

Navajo, 1904

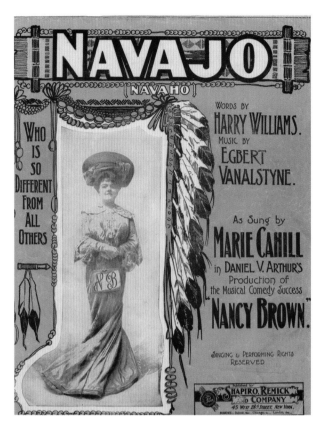

Navajo, words by Harry Williams, music by Egbert Van Alstyne (New York: Shapiro, Remick, 1903). Sheet music from author's collection.

Navajo (Indian characteristique), music by Egbert Van Alstyne (New York: Shapiro, Remick, 1903). Sheet music from author's collection.

In 1904 the musical comedy *Nancy Brown* became popular, in part because it featured the edgy Indian love song *Navajo*. Written by Harry Williams with music by Egbert Van Alstyne, the song is a love story between a Navajo woman and an African American man.[1] Although actress Marie Cahill made *Navajo* a hit on stage, over the next few years recording artists made it a national hit that transformed the genre, propelled its composers to stardom, brought songs about the West to a wider audience, and made lyrics featuring racial stereotypes common practice in western music.

Williams was born on a farm outside St. Paul,

Minnesota, and Van Alstyne hailed from Illinois. While playing in the vaudeville circuit in 1900, the two joined forces and soon found their way to the Tin Pan Alley publisher Shapiro and Remick, later the Jerome H. Remick Company. According to one source, they arrived in New York nearly broke with several published, but mostly unsuccessful, ragtime songs in hand. They had already written *Navajo* but found no one interested in the song because the "subject, style, and music of their song were utterly strange to the New York publishers." Despite several difficult months, they had the "breeziness and pluck of the Western soil" and persevered. Their luck changed in 1903 when the song was adopted in *Nancy Brown* and then became a big hit.[2]

Theater reviews described *Nancy Brown* as having a "record-breaking run of five months" at New York's Bijou Theater with the "unanimous approval of New York, Chicago, St. Louis, Washington, and Boston"; it was "filled with whistleable songs." Marie Cahill played the title role and one reviewer wrote that "her whole personality radiates jollity and mirth. One glance ought to drive away the blues." Another suggested that *Navajo* was "among the accepted masterpieces of their kind, and as sung by the clever comedienne are irresistible."[3]

But *Navajo* was different from other songs of the era in important ways. *Hiawatha* and *Anona* had been imagined love stories of generic noble savages. *Navajo* also told a fictional tale, but it did so using a real western tribe that brought a sense of the authentic to the story. At the time, Navajos were well known in the Southwest tourist market, which had been growing since the Fred Harvey Company had begun escorting visitors to the region in the 1890s. Historians suggest that this popularity worked because Harvey sold a primitivist relationship whereby tourists acquired authenticity by purchasing Navajo blankets and jewelry. Harvey Company's 1902 creation of an "Indian department" capitalized on this Indian craze and brought the southwestern tribe to a national audience. The song *Navajo* also capitalized on this popularity and opened the door for more songs about the region.[4]

More important, the song's lyrics imposed clear racial overtones for the Indian song market. This created another place to introduce racial stereotypes. The Supreme Court's famous segregation case of *Plessy v. Ferguson* was just eight years old when *Navajo* debuted, and Jim Crow was still working its way into American life. So-called coon songs of the ragtime era, direct descendants of blackface and minstrel shows, embodied segregation in popular music. In *Navajo* the singers' question of whether or not the Navajo maiden could have a "coon for a beau" linked second-class African Americans to Native Americans—thus reaffirming white America by denigrating blacks and Indians.[5] Several period newspapers caught on to this and described the song as an "Indian coon song."[6]

Navajo also reflected racial and gender stereotypes. It was the first Indian song to introduce skin color as a descriptor when it described the Navajo maiden as being of a "copper shade" and described her African American lover as a "colored man." It then suggested that the African American would provide his love with feathers if there were chickens near so that the maiden would have "lots to wear" including laces, blankets, and jewels. The *Minneapolis Journal* noted this when it suggested that "some of the numbers have the barbaric color so much affected now in songs ambitious to become 'popular,' but these—as, for instance, Miss Cahill's 'Navajo' song—are interpolations by other authors."[7]

Here are the full lyrics:

Down on the sand hills of New Mexico
There lives an Indian maid,
She's of the tribe they call the Navajo
Face of a copper shade,
And ev'ry evening there was a coon,
Who came his love to plead,
There by the silv'ry light of the moon,
He'd help her string her beads,
And when they were all alone,
To her he would softly crone.

Chorus
Na-va Na-va my Navajo
I have a love for you that will grow
If you'll have a coon for a beau,
I'll have a Navajo.

This Indian maiden told the colored man,
She wanted lots to wear.
Laces and blankets and a powder can,
Jewels and pipestone rare,
You bring me feathers dear from the store,
He answered have no fear,
I'll bring you feathers babe by the score
If there are chickens near
With joy then the maiden sighed
When to her once more he cried.

Repeat Chorus

The *Navajo* sheet music cover does not address these racial attitudes but instead uses a mix of generic Native

American symbols surrounding a black-and-white image of Cahill as Nancy Brown. William or Frederick Starmer, English brothers who lived in and around New York City and are estimated to have created one-fourth of all large-size sheet music covers between 1900 and 1919, made the illustration.[8] The photograph shows Cahill wearing a large hat, a floor-length dress, and carrying a purse with the letters *N B* scripted on it. This image is straight out of the publicity shots for the play and would have appealed to those who saw the musical comedy in person.[9] The generic Indian icons include a long thin blanket serving as a backdrop to the song title at the top of the page. Beneath this is the word "Navaho," which most likely was a phonetic guide for those unfamiliar with the correct pronunciation. A line drawing of a beaded necklace frames Cahill's photo, and hanging off its top right corner is a long Indian warbonnet containing ten eagle feathers. Of course, Navajos traditionally did not wear this type of headdress, but its inclusion, at center, could have alerted potential buyers that this music with a white woman on its cover was about Indians.[10] To the left of the Cahill image is another Indianesque object with two eagle feathers and a quote, presumably from Nancy Brown, that hints at the exotic otherness that caught the public's fancy: "Who is so different from all others." The names of the song's lyricist and composer appear on the far right, above a note that mentions Marie Cahill and Nancy Brown. The publisher's stamp is at lower right. On the inside cover is a small sample page of the song described as the "instrumental popular craze of the country."

The sheet music cover for the instrumental march and two-step, also produced by one of the Starmer brothers, similarly plays on generic Indian stereotypes by depicting a Native American woman standing in a forest at the base of some snowy mountains. The clothing worn by the woman in the foreground is not a traditional dress worn by Navajo women. Instead, it appears more like the layered dress of Plains Indian women such as the Assiniboines or Sioux. Similarly, the tepees in the center of the image are not the traditional Navajo abode, the hogan, but a generic type of temporary Plains Indian dwelling. The setting, with its snowy mountains and tall pines, is more complicated. Although most Americans of this era would have encountered Navajos in the desert Four Corners or along

the Santa Fe railroad, the traditional Navajo homeland, Dinétah, is bounded by four sacred mountains ranging in elevation from 11,000 to 13,000 feet. So, although such a scene was possible, the sacredness of these peaks would have been an unlikely place for a tourist encounter.[11]

Navajo's stage success led all three major record companies, Victor, Edison, and Columbia, to make multiple versions of the song. Victor and Edison capitalized on Harry Macdonough's successes with *Hiawatha* and *Anona* by having him record *Navajo* on disc and cylinder.[12] Columbia used popular vaudeville tenor Harry Tally for its version.[13] Tally made all kinds of records, working almost exclusively for Columbia. Orchestras, banjo players, and a trombonist also recorded the song. The record companies also used *Navajo* in compilations. All of these recordings, combined with the stage performances, made *Navajo* the first big hit about a specific Indian group from the American West.

Macdonough's version for Victor and Edison sounds more like the softer, melodic tones of *Hiawatha* and *Anona*, whereas Tally's recording seems racier and evokes later, edgier Indian songs. The Macdonough disc version, recorded in January 1904, begins with a piano playing the melody, then a tom-tom steps in with four quarter notes followed by twice that many eighth notes. Macdonough sings the verse and chorus with piano accompaniment as a ballad, including another tom-tom before the second verse followed by the chorus repeated twice at the end. The trade journal *Edison Phonograph Monthly* called this version a "fine rendering of this popular song" and suggested that it was being listed at a "most opportune time" because it was being "sung and played everywhere. It is so well known that there cannot fail to be a great demand for it in Edison Records."[14]

Harry Tally's Columbia two-minute cylinder, on the other hand, includes a much more assertive orchestrated tom-tom at the very beginning followed by a strong tom-tom beat throughout the song. Perhaps because the cylinder was more than a minute shorter than the disc, Tally sings the song faster and more boldly.

In addition to these vocals, instrumentals and medleys kept *Navajo* alive in a variety of forms. The Victor Dance orchestra made a rare twelve-inch recording of *Navajo* in 1904. This larger size made the song just over three and half minutes long. Banjo player Vess Ossman also made a version of the song for Victor that same year. In addition, both Edison and Victor included *Navajo* in Indian-themed medleys, with the Edison Military band playing it on a record called the *Navajo Medley* and Victor including it in its *Indian Medley* along with instrumental versions of *Hiawatha* and *Anona*.[15]

With these many versions in circulation, it should come as no surprise that *Navajo* was a major hit. Gardner lists the song in his monthly top twenty for eight straight months from January to August 1904. Within this time, the song made number one for both March and April and appeared in the top ten from February to August.[16]

Stories from newspapers across the country also hinted at the song's popularity. According to one in a 1904 issue of the *Cincinnati Enquirer*, before the second game of the season between the Chicago Cubs and the hometown Reds the "palace of the fans was choked with enthusiasts and every box and reserved seat filled" as Weber's Military Band entertained the crowd with "popular airs" such as *Navajo*. That same week, the *Wichita Beacon* reported that the editor of the *Atchison Globe* apparently had heard a lot of Indian songs when he sarcastically told his readers to "go out in the woods these days. You will find much to be thankful for; the birds don't sing '*Hiawatha*' or '*Navajo*.'" Two months later, the Indianapolis Shortridge High School band's version of *Navajo* was "heartily encored" as part of the high school graduation ceremony.[17]

Navajo's great popularity transformed western music in the talking machine era. Within a year, its composing team of Williams and Van Alstyne had introduced *Cheyenne*, another hit song about the West that jump-started the cowboy music craze that soon swept the country for over a decade. At the same time, *Navajo*'s success encouraged other composers to write more Indian love songs, continuing that genre's popularity for another decade. Finally, the racial overtones of *Navajo* also pushed composers and lyricists to include even edgier songs that incorporated ever more ethnic and racial stereotypes, appealing to still another side of Jim Crow America. These three themes—cowboy and cowgirl love songs, Indian love songs, and ethnic and racial stereotypes—became the three dominant forms of western music during the talking machine era.

NOTES

1. Harry Williams and Egbert Van Alstyne, *Navajo* (New York: Shapiro, Remick, 1903).

2. Tinsley, *For a Cowboy*, 1–2; Phillip Robert Dillon, "Princely Profits from Single Songs," *Scrap Book, First Section* 4, no. 2 (August 1907), 184–85; this source notes that by 1907 Williams had a 1,280-acre ranch in "Dakota." *The Parlor Songs Academy*, http://parlorsongs. com, s.v. "Egbert Van Alstyne"; "Egbert Anson Van Alstyne," *RagPiano*, http://ragpiano.com/comps/vanalsty.shtml.

3. "Big Events This Week," *Fort Wayne (Ind.) News*, January 26, 1904, 9; "List of Excellent Theatrical Events Next Week," *Fort Wayne News*, January 30, 1904, 9; "News of the Theaters," *Chicago Daily Tribune*, November 30, 1903; "Amusements," *Indianapolis News*, January 1, 1904.

4. See Rothman, *Devil's Bargains*; Dilworth, *Imagining Indians*; and Hutchinson, *Indian Craze*.

5. See C. Vann Woodward, *Strange Career*; Meeks, *Border Citizens*; Gordon, *Great Arizona Orphan Abduction*; Schroeder, "Passing for Black."

6. "Portable Dressing Room," *Fort Wayne (Ind.) Journal-Gazette*, January 21, 1904, 3; "At the Theaters," *Minneapolis Journal*, January 15, 1904, 4.

7. "At the Theaters," *Minneapolis Journal*, January 15, 1904, 4.

8. Bill Edwards, "William Starmer and Frederick Starmer," *RagPiano*, www.perfessorbill.com/artists/starmer.shtml.

9. "News of the Theaters," *Chicago Daily Tribune*, November 30, 1903, 15, carries the same photograph.

10. This type of headdress has been in the news of late: Dorian Lynskey, "This Means War: Why the Fashion Headdress Must Be Stopped," *Guardian*, July 30, 2014, www.theguardian.com/fashion/2014/jul/30/why-the-fashion-headdress-must-be-stopped.

11. "Navajo Culture: Clothing," *Miss Navajo, a Documentary by Billy Luther*, www.pbs.org/independentlens/missnavajo/clothing.html; National Museum of the American Indian, "A Life in Beads: The Stories a Plains Dress Can Tell (Washington, D.C.: NMAI Education Office, n.d.), www.nmai.si.edu.

12. Harry Macdonough, *Navajo* (New York: Victor Talking Machine, 1904), 78 disc; Harry Macdonough, *Navajo* (Orange, N.J.: National Phonograph, 1904), Edison Gold Moulded Record #8640. This version can be found at *UCSB Cylinder Audio Archive*, http://cylinders.library.ucsb.edu.

13. Tim Gracyk, "Harry Tally—Tenor," *Tim's Phonographs and Old Records*, www.gracyk.com/harrytally.shtml; Harry Tally, *Navajo* (New York: Columbia Record, 1904), Indestructible cylinder #32363.

14. "Comments on March Records," *Edison Phonograph Monthly* 1, no. 12 (February 1904), 9.

15. Victor Dance Orchestra, *Navajo* (New York: Victor Talking Machine, 1904), disc #1090; Vess Ossman, *Navajo* (New York: Victor Talking Machine, 1904), disc #1196; Arthur Pryor, *Navajo* (New York: Victor Talking Machine, 1904), disc #960; Edison Military Band, *Navajo Medley* (Orange, N.J.: National Phonograph, 1904), Edison Gold Moulded Record #8673; Victor's Orchestra, *Indian Medley* (New York: Victor Talking Machine, 1904), disc #1090.

16. Gardner, *Popular Songs*, 50–51.

17. "Before the Game," *Cincinnati Enquirer*, April 15, 1904, 4; "Atchison Philosophy," *Wichita (Kans.) Beacon*, April 20, 1904, 4; "Diplomas Given to 173 by Shortridge School," *Indianapolis News*, June 9, 1904, 3.

Tammany, 1905

Tammany, words by Vincent Bryan,
music by Gus Edwards (New York:
M. Witmark and Sons, 1905). Sheet
music from author's collection.

In 1905, *Tammany* became the first of the so-called comic songs about Indians made popular in the wake of *Navajo*. Interestingly, the song was not about Native Americans but about whites who appropriated Indianness. *Tammany* tells a sort of history of the Tammany Society, an organization founded after the Revolutionary War as a "fraternity of patriots" to counter Alexander Hamilton's Tory supporters. The organization's name came from Leni Lenape chief Tammany, who in 1683 sold what would become Pennsylvania to William Penn. Organized into thirteen "tribes" for each of the original states, Tammany societies used supposed Indian symbols and ceremonials,

including the wigwam as meeting place and "Big Chief" as the organization's leader. In this sense, Tammany societies became an early form of playing Indian, the idea that white American men used symbols of Indians to construct their own national identities at the same time that they denigrated Native Americans as savages.[1] During the massive Irish immigration of the 1840s, Tammany Hall became a place to help poor immigrants and, in turn, garner political support. Tammany is best known as the stronghold of New York's Democratic Party and the center of boss rule under William Tweed, from his election as "grand sachem" in 1858 to his downfall fourteen years later. After a brief downturn, the organization rebounded in the 1890s to control city and state Democratic politics under the leadership of Charles Francis Murphy and Timothy Sullivan.[2]

Lyricist Vincent Bryan composed the words to *Tammany*, with Gus Edwards providing the music. According to one story, the two wrote the song as a spoof on popular Indian songs, with its references in the first line to *Hiawatha* and *Navajo*, during a smoker at the National Democratic Club, where it was very well received.[3] Bryan also wrote the Indian song *Sitting Bull* as well as many ragtime songs including *In My Merry Oldsmobile* before going on to work as an editor in Hollywood for Charlie Chaplin and "Fatty" Arbuckle. He died in 1937.[4] Gus Edwards wrote ragtime music, including *School Days*, but was best known as the star maker who discovered Groucho Marx, Eddie Cantor, and Walter Winchell. Born in Prussia, Edwards immigrated with his family to New York City, where he worked as a singer and song plugger. He later formed his own music publishing firm, performed in vaudeville, and in 1928 moved to Hollywood to work in movies. In 1939, Bing Crosby starred in a biopic about Edwards called *The Star Maker*. Edwards died in 1945.[5]

Tammany's lyrics feature eight verses with the same variety of choruses to make jabs at Native Americans, Italians, Irish, farmers, reformers, and others. "Respectfully dedicated" to Timothy Sullivan, the New York politician and strong boss for Tammany Hall, the song also makes topical references to former New York governor Dave B. Hill, politician Tom Platt, notorious swindler Cassie Chadwick, and publisher William Randolph Hearst. The full lyrics are as follows:

> Hiawatha was an Indian, so was Navajo,
> Paleface organ grinders killed them many moons
>   ago.
> But there is a band of Indians, that will never die,
> When they're at the Indian club, this is there battle
>   cry:

Tammany, Tammany,
Big Chief sits in his tepee, cheering braves to
      victory.
Tammany, Tammany,
Swamp 'em, Swamp 'em, get the "wampum,"
      Tammany.

On the Isle of Manhattan, by the bitter sea
Lived this tribe of noble Red men, Tribe of
      Tammany.
From the Totem of the Greenlight Wampum they
      would bring,
When their big Chief Man Behind, would pass the
      pipe and sing:

Tammany, Tammany,
Stick together at the poll, you'll have long green
      wampum rolls.
Tammany, Tammany,
Politicians get positions, Tammany.

Chris Colombo sailed from Spain, across a deep
      blue sea,
Brought along a Dago vote to beat out Tammany
Tammany found Colombo's crew were living on a
      boat,
Big Chief said: "They're floaters," and would not let
      them vote, Then to the tribe he wrote:

Tammany, Tammany,
Get those Dagoes jobs at once, they can vote in
      twelve more months.
Tammany, Tammany,
Make those floaters Tammany voters, Tammany.

Fifteen thousand Irishmen from Erin came across,
Tammany put these Irish Indians on the Police
      force.
I asked one cop, if he wanted three platoons or
      four,
He said: "Keep your old platoons, I've got a
      cuspidor, What would I want with more?"

Tammany, Tammany,
Your policeman can't be beat, They can sleep on
     any street.
Tammany, Tammany,
Dusk is creeping, they're all sleeping, Tammany.

When Reformers think its time to show activity,
They blame everything that's bad on poor old
     Tammany.
All the farmers think that Tammany, caused old
     Adam's fall,
They say when a bad man dies he goes to
     Tammany Hall, Tammany's blamed for all.

Tammany, Tammany,
When a farmer's tax is due, he puts the blame on
     you.
Tammany, Tammany,
On the level you're a devil, Tammany.

Doctor Osler says all men of sixty we should kill
That would give old Tammany a lot of jobs to fill.
They would chloroform old Doctor Parkhurst first
     I know
After that they'd fix Tom Platt, because they love
     him so. And then Depew would not go.

Tammany, Tammany,
When you chloroform to kill, don't forget old Dave
     B. Hill.
Tammany, Tammany,
Rope 'em, Rope 'em, and we'll dope 'em, Tammany.

If we'd let the women vote, they would all get rich
     soon,
Think how old man Platt gave all his money to a
     coon.
Mrs. Chadwick is a girl, who'd lead in politics,
She could show our politicians lots of little tricks,
     the Wall street vote she'd fix.

Tammany, Tammany,
Cassie Chadwick leads them all, she should be in
     Tammany Hall.
Tammany, Tammany,
Who got rich quick? Cassie Chadwick, Tammany.

Tammany's chief is digging out a railroad station
     here,
He shut off the water mains, on folks who can't buy
     beer,
He put in steam shovels, to lay off the workingmen,
Tammany will never see a chief like him again,
     He's the poor man's friend.

Tammany, Tammany,
Murphy is your big Chief's name, he's a Rothschild
     just the same.
Tammany, Tammany,
Willie Hearst will do his worst to Tammany.

Like the lyrics, the sheet music cover and the recordings capitalized on the popularity of Native American songs. The cover art features a pale blue background with an orange-red circle in the center, the words "Tammany" across the top, and "A Pale Face Pow Wow" to the right. In the center of the circle is a profile of an Indian wearing an eagle headdress with one long braid trailing down to the bottom of the page. The composers' names are below the chin of the figure, and to the left is a small photograph of a man with the words "Sung with Great Success by Jefferson DeAngelis in Sam S. Shubert's Production of 'Fantana.'" The publisher, M. Witmark and Sons of New York, is listed below the testimonial. In the extreme lower left is a small mark with the letters *E* and *K* beside it, perhaps the illustrator's symbol.

Tammany became a fairly popular song in 1905 even before each of the three main recording companies produced it. Newspaper accounts link the song to New York politics with incidents of both the Democratic and Republican parties singing it to create fervor among their ranks. In another story, rival factions within the YMCA of Washington, D.C., used the song to stir up members. Still another story associated it with New York's American League baseball team, later known as the Yankees, in a game against Washington.[6]

The song became even more popular as a record. Edison included it in its *Bunker Hill Medley* recorded by the Edison Military Band and as a duet by Arthur Collins and Byron C. Harlan; Columbia used Billy Murray as soloist with orchestra in both its cylinder and disc versions. Columbia also featured xylophonist Edward F. Rubsam in another version of the song. Victor produced four different versions on disc including a vocal solo by Frank Kernell, a.k.a. Samuel H. Dudley, a duet by Collins and Harlan, an instrumental by Arthur Pryor's Orchestra and still another by Pryor's band.[7] The Victor recording by Collins and Harlan features a driving tom-tom beat and repeated Indian war whoops that would have made it difficult to distinguish this spoof on New York politics from other popular Indian songs.[8]

Edison Phonograph Monthly went further by suggesting that *Tammany* was both popular and represented authentic Indian songs. It described the Collins and Harlan cylinder as "a topic song that deals humorously with New York's famous political organization in a way interesting to the whole country." It added that the war whoops of the "braves" brought a "striking bit of realism" to the record and noted that the song was "full of ginger" and "keeping with the character of the words and the meaning of the song." Perhaps this is why Gardner lists the song in his top twenty from May to October 1905, including a location in the top ten from May to September and topping out at number two in June and July.[9] These rankings suggest a connection to the most popular Indian songs of the day.

NOTES

1. Deloria, *Playing Indian.*

2. *Encyclopedia Americana*, 30 vols. (New York: Encyclopedia Americana Corp., 1920), s.v. "Tammany Society."

3. Vincent Bryan and Gus Edwards, *Tammany* (New York: M. Witmark and Sons, 1905); *National Museum of American History*, http://americanhistory.si.edu/collections/, s.v. "Tammany Sheet Music"; Louis Sobol, "New York Cavalcade," *Harrisburg (Pa.) Evening News*, November 15, 1945, 18.

4. *Internet Movie Database*, www.imdb.com, s.v. "Vincent Bryan."

5. *Songwriters Hall of Fame*, www.songwritershalloffame.org/search/, s.v. "Gus Edwards"; Daniel L. McNamara, "Personalities in Music: Gus Edwards Columbus of the Theater," *Alton (Iowa) Democrat*, November 4, 1938, 12; Louis Sobol, "New York Cavalcade," *Harrisburg (Pa.) Evening News*, November 15, 1945, 18.

6. "Mayor Cites Jefferson in Denouncing Greed," *New York Times*, April 14, 1905, 1; "Tammany Wouldn't Down," *New York Times*, June 28, 1905, 9; "Contest in Y.M.C.A.," *Washington Post*, November 7, 1905, 10; "New Nationals Lose," *Washington Post*, April 23, 1905, 1.

7. Information derived from the *Discography of American Historical Recordings*, http://adp.library.ucsb.edu, and the *UCSB Cylinder Audio Archive*, http://cylinders.library.ucsb.edu.

8. Arthur Collins and Byron C. Harlan, *Tammany* (New York: Victor Talking Machine, 1905), disc #4373. This disc also contains an alternative set of verses with the "Swamp 'em, Swamp 'em, get the wampum" chorus repeated several times.

9. "Edison Gold Moulded Records for May," *Edison Phonograph Monthly* 3, no. 2 (April 1905), 8; Gardner, *Popular Songs*, 52–53.

Lasca, 1905

The first cowboy recording, Edgar L. Davenport's *Lasca*, was not a song but the recitation of a cowboy poem. Written by British immigrant Frank Depresz in 1882 after a three-year stay in Texas, "Lasca" first appeared in a London literary magazine that same year before American newspapers reprinted it a few years later.[1] Set during a cattle drive on the Rio Grande in Texas, the poem tells the story of a Mexican girl named Lasca and her cowboy sweetheart. Its opening stanza befits any western story: "I want free life and I want free air, and I sigh after the canter of cattle." The story then describes the couple's meeting and a glimpse into life on a cattle drive. Caught in a stampede, the lovers attempt to outrun the herd on a mustang but fail. In desperation, the cowboy kills his horse to use its body as a shield from the stampeding cattle. But as the horse falls, Lasca is caught beneath the steed and falls dead as well. The poem ends after the cowboy has buried Lasca, "in Texas, down by the Rio Grande."[2]

The full poem reads:

I want free life and I want fresh air;
And I sigh for the canter after the cattle,
The crack of the whips like shots in a battle,
The medley of horns and hoofs and heads
That wars and wrangles and scatters and spreads;
The green beneath and the blue above,
And dash and danger, and life and love—
And Lasca!

Lasca used to ride
On a mouse-gray mustang close by my side,
With blue serape and bright-belled spur;
I laughed with joy as I looked at her!
Little knew she of books or of creeds;
An Ave Maria sufficed her needs;
Little she cared, save to be by my side,
To ride with me, and ever to ride,
From San Saba's shore to LaVaca's tide.
She was as bold as the billows that beat,
She was as wild as the breezes that blow;
From her little head to her little feet
She was swayed in her suppleness to and fro
By each gust of passion; a sapling pine
That grows on the edge of a Kansas bluff
And wars with the wind when the weather is rough
Is like this Lasca, this love of mine.

She would hunger that I might eat,
Would take the bitter and leave me the sweet;
But once, when I made her jealous for fun,
At something I'd whispered, or looked, or done,
One Sunday, in San Antonio,
To a glorious girl in the Alamo,
She drew from her garter a dear little dagger,
And—sting of a wasp!—it made me stagger!
An inch to the left, or an inch to the right,
And I shouldn't be maundering here tonight;
But she sobbed, and, sobbing, so swiftly bound
Her torn reboso about the wound,
That I quite forgave her.
Scratches don't count In Texas, down by the Rio
     Grande.

Her eye was brown—a deep, deep brown;
Her hair was darker than her eye;
And something in her smile and frown,
Curled crimson lip and instep high,
Showed that there ran in each blue vein,
Mixed with the milder Aztec strain,
The vigorous vintage of Old Spain.
She was alive in every limb
With feeling to the finger tips;
And when the sun is like a fire,
And sky one shining, soft sapphire,
One does not drink in little sips.
The air was heavy, and the night was hot,
I sat by her side, and forgot—forgot;
Forgot the herd that were taking their rest,
Forgot that the air was close opprest,
That the Texas norther comes sudden and soon,
In the dead of night or the blaze of noon;
That, once let the herd at its breath take fright,
Nothing on earth can stop the flight;
And woe to the rider, and woe to the steed,
Who falls in front of their mad stampede!

Was that thunder?
I grasped the cord
Of my swift mustang without a word.
I sprang to the saddle, and she clung behind.
Away! On a hot chase down the wind!
But never was fox hunt half so hard,
And never was steed so little spared,
For we rode for our lives,
You shall hear how we fared
In Texas, down by the Rio Grande.

The mustang flew, and we urged him on;
There was one chance left, and you have but one;
Halt, jump to ground, and shoot your horse;
Crouch under his carcass and take your chance;
And, if the steers in their frantic course
Don't batter you both to pieces at once,
You may thank your star; if not, goodby
To the quickening kiss and the long-drawn sigh,
And the open air and the open sky,
In Texas, down by the Rio Grande.

The cattle gained on us, and just as I felt
For my old six-shooter behind in my belt,
Down came the mustang, and down came we,
Clinging together—and, what was the rest?
A body that spread itself on my brest,
Two arms that shielded my dizzy head,
Two lips that hard on my lips were prest;
Then came thunder in my ears,
As over us surged the sea of steers,
Blows that beat blood into my eyes,
And when I could rise—
Lasca was dead!

I gouged out a grave a few feet deep,
And there in Earth's arms I laid her to sleep;
And there she is lying, and no one knows;
And the summer shines and the winter snows;
For many a day the flowers have spread
A pall of petals over her head;
And the little gray hawk hangs aloft in the air,
And the sly coyote trots here and there,
And the black snake glides and glitters and slides
Into a rift in a cottonwood tree;
And the buzzard sails on,
And comes and is gone,
Stately and still like a ship at sea.
And I wonder why I do not care
For the things that are like the things that were.
Does half my heart lie buried there
In Texas, down by the Rio Grande?

Davenport, a member of a famous acting family, recorded a shortened version of "Lasca" for a two-minute Edison cylinder in the summer of 1905 and a slightly longer one for a Victor disc a year later. The National Jukebox at the Library of Congress notes that Davenport possessed a "powerful baritone that registered quite well with the acoustical [recording] process," and he used that voice, recording twenty-one different pieces for Edison, Victor, and Columbia between 1905 and 1913. The August 1905 issue of *Edison Phonograph Monthly* called it a "pathetic poem" that told of the girl's affection for "her lover of the plains." It then recounted the story line, noted Davenport's effectiveness as a speaker, and observed that Chopin's Funeral March plays at the end of the recording.[3] Four years later, when Edison had perfected his four-minute Amberol cylinders, Davenport recreated the poem in a longer version with incidental music included. This time the *Monthly* hinted at its great popularity when it noted that the poem was "familiar to every high-school boy and girl in the country . . . and a great help in their study of elocution."[4]

NOTES

1. The earliest publication listed at Newspaper.com is "Lasca," *Newark (Ohio) Advocate*, January 29, 1883, 2.

2. *All Poetry*, http://allpoetry.com/poems/, s.v. "Lasca" (by Frank Desprez).

3. *Library of Congress, National Jukebox*, www.loc.gov/jukebox/, s.v. "Lasca"; *Discography of American Historical Recordings*, http://adp.library.ucsb.edu, s.v. "Lasca" (Edgar L. Davenport); *UCSB Cylinder Audio Archive*, http://cylinders.library.ucsb.edu, s.v. "Lasca"; "Comments on Edison Gold Moulded Record for September 1905," *Edison Phonograph Monthly* 3, no. 6 (August 1905), 10.

4. Edgar L. Davenport, *Lasca* (Orange, N.J.: National Phonograph, 1909), Edison Amberol #296; "Edison Amberol Records for November," *Edison Phonograph Monthly* 7, no. 9 (September 1909), 16.

Sitting Bull, 1905

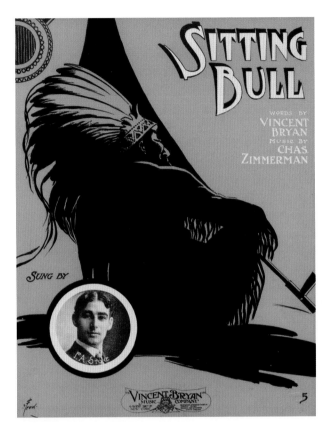

Sitting Bull, words by Vincent Bryan, music by Chas. Zimmerman (New York: Vincent Bryan Music, 1905). Sheet music courtesy Frances G. Spencer Collection of American Popular Sheet Music, Crouch Fine Arts Library, Baylor University Libraries Digital Collections, Baylor University, Waco, Texas.

Tammany composer Vincent Bryan also wrote the lyrics to the 1905 song *Sitting Bull*, another early comic Indian tune that ridiculed the name of the Hunkpapa Sioux leader in an early musical stage production of *The Wizard of Oz*. Oz creator L. Frank Baum had collaborated with composer Paul Tietjens to turn the popular book into a musical play, which debuted in 1901.[1] After several years of success, it was revived in 1904 with new songs and dances. More numbers were added the following year, including

Sitting Bull, written by Bryan and composer Charles Zimmerman.[2] The real Sitting Bull, or Tatanka-Iyotanka, was the Hunkpapa holy man who had participated in the Battle of the Little Bighorn, fled to Canada, and worked for Buffalo Bill in his Wild West exhibition before Indian police arrested and killed him during the 1890 Ghost Dance movement.[3]

For the 1905 version of *The Wizard of Oz*, costar Fred Stone, who played the Scarecrow, added *Sitting Bull* to

"The Dance of All Nations" number in which he sang the tune while dressed as an Indian chief surrounded "by a chorus of girls dressed as Mexicans, cowgirls, and squaws." Following this, Stone performed the "Green Corn Dance," a very strenuous, "spineless, or loose-limbed dance" that became popular with the public and boosted the song with it.[4] The December 3, 1905, issue of the *Boston Globe* described the bit as a "remarkable achievement in acrobatic dancing" and added, "Fred Stone's Indian song 'Sitting Bull' taxes the staying power of this tireless dancer to the utmost. It is a most arduous and terpsichorean 'stunt,' and so numerous are the encores it wins nightly that the comedian is thoroughly exhausted at the conclusion of the performance."[5]

Another newspaper the next spring described the piece as an "Indian war dance in which he [Stone] impersonates Sitting Bull with a scintillating background of pretty girls, garbed as cowboy and Indian squaws."[6] Bryan's lyrics poke fun at the name "Sitting Bull," connect scalping to barbering, suggest he hated the Indian police, and say that his portrait adorns the penny. The song goes like this:

> Mary Cow, an Indian maiden, married "Standing
>   Steer!"
> Mary had a little lamb, she said he was a "Deer!"
> Mary's kid would do no work, he seemed to have
>   a pull,
> He sat 'round the camp so much they called him,
>   "Sitting Bull!"
>
> Bull became a barber and employed a thousand men.
> Once they'd cut your hair, you'd never need it cut
>   again!
> He disliked bald headed men, they chased him
>   everywhere;
> They knew Sitting Bull was very good at raising hair.

> Sitting Bull, just hated all the Indian Police!
> He would follow on their track, they could not
>   make him cease.
> He could scent policemen out no matter where
>   they went.
> Though he's dead, his head is still upon the copper
>   cent.
>
> *Chorus*
> Old Sitting Bull, he was no fool;
> He was a well-read man, although he never went
>   to school,
> He would not walk when he was full,
> He sat on all the other chiefs, did Sitting Bull.

John Frew illustrated the sheet music cover for *Sitting Bull*, and its simplicity reflects the artist's style. Frew was born in 1875 in Ireland and immigrated to the United States at age twenty but retained his Irish citizenship and frequently traveled back home. He worked for several different publishing companies from his Manhattan home from the 1890s to the 1930s. According to sheet music historian Bill Edwards, Frew illustrated a variety of covers, with his best-known work probably being that for *Alexander's Ragtime Band.* Edwards notes that Frew often placed detailed figures in the foreground set against simple backgrounds.[7] This is true of the *Sitting Bull* cover. Colored in orange and black, the image features the dark figure of an Indian sitting against a tepee opening. His face is turned away, with only the buckskin fringes of his clothing, a pipe, and his feather headdress clearly visible. To his back are the words "Sung by" and a cameo image of F. A. Stone. The song's title and credits are in white, set to the right against the tepee.

Despite the popularity of the Oz play, Edison did not record *Sitting Bull*, and the only recordings that I can locate are references to discs made by Columbia,

Zon-o-phone, and the International Record Company. For Columbia, Frank Williams recorded the disc for an April 1906 release, and Arthur Collins and Byron G. Harlan sang it for Zon-o-phone around that same time. Despite the success of the *Wizard of Oz*, Gardner does not include the song in his charts.[8]

NOTES

1. Matz, "Images of Indians," 254–57; Swartz, *Oz before the Rainbow*.
2. Vincent Bryan and Chas. Zimmerman, *Sitting Bull* (New York: Vincent Bryan Music, 1905). This can be found online at the Frances G. Spencer Collection of Popular Sheet Music site at Baylor University, http://digitalcollections.baylor.edu/cdm/ref/collection/fa-spnc/id/5531.
3. Utley, *Lance and the Shield*.
4. Swartz, *Oz before the Rainbow*, 144.
5. "Plays and Players," *Boston Globe*, December 3, 1905, 53–54.
6. "News of the Theater," *Scranton (Pa.) Republican*, May 6, 1906, 7.
7. Bill Edwards, "John Frew," *RagPiano*, www.perfessorbill.com/artists/frew.shtml.
8. *Discography of American Historical Recordings*, http://adp.library.ucsb.edu, s.v. "Sitting Bull"; "Record Bulletins for April 1906," *Talking Machine World* 2, no. 3 (March 15, 1906), 29; *Talking Machine World* 2, no. 4 (May 15, 1906), 39.

Feather Queen, 1905

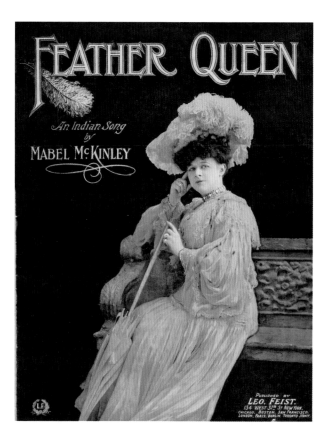

Feather Queen, **words and music by Mabel McKinley (New York: Leo Feist, 1905).** Sheet music from author's collection.

The first Indian love song after *Navajo* was Mabel McKinley's 1905 song *Feather Queen*.[1] McKinley was the niece of President William McKinley and had first hit it big in western music with *Anona*, which she published in 1903 under the pseudonym Vivian Grey. Although contemporary reports suggest that McKinley often sang the lyrics, *Feather Queen* apparently was never recorded as anything but an instrumental intermezzo or two-step.

Nevertheless, an examination of the sheet music suggests a love song around ideas of assimilation in which a beautiful chieftain's daughter called the Feather Queen tells the brave who is courting her that she loves "pale face ways." Then, when the young man goes to town and buys a suit of clothes to prove his love, the Feather Queen relents, telling him, "You can't make a pale face man, of a true born Indian." The full lyrics are as follows:

Once an Indian loved a chieftain's daughter,
Sweet sixteen, quite serene, an Indian queen
Though she liked the brave who came to court her,
Feather Queen was a sad coquette, like girls I've
    seen!
She said "It's try, you've come to woo, and I love you!
But still, you see, the man for me, a swell must be;
Tis the pale face ways I love"
Then he vowed by stars above
That none but he should win this pretty Feather
    Queen!
When day is ended
And sunset splendid
Bathes all the prairie
In gold and green!
Then I'll come to you
To fondly woo you,
Dear prairie fairy,
My Feather Queen!

Then the Indian caught his fleetest pony
Rode away, without delay, to town that day
Bought some clothes that made him look real "tony"
Then returned, to his Feather Queen, for whose
    love he yearned.
But, what a shame, for when he came, she took the
    blame
And in distress, cried "change that dress, for I
    confess"
You can't make a pale face man, Of a true born
    Indian!
You've won my heart, I'll be your little Feather
    Queen!

Like the sheet music cover for *Anona*, the one for *Feather Queen* places more significance on McKinley's celebrity than on an idealized Indian maiden. In a simple black-and-white image, McKinley, dressed in a long flowing gown, holds a parasol and wears an elaborate hat of feathers. She sits on a bench looking straight into the camera. The title "Feather Queen" sits atop the sheet with a single feather crossing the *F* and underlining the *ea* of the first word. "An Indian Song by Mabel McKinley" stands below the feather hat, level with the composer.

Both Edison and Victor recorded versions of *Feather Queen* in late 1905, though both did so only as instrumental dance songs. *Edison Phonograph Monthly* for March 1906 suggested that the cylinder was becoming very popular. The Victor disc plays the tune at a lively speed, with lots of flourishes, and it sounds a lot like the instrumental versions of *Hiawatha* or *Anona*.[2]

Contemporary accounts suggest that McKinley also sang versions of *Feather Queen* on stage, contributing to her becoming a popular composer. A Missouri newspaper reported that she appeared in late 1905 in New York in the four-act play *The Parson's Wife*, in which she played the daughter of a Virginia family who sings to pay off the family mortgage. This play allowed McKinley to perform three of her own songs including *Anona* and *Feather Queen* and gave her "ample scope for displaying her pleasing vocal ability." The *Washington Post* remarked later that year that McKinley was a vaudeville favorite and that the International Dancing Masters' Association had accepted *Feather Queen* as a ballroom dance. Another story in that paper in early 1906 announced her as the leading attraction at Chase's "Polite Vaudeville" and suggested that the talented McKinley had "overcome the most discouraging of obstacles, the chief of which was the unexpressed public suspicion that she was perhaps trading upon the advantage of a name that the American people will always revere and honor." A Chicago paper similarly remarked that McKinley was a star and that her original compositions such as *Feather Queen* had "netted her a tidy sum."[3]

Other articles specifically connected the song to images of Native Americans. The *Philadelphia Inquirer* included in a December 1905 story three lines of music of *Feather Queen* and a picture of the composer. It then suggested a primitivist view of the exotic:

> The fad of any American girl for anything in the musical line bearing on Indian flavor, particularly that which pertains to the ballroom, has induced dancing masters of recent days and composers of the new style of two-step to emulate each other in the glorification of the red man.
>
> So pronounced has this crotchet become that no title embodying the characteristics of the

aborigine has been left undiscovered by modern writers, the latest and most unique of which is the new intermezzo by Miss Mabel McKinley known as the "Feather Queen." It is essentially an American work in text and purpose, possessing, however, a theme, the originality of which is coexistent with the native Indian in all his quaint and eccentric individuality.[4]

Another story the following summer reported that McKinley and a maid drove a huge car, specially outfitted for her by music publisher Leo Feist and complete with wardrobe, a bed for two, and kitchen complete with icebox, from New York to Pittsburgh. It reported that it was "probably the only case on record where a public singer has made single-handed a journey by automobile of five hundred miles or more." Once in the "soot laden city," McKinley sang *Feather Queen* and other Indian songs for the "Red Men council" at the opening of the new Luna amusement park on Independence Day.[5]

This "council" was not an Indian meeting but a conference of the fraternal organization known as the Improved Order of Red Men, a group of white men who played Indian as part of their goal of "perpetuating the beautiful legends and traditions of a once-vanishing race and the keeping alive some of the traditional customs, ceremonies, and practices." The fact that McKinley made

such an unprecedented drive to Pittsburgh to perform her "authentic" Indian songs to a group of white fraternal brothers playing Indian suggests how deeply authentic some believed these Indian love songs to be.[6] Despite such sentiments, Gardner does not include *Feather Queen* in any of his top-twenty lists.

NOTES

1. Mabel McKinley, *Feather Queen* (New York: Leo Feist, 1905).
2. "Comments on Edison Gold Moulded Records for April 1906," *Edison Phonograph Monthly* 4, no. 1 (March 1906), 9; *Discography of American Historical Recordings*, http://adp.library.ucsb.edu, s.v. "Feather queen."
3. "Mabel McKinley a Star," *Sedalia (Mo.) Democrat*, November 28, 1905, 3; "Notes of the Stage," *Washington Post*, December 31, 1905, 2; "Coming to the Theaters," *Washington Post*, March 15, 1906, 4; "Vaudeville Stars," *Chicago Inter-Ocean*, May 6, 1906, 38. Chase's unusual title for his theater can be found in "Chase's Polite Vaudeville," *Army and Navy Register* 34, no. 1370 (Washington, D.C.), March 17, 1906, 18.
4. "New Ball Room Dance by Mabel McKinley," *Philadelphia Inquirer*, December 10, 1905, 16.
5. "Mabel M'Kinley's Novel Automobile Tour," *El Paso Herald*, July 11, 1906, 7; Meg O'Malley, "Luna Park," *Popular Pittsburgh*, www.popularpittsburgh.com/pittsburgh-info/pittsburgh-sportsandrec/amusement-parks/lunapark.aspx.
6. Deloria, *Playing Indian*, 62–71; *The Improved Order of Red Men*, http://redmen.org/redmen/info/; Elliott Young, "Red Men, Princess Pocahontas, and George Washington: Harmonizing Race Relations In Laredo at the Turn of the Century," *Western Historical Quarterly* 29 (Spring 1998): 48–85.

Silver Heels, 1905

Silver Heels, words by James O'Dea, music by Neil Moret (New York: Jerome H. Remick, 1905). Sheet music from author's collection.

Silver Heels (march two-step), music by Neil Moret (New York: Jerome H. Remick, 1905). Sheet music from author's collection.

Following on his success with *Hiawatha,* composer Neil Moret produced another popular Indian love song, *Silver Heels,* in late 1905. Although Moret had originally written *Hiawatha* as an instrumental love song for his girlfriend in Hiawatha, Kansas, when he sold the tune to Jerome Remick for $10,000 the publisher hired lyricist James O'Dea to recast the song as an Indian love song based on the Longfellow poem. After the recordings by Harry Macdonough and John Philip Sousa went big, Remick rewarded Moret with a job as a publishing executive and encouraged him to find more such songs. The firm published *Navajo* in 1904, and then in 1905, caught up in the growing Indian craze he had helped start, Moret teamed again with O'Dea to write *Silver Heels.*[1]

In place of the interracial ambiguities of *Navajo,* the *Silver Heels* love story between an "Indian brave" and the "sweetest and neatest little girl" clearly has overtones of assimilation and domesticity. During the chorus, for example, Young Chief suggests that he will build Silver Heels "a big teepee" if she will come and cook his meals. Then, during the second verse, he suggests that the two of them will be "right at home" with a "hubby and chubby little papoose on her knee." Along with assimilation, the song's use of "fake Indian speech" in lines such as "heap much kissing" suggests a derogatory attitude toward Native Americans rather than Moret's purported admiration.[2]

Period accounts suggest the supposed authenticity Moret brought to his Indian songs. One story, reproduced in various forms across the country in, among others, the *Washington Post, Minneapolis Journal*, and *Santa Cruz Sentinel*, described the song and several lines of the intermezzo:

> The text of the "Silver Heels" composition is founded upon the Sioux style of chant, and its Indian aroma is pregnant with all the glamor of the Wigwam— the fire dance, the holocaust, and the triumphal march of conquest. The opening measures of the composition bespeak the conclave of the pipe of peace, merging into strains of hilarity and joy, and culminating with the glory of battle. . . . The author of "Hiawatha" looks forward to a renown duplicated in the former work through the bold treatment of his present Indian production.[3]

The text, of course, is not Sioux but was born within the fervent imaginations of Moret and O'Dea and suggests not authenticity but the playing Indian of the Improved Order of Red Men (see *Feather Queen*).

The full text of the song goes like this:

Where the cornflow'rs wave once an Indian brave,
All unfettered by the white man's law,
Loved a pretty little crowfoot squaw
Just the sweetest and the neatest little girl he ever saw.
She was always coy to this Indian boy,
To his heart she didn't do a thing,
When the moonbeams on the river set the
    shadows all a quiver, then he'd sing:

I love you and you love me,
Pretty little Silver Heels
I'll build you a big teepee,
If you will come and cook my meals
Young Chief's blue and all for you,
Plenty heap he love-sick feels
Don't be missing, heap much kissing, Silver Heels.

When the summer goes and the north wind blows
In a cozy little wigwam we,
"Will be always right at home." said he
"With a hubby and a chubby little papoose on your
    knee."
But the maiden shy only dropped her eye,
As a tender little sigh she sighed
While her copper colored lover 'neath the silv'ry
    stars above her, once more cried:

I love you and you love me,
Pretty little Silver Heels
I'll build you a big teepee,
If you will come and cook my meals
Young Chief's blue and all for you,
Plenty heap he love-sick feels
Don't be missing, heap much kissing, Silver Heels.

The sheet music covers for the *Silver Heels* song and intermezzo two-step also suggest authenticity. For the song, artist Bertha Young painted a background reminiscent of a birch tree and then inserted into its center a cameo head-and-shoulders painting of a Caucasian-looking Indian woman.[4] She looks to her left and wears her hair in two braids at her shoulders. The song's title is curved over the top of the cameo and a beaded necklace. Below the insert is the tag "An Indian Ballad" and the credits "Poem by Jas. O'Dea, Melody by Neil Moret." The publishing information is located at the bottom of the page. Young also illustrated the instrumental, this time painting a young Native American woman dancing. She wears a Plains Indian buckskin dress and tall moccasins. "Silverheels" is written in white across the top with "Indian Intermezzo-Two Step" in gold beneath against a dark green forest background. At the lower right are the song and publisher credits including "By Neil Moret, Composer of 'Hiawatha,' 'Moonlight,' etc."

Like many of these Indian love songs, recording companies issued both instrumental and vocal versions of *Silver Heels*. A Victor disc sung by Harry Tally in 1906 follows the lyrics except for not singing the words "hubby or chubby" in the second verse. The Harmony Disc Record company, a subsidiary of Columbia, also released a disc. The Edison cylinder featured the Edison Military Band in an instrumental version that *Edison Phonograph Monthly* suggested "will be extremely popular and much asked for, [it] goes without saying, even if it had to depend on its catchy musical merit alone, without the added boom it will get from its very much alive publishers and the reputation from its famous composer."[5] Later that fall, the trade journal listed the title among its "Jobber's List of 250 Good Selling Edison Records." Gardner lists *Silver Heels* among his top-twenty songs from December 1905 to April 1906, peaking at number six in February 1906.[6]

NOTES

1. James O'Dea and Neil Moret, *Silver Heels* (New York: Jerome H. Remick, 1905); Neil Moret, *Silver Heels* (New York: Jerome H. Remick, 1905). Pisani, *Imagining Native America*, 248–54, discusses Moret's story.

2. Pisani, *Imagining Native America*, 256–57, also discusses the significance of what he calls "fake Indian speech."

3. "New Musical Work by 'Hiawatha's' Author," *Washington Post*, September 24, 1905, 3; "A Musical Hit," *Minneapolis Journal*, November 26, 1905, 5; "New Musical Composition," *Santa Cruz (Calif.) Sentinel*, December 20, 1905, 11.

4. Except for about a dozen other period sheet music examples of her cover art, I could find nothing else about artist Bertha Young other than that she appears to be one of the very few women in this business at this time.

5. Harry Tally, *Silver Heels* (New York: Victor Talking Machine, 1906), disc #4579; Harmony Disc Record, *Silver Heels* (Chicago: Great Northern Mfg., ca. 1907), disc #2044; "Comments on Edison Gold Moulded Records for February 1906," *Edison Phonograph Monthly* 3, no. 11 (January 1906), 9.

6. "A Jobber's List of 250 Good Selling Edison Records," *Edison Phonograph Monthly* 4, no. 9 (November 1906), 20; Gardner, *Popular Songs*, 53–54.

Cheyenne, 1906

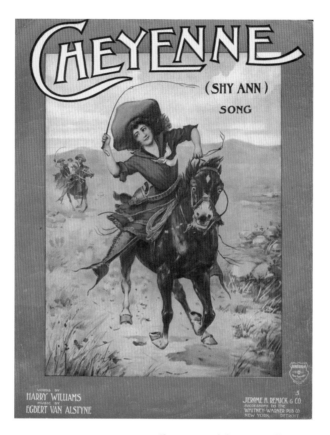

Cheyenne, words by Harry Williams,
music by Egbert Van Alstyne (Detroit:
Jerome H. Remick, 1906). Sheet music
from author's collection.

Although *Lasca* was the first recording to depict cowboys, Harry Williams and Egbert Van Alstyne's *Cheyenne* started the cowboy music craze in 1906. Written by the *Navajo* composers, *Cheyenne* also first gained fame on stage in the two-act music comedy *The Earl and the Girl*, which ran in England between December 1903 and September 1904 before adding new songs, including *Cheyenne*, in 1905. It then played in both England and New York, where comedian Eddie Foy starred.[1]

Within a year, newspapers reported that *Cheyenne*, as sung by J. Bernard Dyllyn, was the hit song of the play. An interesting story from a Washington, D.C., newspaper reported that during the acting troupe's goodwill trip to the "Government Hospital for the Insane" in April 1906, "J. Bernard Dyllyn, with a bevy of cow-girls," sang *Cheyenne*, "and the shouting of the chorus was greatly augmented by the whoops of many of the male auditors, who were unable to restrain their desire to have a part in the success of the number." The *Harrisburg Telegraph* similarly commented on "the dashing cowboy and girl feature, 'Cheyenne,'" with its beautiful and artistic costumes.[2]

Although sometimes mistaken as part of the Indian song craze, *Cheyenne* does not include any reference to the Cheyenne tribe but is instead a love story between a cowboy and a cowgirl known as Shy Ann.[3] In fact, the story line clearly recounts the meeting between the Virginian and Molly Stark Wood from Owen Wister's novel after her stagecoach got stuck midstream and the cowboy carried her out on his horse. Describing this action, Wister wrote, "a tall rider appeared so close against the buried axles, and took her out of the stage on his horse so suddenly that she screamed."[4] Also set in Wyoming, the characters in *Cheyenne* meet sixty-seven miles from the capital city, where the cowboy picks up Shy Ann and rides off with her.

The Jerome H. Remick music company, the same that had printed *Navajo*, published the sheet music version of *Cheyenne* in 1905.[5] The cover depicts neither the Wister story nor the song's lyrics. It has a bright red border around a western scene with the word "Cheyenne" in white letters crossing through the border and illustration at the top. The composers are listed at the lower left and the publishing company on the lower right. Interestingly, above the title on the music page is a dedication "to our mutual friend Danny Maher," the top American jockey then working in England.[6] On the top right of the cover illustration are the words "Shy Ann" in parentheses and "song" below them. The illustration itself has a western setting with dirt, a little grass, and rocks in the foreground and distant mountains in the background. In the center a dark-haired cowgirl rides a mad, dashing horse whose eyes bulge out. The woman, presumably Shy Ann, is no eastern spinster but sits astride the horse, holding the reins in her left hand and a whip in her right. She wears a large cowboy hat, a red blouse with sleeves rolled up to her elbows, and a kerchief around her neck. A six-gun is holstered around the top of her blue knee-length skirt, and tall leather boots with fringes wrap her legs. Although the girl's face is forward, her eyes look back to a group of three mounted cowboys in hot pursuit, one with a similar whip held high in the air.

The song's lyrics begin with three "yips!" then go:

Way out in Old Wyoming long ago,
Where coyotes lurk while night winds howl and
    blow,
A cowboy's lusty voice rang out "Hello"
And echoed thro' the valley down below

Then came back a maiden's answer sweet and
    clear,
Cowboy tossed his hat up in the air
Said he "I've come to take you right away from
    here,
Cheyenne, they say, is miles away but they've a
    preacher there."

Then She just drooped her eye,
She was so very shy,
So shy, oh my, and then he made reply.
Oh! Oh! Oh!

Chorus
Shy Ann, Shy Ann, hop on my pony,
There's room here for two dear,
But after the ceremony,
We'll both ride back home dear, as one,
On my pony from old Cheyenne.

They rode that night and nearly half the day,
Cheyenne was sixty seven miles away,
But when at last they galloped up the street,
The cowboy's pride was really hard to beat,
On his arm his future bride a carrying,
But beneath the little churches dome,
Said she "I feel like turning back, not marrying,
His face got red, and then he said, "You will or
    you'll walk home,"
If you ride back today, you'll honor and obey,
I do, I do, then he was heard to say, Oh! Oh! Oh!

Repeat Chorus

The cowboy record craze began when Billy Murray made his Victor disc of *Cheyenne* on April 27, 1906, in Philadelphia.[7] Murray was the most popular singer in the acoustic talking machine era and was well known for covering the songs of George M. Cohan such as *Give My Regards to Broadway* and *Yankee Doodle Boy*. Although he had been raised in the Mile High City, the "Denver Nightingale"—as he was known—had not yet recorded any songs about his native West, although a close friend suggested that Murray was "well acquainted with both Indians and Cowboys."[8]

Murray's version of *Cheyenne* was the first record

to be listed as a "cowboy song," and it soon became the biggest hit of the year and then was remade repeatedly by competing recording companies. All told, twenty-one different outfits recorded the song: an American Record Company disc, a Columbia two-minute cylinder, two Columbia discs, a D&R disc, a Faultless Concert disc, a Columbia Master disc, an Indian seven-inch disc, an International disc, a Kalamazoo disc, a Lyric disc, a Marconi disc from a Columbia pressing, an Oxford disc, Silvertone, Standard, and Star discs from a Columbia pressing, ten-inch and eight-inch Victor discs, another Victor disc, and two Zon-o-phone discs.[9]

Edison is notably absent from this list. Historian Jim Walsh suggests that perhaps "Mr. Edison did not like the number!"[10] Others argue that the New Jersey company appealed more to rural America than to urban dwellers, so perhaps the "postfrontier" nostalgia of *Cheyenne* was more prevalent among the increasingly urban population, patrons of Victor, Columbia, and the others. That said, Edison jumped on the cowboy bandwagon soon enough with its cylinder *Broncho Bob and His Little Cheyenne*, which basically offers the *Cheyenne* lyrics as a two-person skit and features an upbeat version of its chorus sung by Ada Jones. Edison also released its own version of nearly every cowboy song produced before World War I included in this catalogue. This suggests that if Edison did not recognize the potential cowboy interest in *Cheyenne* in 1906 it quickly understood the song's resonance with the American market and worked to supply its own product to satisfy this demand for frontier nostalgia.[11]

Of these various recordings, two versions by Murray best represent the song. The first, which appeared on the Columbia cylinder, discs, and other company recordings made from the Columbia pressings, was issued in June 1906 and is a fairly straight performance with Murray singing it with a band accompaniment. Although the sheet music calls for an *allegro moderato* tempo, roughly 116–120 beats per minute, Murray sings it a bit slower, more like 90 beats per minute. Prominent throughout is a tom-tom beating through both the verse and the chorus. This feature, most associated with Native American music, is perhaps why *Cheyenne* has been characterized as an Indian song.[12]

Billy Murray made his more famous recording with Victor in July 1906. It also features a prominent tom-tom, a band accompaniment, and western sound effects. The record also has a faster pace at about 120 beats per minute, as the tempo markings indicate. Then, accompanying the opening notes, war whoops and yells are heard before Murray ever sings a note. As he sings the first line a shot rings out, and as he finishes the second line of the verse about howling winds a slide whistle sounds. The whoops and yells, as well as the tom-tom, return between the chorus and the second verse, which features the sound of galloping horses. The cries return after the second chorus as the band plays the melody for the last time.[13]

These many recordings made *Cheyenne* quite popular. Gardner lists the song as first making it into the top twenty in April 1906, cracking the top ten the following month, and then rising to number three in June that year. It remains in his top five throughout the summer and leaves his charts in November.[14]

The trade journal *Talking Machine World* ran an advertisement for the American Record Company's release, made from the Victor pressing, with the picture of a cowboy and Native American woman (sitting sidesaddle) in a cameo illustration. The adjacent text simply says "Cheyenne" in large letters at the top and lists the record number and that it was sung by Billy Murray. It then states "One of Our Latest Records—A Decided Hit! A cowboy romance, depicting life on the Western Plains. Introducing the hoof-beats of the pony, Indian yells, and other effects." Later, the same issue describes *Cheyenne* in one of its song lists as "the biggest hit this year." The following month, in an article on the difficulty of predicting which songs will be most popular with the public, the head of the American Record Company's laboratory remarked, "Cheyenne is another song which looks good. We listed this last month in our bulletin . . . by Billy Murray, and already it is going big." Finally, the July issue, in an article on the value of window displays, wrote: "We will take, for example, 'Cheyenne,' the cowboy love song which is so popular just now. A window filled with the regalia of the western plains, saddles, spurs, rifles and revolvers, and if the Indian side is to be represented, Navajo blankets, bows and arrows arranged in an artistic manner will collect a crowd of the curious immediately."[15]

Like today's reality and talent show television programs, the success of *Cheyenne* spurred the creation of similar songs almost immediately. *Talking Machine World* lists a *Cheyenne March and Two-Step* recorded on Zon-o-phone records in its July 15, 1906, edition, and two months later it listed another recording simply called *Cheyenne Medley.* On December 5, 1906, none other than Billy Murray recorded by far the strangest take-off on the hit cowboy song. Inspired by Upton Sinclair's popular muckraking novel *The Jungle* set in Chicago's meatpacking area, Murray sang *Cheyenne: Parody,* which tells the tale of a sick horse bound for the slaughterhouse.[16] Murray, accompanied by orchestra but thankfully without sound effects, sings on Victor records:

> Way out in old Wyoming lives a man,
> Who owned a sick old pony named Shy Ann
> This pony was so old it couldn't stand
> And it had every sickness in the land.
>
> But one day the beef trust sent its agent down
> He paid thirty cents for old Shy Ann
> Said he we'll ship this pony off to Packingtown
> She may be sick
> But she'll look slick
> When packed into a can
> We'll take poor old Shy Ann
> We'll put her in a can
> We'll can Shy Ann, she'll look like potted ham. Oh,
>   Oh, Oh,
>
> Cheyenne, Cheyenne, you sick old pony
> We'll take you,
> And bake you
> And make you into baloney
> And the folks who eat you won't know
> You're that pony from old Cheyenne.

This version surely tested the old saying that imitation is the sincerest form of flattery.

NOTES

1. Fields, *Eddie Foy*, 161–64; *Wikipedia*, s.v. "The Earl and the Girl."

2. "Special Sale of Sheet Music," *Brooklyn Daily Eagle*, March 18, 1906, 5; "Actors Dance and Sing for the Amusement of the Insane," *Washington Post*, April 4, 1906, 11; "Actors at the Hospital," *Washington (D.C.) Evening Star*, April 4, 1906, 22; "Shylock and Co. A Success," *Harrisburg (Pa.) Telegraph*, April 16, 1906, 8.

3. The inside cover of the March 15, 1906, issue of *Talking Machine World* ran an advertisement for the American Record Company's version of *Cheyenne* depicting a cowboy and an Indian maiden riding on a horse; see issue at http://archive.org/details/talkingmachinewo2bill.

4. Owen Wister, *The Virginian: A Horseman of the Plains* (New York: MacMillan, 1902), 101–2.

5. Harry Williams and Egbert Van Alstyne, *Cheyenne* (New York: Jerome H. Remick, 1905).

6. "Daniel A. Maher," *National Museum of Racing and Hall of Fame*, www.racingmuseum.org/hall-of-fame/daniel-maher.

7. Murray had recorded *Cheyenne* on January 19, 1906, for Victor, but the whereabouts of that recording are unknown. See *Discography of American Historical Recordings*, http://adp.library.ucsb.edu, s.v. "Cheyenne" (Billy Murray).

8. Walsh suggests that Victor catalogue editor Sam Rous had asked Murray if he had a nickname that could be published, and Murray "facetiously replied that it might be appropriate to call him a 'Rocky Mountain Canary,'" the name given to mules who worked in western mines. Rous instead thought of Jenny Lind's nickname, "Swedish Nightingale," and started referring to Murray as the "Denver Nightingale." See Walsh, "'Cowboy Song' Recordings, Part 2," *Hobbies*, May 1976, 35–36.

9. Hoffman, Carty, and Riggs, *Billy Murray*, 231–32, 62; "New Columbia Cylindrical Records," *Fitchburg (Mass.) Sentinel*, May 29, 1906.

10. Walsh, "'Cowboy Song' Recordings, Part 1," *Hobbies*, April 1976, 35.

11. Greg Milner, *Perfecting Sound Forever: An Aural History of Recorded Music* (London: Faber and Faber, 2010), 38. Postfrontier nostalgia is discussed in Wrobel, *End of American Exceptionalism*, 69–142.

12. Harry Williams and Egbert Van Alstyne, *Cheyenne (Shy Ann)* (Columbia Phonograph, 1906), cylinder #32944; Harry Williams and Egbert Van Alstyne, *Cheyenne—Cowboy Song* (Columbia Phonograph. 1906), 78 disc #3389.

13. Harry Williams and Egbert Van Alstyne, *Cheyenne (Shy Ann)* (Victor Talking Machine, 1906), 78 disc #16102-A.

14. Gardner, *Popular Songs*, 54–55.

15. *Talking Machine World* 2, no. 3 (March 15, 1906), inside cover, 30; "Hard to 'Pick the Winner,'" *Talking Machine World* 2, no. 4 (April 15, 1906), 30; "Value of Window Displays," *Talking Machine World* 2, no. 7 (July 15, 1906), 9.

16. Billy Murray, *Cheyenne—Parody* (Victor Talking Machine, 1906) 78 disc #4974; *Library of Congress, National Jukebox*, www.loc.gov/jukebox/, s.v. "Cheyenne: Parody."

Arrah Wanna, 1906

Arrah Wanna, words by Jack Drislane,
music by Theodore Morse (New York:
F. B. Haviland, 1906). Sheet music
from author's collection.

Arrah Wanna (intermezzo two-step),
music by Theodore Morse (New York:
F. B. Haviland, 1906). Sheet music
from author's collection.

Like *Navajo*, *Arrah Wanna* is an interracial love song that played stereotypes against each other, in this case Native American and Irish, as part of an assertion of a favored American ethnicity. The song tells the story of Irishman Barney Carney's love for Indian maiden Arrah Wanna (Arrah was a stereotypical name for an Irish girl). Although this may seem like an odd pairing, period songs about the Irish were as popular as songs about Indians, so bringing the two together in what the songwriter called "An Irish Indian Matrimonial Venture" made sense.[1]

Indeed, something about the song resonated with the American public. According to Gardner, *Arrah Wanna* may have been one of the most popular Indian songs of the era. In his reconstructed history of top-twenty song charts, Gardner indicates that *Arrah Wanna* first made the list in November 1906, the last time that *Cheyenne* did so, and stayed in the top twenty for the next eight months, hitting the top ten for six of those and climbing to number one in January and February 1907.[2]

Arrah Wanna represented eastern views of western racial mixing. Whereas *Navajo* uses a "colored man" to court an Indian maiden, in *Arrah Wanna* Barney Carney serenades Arrah Wanna outside of her "tent" with his bagpipes. Of course there were Irish in the American West going back at least a century, most certainly Irish-Indian marriages, and dozens of popular songs about the Irish and Ireland during the Tin Pan Alley era. Nevertheless, historian Mick Molony suggests that "as mainstream as the Irish in America had become, they were still not members of the establishment." Songs like *Arrah Wanna* thus appropriated western peoples into eastern ideals of Jim Crow America and "placed the Irish in incongruous situations with exotic 'others.'" But as historian Linda Gordon and others suggest, this view of the Irish resided mostly in the metropolitan east, whereas many westerners considered the Irish white.[3]

The song's lyrics intermix stereotypical identities, calling the Indian maid a "queen of fairies" and the Irish laddie a "buck" in the first verse. In the chorus, the song also plays with gender norms when the Irishman promises to build her a "wigwam made of shamrocks green" that will "make those redmen smile." Then in the second verse, Arrah Wanna makes a plea for racial superiority, suggesting that before she will marry Barney Carney "some great race must call you Big Chief," only to have the Irishman cleverly change the meaning by suggesting that his family all are great runners and "first in every race." The full lyrics go like this:

> 'Mid the wild and wooly prairies lived an Indian
>   maid,
> Arrah Wanna queen of fairies of her tribe afraid
> Each night came an Irish laddie buck, with a
>   wedding ring
> He would sit outside her tent and his bagpipes
>   loudly sing.

Chorus
> "Arrah Wanna, on my honor, I'll take care of you,
> I'll be kind and true
> we can love and bill and coo
> In a wigwam made of shamrocks green, we'll
>   make those red men smile,
> When you're Misses Barney, heap much Carney,
>   from Killarney's Isle."

> While the moon shone down upon them Arrah
>   Wanna sighed
> "Some great race must call you Big Chief, then I'll
>   be your bride."
> "Sure that's easy" whispered Barney, with a
>   smiling face,
> "All my fam'ly were good runners and were first in
>   every race."

Repeat Chorus

Theodore Morse composed the music for *Arrah Wanna* and Jack Drislane penned the lyrics.[4] Little is know about Drislane other than that he wrote several popular songs of the period with Morse, including more than three dozen that were recorded by various artists. According to one period newspaper ad, he worked with Morse and another man as a singer, dancer, and humorist. Morse was born in Washington, D.C., in 1873, studied piano and violin as a boy, and then left the Maryland Military Academy for New York City at age fourteen. He worked for various music publishers as a clerk, song plugger, and composer, publishing his first song in 1895. After failing to operate his own music publishing house, Morse settled into life as a composer and arranger for the firm Howley, Haviland, and Dresser, eventually becoming chief composer and a partner in the firm. A year after *Arrah Wanna* appeared, he married Alfreda Theodora Strandberg, and the couple became a song-writing team, producing several popular rags including *Blue Bell* and *M-O-T-H-E-R*. Like many composers of the period, Morse capitalized on the popularity of ethnically charged humor in the years before the Great War, producing songs that denigrated Jews (*When Mose with His Nose Leads the Band*), Irish (*Arrah Wanna*), African Americans (*Down in Jungle Town*), and Germans (*The Leader of the German Band*). He died in 1924. Morse was a founding member of ASCAP and was elected to the Songwriters Hall of Fame in 1970.[5]

André De Takacs created the dramatic sheet music covers for both the song and the intermezzo versions of *Arrah Wanna* for F. B. Haviland music publishers. De Takacs, the son of a Hungarian count, immigrated to the United States in 1901 and established an art studio in New York City. He created sheet music covers for many songs between 1906 and 1919—including westerns *Iola*, *My Pony Boy*, and *Ragtime Cow Boy Joe*—and also illustrated a couple of books, commercial art, and postcards. He was noted for his bold color schemes. He died of a heart attack at age thirty-nine.[6]

For *Arrah Wanna*, De Takacs divided the cover into three vertical sections, with the two outer thirds colored in a bold cherry red serving to frame the middle green section containing a scene from the song. In this view, Carney—dressed in traditional Irish costume of knickers, long hose, buckled shoes, a long coat, ruffled shirt, and top hat—plays his bagpipes outside the tepee of Arrah Wanna, who wears a long dress, long braids, and a single feather in her hair. Historian William H. A. Williams notes that the bagpipe pictured is the continental style pipe, not the Irish lap pipe.[7] To the left of the scene are Irish symbols including a harp and shamrocks placed above cameos of the composer and lyricist. To the right are Native American symbols including a shield, knife, spear, and peace pipe placed above a cameo of vaudeville singer Flossie Allen. I can find no source connecting her to this song. In the bottom right corner is the publisher information.

The intermezzo cover focuses on an image of Arrah Wanna peeking her head out of a tepee. She is fair, with parted hair, a head band with single feather, and two braids falling over her shoulders to her buckskin dress. Across her tepee are small bands at the top and bottom containing pictographs of deer, horses, birds, buffalo, canoes, and Indians. These are placed on bright green shamrocks. In green letters seemingly stitched to the skin wall is the title "Arrah Wanna," with Theodore Morse's cameo below. The publisher information is at the center bottom.

Period newspapers suggest that *Arrah Wanna* was popular with the public across the country before it ever became a recording. An ad selling the sheet music for nineteen cents in a Pennsylvania newspaper stated, "Arrah Wanna is a new Irish Indian matrimonial song that is becoming very popular wherever sung. Get it before it becomes worn out here." Two months later, a Fort Wayne paper reported that a man sang the song during a minstrel show "with jumping jack accompaniments . . . and spent the next

ten minutes mopping inky perspiration." A year after that, a comedian performed the song in blackface in Leavenworth, Kansas, to rave reviews, and a soprano in Winnipeg, Canada, performed a version of the song with projected illustrations. Meanwhile, newspapers in Missouri and Kansas called the song "one of the four most popular pieces of the day" and the "great Indian Intermezzo" and noted that its "success is assured because it has made a hit in the East." The next month a paper in Abilene, Texas, confirmed this, reporting that the song was "one of New York's latest hits," and an Arizona Territory rag suggested that "everyone is whistling it and Keith sings it tonight at the Iris for the last time."[8]

Such popularity ensured success for the recordings. All told, Edison produced three versions of the song in its two-minute, gold-moulded cylinders: a 1906 recording by the Edison Military Band, a 1907 version by comedians Arthur Collins and Byron G. Harlan, and a strange instrumental version performed on a street piano—a hand-cranked hurdy-gurdy instrument that was part music box and part piano.[9] In the latter version, Billy Murray talks with Italian immigrant August Molinari, who plays the song as part of a medley. In other words, an Irish American singer talks to an Italian American organ-grinder about an Irish Indian love song! *Edison Phonograph Monthly* described the Collins and Harlan cylinder as a "combination of music generally set down as typical of the Indian and the Irish. Both words and music are catchy and the song can hardly fail to make a hit."[10] For the street piano cylinder, the trade journal first introduced Molinari (who made only this single cylinder), whose "talents are of a physical character, for he furnishes the motive power for a street piano. . . . [The unique cylinder medley] will prove to those who do not know how well a street piano can sound on a carefully made Record, a very pleasant surprise." It then added: "There is nothing in the least shrill or unpleasing to the ear. The melody and runs are reproduced, together with the broken Italian talk of the organ grinder with great fidelity. . . . We feel certain that this and other similar succeeding Records will find considerable favor among Edison Phonograph Owners."[11]

That same year, Thomas Edison celebrated his

sixtieth birthday, and *Talking Machine World* reported that at his company party singers Collins and Harlan sang a version of the song about National Phonograph Company president and general manager William E. Gilmore that included this first chorus:

Mr. Gilmore, Mr. Gilmore, we are proud of you

You are tried and true,

You will never fret and stew.

In an office built of concrete strong,

You could make your henchmen smile,

If you'd only set us rules to let us smoke a little
while.[12]

When Edison re-released the song on its new, longer-playing Amberol records in 1909, the *Monthly* stated the song was "even more popular to-day than it was when first published. . . . Many thousand two-minute Records of it have been sold and no doubt exists that many thousands more will be sold in Amberol form." It then noted that the longer record included more of the song and new features, making it worthy of the higher Amberol price.[13]

Victor also made multiple versions of the Irish-Indian hit including 1906 discs featuring Murray and the Haydn Quartet as well as another performed by Collins and Harlan. The Victor Dance Orchestra also made an instrumental version in 1907. Columbia likewise featured Collins and Harlan in a disc recording as well as Prince's Military Band in an instrumental medley that included *Arrah Wanna*. Finally, Oxford Records, a Sears imprint that used Columbia masters, produced a Collins and Harlan disc as well.[14]

NOTES

1. Williams, *'Twas Only an Irishman's Dream*; Molony, "Irish-American Popular Music"; Jack Drislane and Theodore Morse, *Arrah Wanna* (New York: F. B. Haviland, 1906).

2. Gardner, *Popular Songs*, 53–55.

3. Williams, *'Twas Only an Irishman's Dream*, 193; Molony, "Irish-American Popular Music," 395. See also Gordon, *Great Arizona Orphan Abduction*, 11–13; and Emmons, *Butte Irish*.

4. Jack Drislane and Theodore Morse, *Arrah Wanna* (New York: F. B. Haviland, 1906); Theodore Morse, *Arrah Wanna* (New York: F. B. Haviland, 1906).

5. *Discography of American Historical Recordings*, http://adp.library.ucsb.edu, s.v. "Jack Drislane" (lyricist); *The Parlor Songs Academy*, www.parlorsongs.ac, s.v. "Jack Drislane"; "Bert Fitzgibbon, Theodore Morse, and Jack Drislane," *Boston Daily Globe*, November 19, 1905, 25; *Allmusic*, www.allmusic.com, s.v. "Theodore Morse"; *Songwriters Hall of Fame*, www.songwritershalloffame.org/search/, s.v. "Theodore Morse"; *The Parlor Songs Academy*, www.parlorsongs. ac, s.v. "Theodore Morse."

6. Bill Edwards, "André De Takacs," *RagPiano*, www.perfessorbill. com/artists/detakacs.shtml.

7. Williams, *'Twas Only an Irishman's Dream*, 193.

8. "Arrah Wanna," *New Castle (Pa.) News*, November 2, 1906, 3; "The Elks' Minstrels," *Fort Wayne (Ind.) Daily News*, January 25, 1907, 6; "The Orpheum," *Leavenworth (Kans.) Times*, March 19, 1907, 8; "Review of Week's Events," *Winnipeg (Manitoba, Canada) Tribune*, March 23, 1907, 8; "Most Popular Music," *Kansas City Star*, April 3, 1907, 3; "Band Concert at Chilocco," *Arkansas City (Kans.) Daily Traveler*, April 6, 1907, 3; "Arrah Wanna," ad, *Kansas City Star*, April 16, 1907, 7; "Reports from Texas Are the Best of All," *Abilene Daily Reporter*, May 8, 1907, 4; *Daily Arizona Silver Belt* (Globe, Ariz. Terr.), May 19, 1907, 8.

9. This information is gleaned from *UCSB Cylinder Audio Archive*, http://cylinders.library.ucsb.edu; examples of "street piano" or "barrel piano" can be found on YouTube.com.

10. "Gold Moulded Records for January 1907," *Edison Phonograph Monthly* 4, no. 9 (November 1906), 11.

11. "Comments on Edison Gold Moulded Records for August," *Edison Phonograph Monthly* 5, no. 4 (June 1907), 12–13.

12. "Honoring Thomas Edison," *Talking Machine World* 3, no. 2 (February 15, 1907), 47.

13. "Edison Amberol Records," *Edison Phonograph Monthly* 7, no. 6 (June 1909), 27.

14. Recording information from *Discography of American Historical Recordings*, http://adp.library.ucsb.edu. Information on Oxford Records can be found at Allan Sutton, "American Record Labels and Companies: The Sears, Roebuck and Company Record Labels (1905–1950)," *Mainspring Press*, www.mainspringpress.com/sears-labels.html.

Iola, 1906

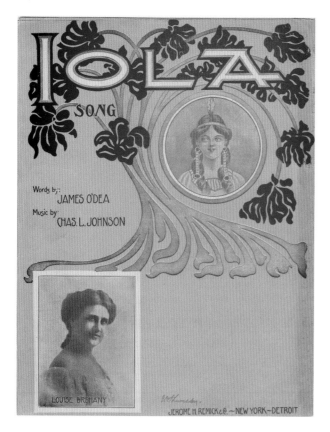

Iola, words by James O'Dea, music by
Chas. L. Johnson (New York: Jerome
H. Remick, 1906). Sheet music from
author's collection.

Iola (intermezzo), music by Chas. L.
Johnson (New York: Jerome H.
Remick, 1906). Sheet music from
author's collection.

Iola represents the effort by songwriters to spin off another hit within the Indian love song genre. Charles L. Johnson, a Kansan and one of the most prolific ragtime composers, wrote the intermezzo in 1904 with words by Karl Knappen.[1] Apparently, like *Hiawatha*, Johnson wrote the original score about a Kansas town, this time the village of Iola.[2] The sheet music for this version depicts a tree full of leaves against a peach-colored background. The title "IOLA," in white, is set in among the branches. Below the "LA" and framed by the curving tree trunk is a cameo drawing of an Indian woman with long flowing hair and a headband with two feathers. She looks down at a small bouquet of flowers. Two years later, James O'Dea, the lyricist who wrote the words for *Hiawatha* and *Silver Heels,* rewrote the words for *Iola* and the tune became a minor hit.[3] And what words! Iola is described as an "Injun Queen of sweet sixteen"; her beau who came to "her lodge beneath a tree" is depicted as a "copper colored aboriginee." Then, after singing his love song to his bride, the song suggests "To that ditty singing brave, not a shadow of encouragement she gave." The full, convoluted text is as follows:

Many, many years ago,

In a valley where the prairie roses grow

Once there lived an Injun Queen of sweet sixteen.

Who never knew a care.

To her lodge beneath a tree,

Came a copper collored aboriginee,

To this maiden sightly, He would nightly warble
    there.

Refrain

My sweet Iola, Iola list to me

My dream of bliss to me

Come throw a kiss to me

For you, I'm waiting,

Here 'neath the stars ashine

My love please don't decline

Iola Mine.

To that ditty singing brave

Not a shadow of encouragement she gave,

Nightly he would sigh for hours and send her
    flow'rs,

The while his love he told,

And he persevered so well

That at last he won his copper colored belle,

With this serenade he woos lady of old.

The Jerome H. Remick company of New York published the revised sheet music for the O'Dea and Johnson intermezzo and song versions. André de Takacs, the company illustrator who created the *Arrah Wanna* cover, repeated the image of the curving tree for the *Iola* cover sheet but changed the cameo Indian girl to a straight-on head-and-shoulders view of a young lady with long earrings, parted hair down to her shoulders, and a small headband with one feather in back. She looks somewhat like the girl in *Silver Heels.* The cover of the redrawn *Iola* intermezzo cover, by an unknown named Merrian, shows a head-and-shoulders image

of a exotic woman with dark hair, a flowing dress, and ornamented with an interesting headband that covers her right ear, earrings, necklace, and a snake-shaped bracelet.[4]

Victor, Columbia, and Edison each made versions of *Iola*. John Philip Sousa's band recorded the intermezzo in September 1906. The duo of Harry Macdonough and Frank C. Stanley made the song version into a record the following month. In January 1907, Stanley teamed with Byron G. Harlan for another disc for Victor. For Columbia, xylophonist Thomas Mills recorded the intermezzo in 1906 before Stanley teamed with Henry Burr and Irving Gillette for a trio version of the song in early 1907. None of these recordings are mentioned in *Talking Machine News* other than being included within a company listing of songs. Edison's only recording was a cylinder made by the Edison Military Band in December 1906.[5] For that version, *Edison Phonograph Monthly* described it as "an intermezzo on the order of 'Hiawatha.'" It noted that it had the same publisher as *Hiawatha* and that the band made a "splendid Record of it." All of these recordings had some impact, for Gardner lists *Iola* as the number five song for December 1906 and in the top twenty for the next two months.[6]

NOTES

1. Charles L. Johnson, *Iola* (intermezzo) (Kansas City: Central Music, 1904). A copy of this version can be found at *IN Harmony: Sheet Music from Indiana*, http://webapp1.dlib.indiana.edu/inharmony/welcome.do/, s.v. "Iola."

2. Ted Tjaden, "The Rags of Charles L. Johnson," *Classic Ragtime Piano*, www.ragtimepiano.ca.

3. James O'Dea and Chas. L. Johnson, *Iola* (New York: Jerome H. Remick, 1906).

4. Chas. L. Johnson, *Iola* (intermezzo) (New York: Jerome H. Remick, 1906).

5. This is based on *Discography of American Historical Recordings*, www.library.ucsb.edu, s.v. "Iola."

6. "Edison Gold Moulded Records for December 1906," *Edison Phonograph Monthly* 4, no. 8 (October 1906), 8; Gardner, *Popular Songs*, 55–56.

Ida-Ho, 1907

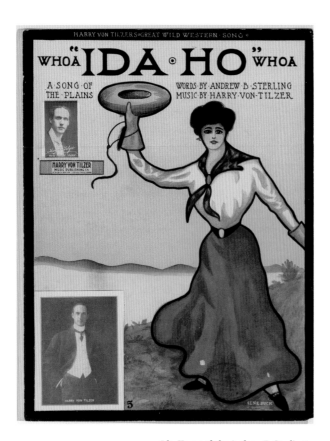

Ida-Ho, words by Andrew B. Sterling, music by Harry Von Tilzer (New York: Harry Von Tilzer Music, 1906). Sheet music from author's collection.

Ida-Ho (fantasia), music by Harry Von Tilzer (New York: Harry Von Tilzer Music, 1906). Sheet music from author's collection.

Cheyenne's success encouraged other Tin Pan Alley songwriters to write similar cowboy songs. In fact, just a week after he had recorded the *Cheyenne* parody, Billy Murray recorded for Victor *Ida-Ho*, another cowboy love song. A quick comparison to *Cheyenne* brings out several interesting points. *Ida-Ho* was neither written for nor performed on stage but instead was written specifically for the sheet music and recording industries. This is significant because it shows that *Cheyenne*'s popularity resonated so much with these home-based audiences that the new song could bypass the theater and go directly to the consumer phonograph market. On the other hand, the new song repeated basically the same story line of a cowboy pursuing his cowgirl and once again made a pun out of the girl's name—Ida instead of Shy Ann—by linking it to a real western place. Finally, the Edison company, which had never recorded *Cheyenne*, entered the cowboy craze when Murray recorded a copy of *Ida-Ho*, accompanied by the Edison Male Quartet, on cylinder.[1]

At the same time, the writer and publisher of *Ida-Ho*, Harry Von Tilzer, released several versions of the sheet music with a full-color illustration of a beautiful cowgirl waving her hat against a yellow background.[2] It carries the description "A song of the Plains," with lyrics by Andrew B. Sterling and music by Von Tilzer. On one version, Von Tilzer is pictured twice on the cover, a small head-and-shoulders view near the top left and a larger image at lower left. Other covers include Von Tilzer's cameo at the top and pictures of noted singers Ethel Robinson or Mabel Russell at the bottom. The top of the cover page boasts that this is "Harry Von Tilzer's Great Wild Western Song" and features the title framed by the words "Whoa" so that it looks like "Whoa 'Ida Ho' Whoa."

Von Tilzer was the oldest of five brothers who all became Tin Pan Alley songwriters. Born Harry Gumm (or Gummblinsky) in Detroit in 1872, Harry took his mother's maiden name because it sounded better. At age fourteen, he left home to join a circus as a singer and tumbler. He soon became a stage actor, singer, and songwriter. He published his first song in 1892 and that year moved to New York, where he worked as a saloon pianist and singer for the next six years. He and lyricist Sterling worked vaudeville together and became a composing team. In 1898 the Shapiro music publishing company hired Von Tilzer to write songs for them, and he soon became a partner. By 1902 he was successful enough to start his own publishing firm, and over the next dozen years he produced hundreds of popular songs—many, like *Ida-Ho*, featuring cover illustrator Gene Buck. After patriotic songs grew popular during the Great War and jazz became the symbol of the 1920s, Von Tilzer's popularity waned. He died in 1946 and was later inducted into the Songwriters Hall of Fame.[3]

Artist Gene Buck studied art at the Detroit Art Academy and then went to work as a staff illustrator for the Jerome Remick company in New York. Although his peak years were in the decade after 1904, Buck is reported to have produced more than five thousand music covers over his career. During this period his work, like that on *Ida-Ho*, was known for a minimal use of the color palette. He later turned to songwriting and in 1914 became one of the founders of ASCAP, serving as its president from 1924 to 1941.[4]

The sheet music covers of *Cheyenne* and *Ida-Ho*, both of which feature images of the twentieth century's emerging New Woman, make for an interesting comparison. *Cheyenne* pictures a wild, independent cowgirl, whip in hand, riding a galloping horse while several cowboys pursue in the distance. *Ida-Ho*, however, depicts more of the sophisticated yet athletic Gibson Girl image, with a cowgirl in long skirt, long-sleeve blouse, kerchief, and leather gauntlets waving a cowboy hat. Neither image depicts its song very well. In the song *Cheyenne*, Shy Ann rides up to the cowboy and they ride away together to get married, and in *Ida-Ho* Ida is described as "wild as any injun" who goes "dashing cross the plains," leaving her cowboy to beg for her not to run away. In fact, it almost makes better sense to reverse the two images for the songs.[5]

The *Ida-Ho* music is set to 2/4 time and "Respectfully Dedicated to IDA." It begins at an *allegro moderato* tempo, accompanied by an imitation of horse hoofbeats. The lyrics then go:

Way out west in Idaho,
There's a gal that I love so,
Ida, my Ida oh, oh,

Wild as any injun she,
when she yells "You can't catch me"
"Whoa! there, my Ida, Whoa!"

On her bucking bronco she goes dashing cross the
    plain
Fast as any train, she drives me insane.
"Shoofly don't you bother me" she yells out once
    again,
Then the prairie rings with her refrain.

Chorus
Ida Ho whoa! whoa! don't go so fast dear
My horse won't last dear, So please go slow
My Ida Ho I'll kiss you if I catch you,
Won't you stay dear, Don't run away dear, My Ida
    Ho.

She's "all wool" and don't forget,
she's a thoroughbred you bet,
Ida, my Ida oh, oh,
I'll catch up to her some day,
take her in my arms and say,
"Whoa! there, my Ida, Whoa!"

She has lassoed ev'ry cowboys heart that's in the
    west
But I'll do my best, put her to the test,
I will capture her someday and hug her to my
    breast,
Then I'll let the parson do the rests.

Repeat Chorus

Another version of *Ida-Ho* appeared in 1906 as a two-step.[6] Also dedicated to "Ida," the sheet music describes the song as a "Wild Western Fantasia" and includes directions at the beginning stanzas to imitate horse hoofbeats. The Gene Buck cover art also features a minimal color palette, this time with a golden sun setting behind mountains of green, yellow, and white, with a blue sky and two white puffy clouds. The title "Ida-Ho" floats above the clouds, and above the border is the description "Harry Von Tilzer's Great Wild Western Hit and Two Step." Von Tilzer's photograph is in the lower right corner.

According to Jim Walsh, this last version became the first recording when Zon-o-phone released it in March 1907. Its supplement said that the song was a "breezy catchy two step typifying the true life of the Western Cowboy" and suggested that the horse's hoofbeats and cowboy yells made it realistic.[7] Edison released its version in April with Billy Murray singing the lead and the Edison Male Quartet providing harmony. Comprising singers John Bieling, Harry Macdonough, S. H. Dudley, and William F. Hooley, this group recorded under different names for each recording company, including the Edison Male Quartette and the Haydn Quartet for Victor.[8] *Edison Phonograph Monthly* for February

1907 described *Ida-Ho* as "a western song, called the 'melodious cyclone' that is sweeping the country." Its more detailed description later that issue included part of the chorus and added that the song was "now popular from coast to coast." That April, in a Spokane newspaper the Columbia Phonograph Company reported that the song was selling "like hot cakes."[9] Despite these accolades, Gardner does not mention *Ida-Ho* in his book as breaking into any top-twenty chart.

NOTES

1. *Discography of American Historical Recordings*, http://adp.library. ucsb.edu, s.v. "Ida-ho"; Billy Murray and the Edison Male Quartet, *Ida-Ho* (Edison Talking Machine Company, 1907), Edison Gold Moulded Record #9520.

2. Harry Von Tilzer, *Ida-Ho* (New York: Harry Von Tilzer Music, 1906). In my sheet music collection, I have two other versions of this music, featuring vaudeville singers Ethel Robinson on one and Mable Russell on the other. David A. Jasen, *A Century of American Popular Music: 2000 Best-Loved and Remembered Songs* (New York: Routledge, 2002), 39, notes that Ethel Robinson had a vaudeville hit with the song *Come Take a Trip in My Air Ship*, and Billy Murray had it on record. The *Winnipeg (Manitoba, Canada) Tribune*, December 13, 1913, noted that Mable Russell's husband Eddie Leonard had been a minstrel singer and that "Miss Russell is an able and attractive partner and the two have a very high class and enjoyable turn."

3. *The Parlor Songs Academy*, www.parlorsongs.ac, s.v. "Harry Von Tilzer."

4. *Allmusic*, www.allmusic.com, s.v. "Gene Buck"; Bill Edwards, "Gene Buck," *RagPiano*, http://perfessorbill.com/artists/buck.shtml.

5. "The Gibson Girl's America: Drawings by Charles Dana Gibson," *Library of Congress, Exhibitions*, www.loc.gov/exhibits/ gibson-girls-america/.

6. Harry Von Tilzer, *Ida-Ho* (two-step) (New York: Harry Von Tilzer Music, 1906).

7. Walsh, "'Cowboy Song' Recordings, Part 4," *Hobbies*, July 1976, 36.

8. Walsh, "'Cowboy Song' Recordings, Part 3," *Hobbies*, June 1976, 126.

9. *Edison Phonograph Monthly* 4, no. 12 (February 1907), 2, 11; "Cheyenne Idaho," *Spokane (Wash.) Spokesman-Review*, April 28, 1907, 7.

Reed Bird, 1907

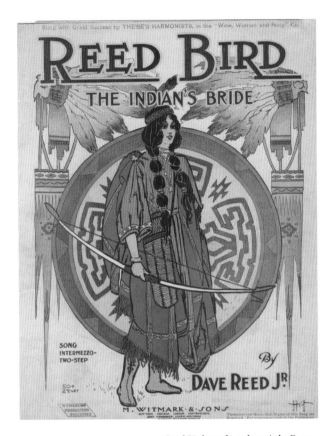

Reed Bird, words and music by Dave Reed Jr. (New York: M. Witmark and Sons, 1904). Sheet music from author's collection.

Reed Bird, written by Dave Reed Jr. in 1904 but not recorded until 1907, is an unusual Indian love song.[1] Reed was the son of Dave Reed, a pioneer minstrel singer whose long career spanned 1844–1903 and included stints in New York, on a Mississippi river boat, and in vaudeville. In fact, the elder Reed and his wife brought their four children into the act in the 1880s as a group called the Reed Birds.[2] Dave Jr. published his first song in the 1890s and then composed many others during this period, including a handful of Broadway musicals and several Indian songs including *My Kickapoo Queen,*[3] *My Chippewa,* and *Maid of the Midnight Moon.*[4]

Perhaps Reed used his family history as the inspiration for this song. Although its lyrics are familiar in tone to other period pieces with its love story between an "Injun brave" and his "little copper colored squaw," the story line follows the kidnapping of the girl by another tribe, her pursuit by her lover and the subsequent intertribal battle, and then her rescue and wedding. Further, unlike most other love songs, *Reed Bird*'s verses are in a minor key, creating a darkened mood. The song also relies on its lines with internal rhymes such as "battling" and "rattling" as well as "creeping," "sleeping," and "sweeping." The full lyrics go like this:

Big bold Injun brave loves a little copper colored
    squaw
His foes capture her along a Highway
He does whoop and rave, calls his mighty tribe to
    go to war;
Heap much scouting, war whoops shouting
Out to do or die, all skulking in a sly way.

Dark night out for fight, swooping down the valley
    from the hill,
Comes that mighty tribe without a warning.
Wigwam, soon they storm fighting with the
    enemy to kill,
Bravely battling, Gunshots rattling,
Big chief rescues squaw and weds her in the
    morning.

Chorus
Creeping on the enemy sleeping, wily warriors
    sweeping
Soon leave those red men dead men, fly away to
    hide and soon the maiden
Neath the moonbeams fading, Little heart love
    laden, is the Indian's bride.

Big bold Injun brave held his little Princess on his
    arm,
Dashed off madly on his little pony
Left his foes to rave, while he took her safely out of
    harm,
Heap quick marrying, no use tarrying
Sweet Miss, big kiss, Just to seal the ceremony
Big row all done now, Ev'ry Injun wears a little
    smile,
Big Chief never ugly any more now.
Wars cease, pipe of peace fire water plenty all the
    while,
Big owls hooting, Each night scooting,
All time make big Injun dream about a pow wow.

Repeat Chorus

Artist Joseph Hirt designed the sheet music for *Reed Bird* for the New York music publisher M. Witmark and Sons. It is one of the most elaborate and beautiful of the period, rivaling *Red Wing*, another Hirt product. Hirt also illustrated the cover for the much later cowboy song *In the Golden West*. He was born in New York City in 1879 to German and Prussian immigrant parents. His first sheet music cover art appeared in 1901, and within a decade he had produced more than two hundred. Around that time he went into commercial art, illustrating advertisements and posters. He later worked in the film industry and as a painter. His cover art is known for its use of multiple colors, and *Reed Bird* definitely fits the bill. The illustration features a Caucasian-looking woman with long black hair wearing a red-and-green dress and tan moccasins and carrying a long bow. She is framed by Indian headdresses with large eagle feathers and other colorful Indian pieces. If cover art had sold music, *Reed Bird* would have been a million seller.[5]

Arthur Collins and Byron G. Harlan recorded *Reed Bird* as a duet for Victor in February 1907 and for Edison two months later. Arthur Pryor's Band made a disc of the intermezzo two-step a few months later for the company. Also in May, J. W. Myers recorded it for Columbia.[6] The Edison cylinder starts with a pounding tom-tom, whoops, music, and then more whoops. Collins and Harlan then sing the verse in deep, staccato voices that create a somewhat grave tone. The chorus then gets warm as it moves to a major key. *Edison Phonograph Monthly* suggested that "songs of the noble Red Man continue to compete with coon songs for the center of the stage of popularity." It then described the song's plot and observed that, "of course, the song is much more attractive than anything actually produced by Indians, but the words are Indian, there are whoops of the braves and the tom tom's beat, therefore it is an Indian song."[7] Such bravado might suggest that a love song about warring Indians with such "accurate" and "attractive" particulars, combined with a colorful and detailed sheet music cover, would be a big seller. On the contrary, the song was not mentioned again in the trade journals, the lists of good sellers, or Gardner's top-twenty charts.

NOTES

1. Dave Reed Jr., *Reed Bird* (New York: M. Witmark and Sons, 1904).

2. A description of this group can be found under "Keith's Union Square" in "Last Week's Bills," *New York Dramatic Mirror*, December 17, 1898, 18.

3. *My Kickapoo Queen* is described as a "Zulu-Indian kind of a coon song. . . . The music is exceptionally catchy and odd." "Edison Gold Moulded Records for April," *Edison Phonograph Monthly* 4, no. 12 (February 1907), 11.

4. An overview of the career of Dave Reed Sr. can be found in Edward LeRoy Rice, *Monarchs of Minstrelry, from "Daddy" Rice to Date* (New York: Kenny, 1911), 67–68; Phillip Robert Dillon, "Princely Profits from Single Songs," *The Scrap Book, First Section* 4, no. 2 (August 1907), 188–89. Reed Jr.'s Broadway performances are outlined at *Internet Broadway Database*, http://ibdb.com, s.v. "Dave Reed, Jr." *Discography of American Historical Recordings*, http://adp.library. ucsb.edu, s.v. "David Reed" (composer) shows more than two dozen recordings of songs written by Reed.

5. Bill Edwards, "Joseph Hirt," *RagPiano*, www.perfessorbill.com/ artists/jhirt.shtml.

6. Zon-o-phone also recorded it in 1907. See www.78discography.com/ Zon010.htm

7. "Comments on Edison Gold Moulded Records for June," *Edison Phonograph Monthly* 5, no. 2 (April 1907), 11. The Victor and Columbia records can be found at *Discography of American Historical Recordings*, http://adp.library.ucsb.edu.

San Antonio, 1907

San Antonio, words by Harry Williams,
music by Egbert Van Alstyne (New
York: Jerome H. Remick, 1907). Sheet
music from author's collection.

Following their success with *Cheyenne*, songwriters Harry Williams and Egbert Van Alstyne returned to the growing cowboy song craze with another tune for the Jerome H. Remick company in 1907 titled *San Antonio*.[1] Like their previous hit, *San Antonio* is a conversation between two cowboys about a girl who has "hopped up on a pony" and left one of them for another man. *Variety* magazine described the song in its March 30 issue as "absolutely the greatest of all cowboy songs. A hit the world over."[2]

   The score calls for *moderato* tempo in 4/4 time with these lyrics:

Just as the moon was peeping o'er the hill
After the work was through
There sat a cowboy and his partner Bill
Cowboy was feeling blue
Bill says "Come down Pal, Down into town Pal,
Big time for me and you,
Don't mind your old gal, you know it's "Cold" Pal,
If what you say is true"
"Where is she know" Bill cried
And his partner just replied

Chorus

San Antoni, Antonio

She hopped up on a pony and ran away with Tony

If you see here just let me know

and I'll meet you in San Antonio.

You know that pony that she rode away

That horse belongs to me

So do the trinkets that she stow'd away

I was the big mark E

I won't resent it I might have spent it

Plunging with Faro Jack

If she's not happy there with her chappie

Tell her I'll take her back

No tender foot like him

Could love her like her boy Jim

Repeat Chorus

The sheet music cover depicts a nighttime campfire scene full of western icons, with one cowboy wearing wooly chaps, a six-shooter, red shirt, neckerchief, and big hat sitting on a tree stump talking to another cowboy standing nearby. The second man is similarly dressed except that he wears leather chaps. A horse grazes in the distance and a coiled rope sits in the right foreground. The blazing fire is in middle foreground, its flames rising to smoke as it wisps upward between the two men. The image contains the signature "Starmer" in the lower left corner, referring to William and Frederick Starmer, two of the most prolific sheet music illustrators in the early twentieth century. The brothers—English immigrants—lived in and around New York City and created one-fourth of all large-format covers, always signing just their last name, between 1900 and 1919. This practice makes it impossible today to know exactly how many covers each brother produced.[3]

Billy Murray recorded *San Antonio* for both Victor and Edison in the spring of 1907. Victor's version includes an orchestra accompaniment and appeared as a one-sided, eight-inch disc on March 8.[4] Then in May, Edison released a two-minute cylinder that featured Murray, backed by the Edison Male Quartet. This prolific group, also known as the Hayden Quartet, featured Harry Macdonough, John Bieling, S. H. Dudley, and William F. Hooley.[5] *Edison Phonograph Monthly* described *San Antonio* as the "new cowboy song . . . [that] has rapidly achieved popularity from coast to coast. As a Record it is exceptionally entertaining and tuneful."[6]

The song's instant popularity might be explained by its inclusion in other formats including what were called "minstrels." These entourage recordings recalled a minstrel or vaudeville show with an announcer and a small group of performers who sang a chorus of a new or popular song or two and told a few jokes. Columbia called its 1907 version simply "Record H" and featured the group called the Rambler Minstrel Company, with Murray singing *San Antonio*. The Rambler Minstrels consisted of popular recording artists Steve Porter, Murray, Arthur Collins, and Byron G. Harlan.[7] The record begins with a group song titled *In the Good Old United States*, and then announcer Porter tells the gentlemen to be seated. Murray then tells a couple jokes and the gang hoots, whistles, and laughs. Porter introduces Murray and *San Antonio*, and the Denver Nightingale belts out one verse before the group joins in for the chorus. Cheers and whistles end the recording. Busy Bee Records released its disc of this same recording, calling it "Minstrel Record G with orchestra accompaniment."[8] Victor's minstrel version of *San Antonio* features Murray and the Haydn Quartet redubbed the Christy Minstrels. The recording also includes gags and two songs, *Yankee Doodle Negros* and *San Antonio*.[9]

Instrumental medleys that contained several songs also contributed to *San Antonio*'s success. Columbia produced an instrumental version as part of its *San Antonio Medley* in July 1907, and the following month Edison released its own band number, the *Poor John Medley*, which includes an instrumental version of *San Antonio*.[10]

All of these recordings kept the cowboy music craze going and aided *San Antonio*'s rise to the top of Gardner's reconstructed charts. Gardner first ranks the song in the top twenty at number ten in March 1907, raises it to number two the next month, and then to number one in May. He has it in the top five through August before removing it from the list in October.[11]

NOTES

1. Harry Williams and Egbert Van Alstyne, *San Antonio* (New York: Jerome H. Remick, 1907).

2. *Variety* 6, no. 3 (March 30, 1907), 20; this is quoted in Tinsley, *For a Cowboy*, 6.

3. Bill Edwards, "William Starmer and Frederick Starmer," *RagPiano*, www.perfessorbill.com/artists/starmer.shtml.

4. *Discography of American Historical Recordings*, http://adp.library.ucsb.edu, s.v. "San Antonio."

5. Gracyk, *Popular American Recording Pioneers*, 178–80.

6. *Edison Phonograph Monthly* 5, no. 1 (March 1907), 9. Twenty-four years later, Columbia Picture animators used *San Antonio* as the opening tune in the Krazy Kat cartoon *Rodeo Dough*, available on YouTube.com.

7. Walsh, "'Cowboy Song' Recordings," Part 3, *Hobbies*, June 1976, 126.

8. The Rambler Minstrel Company (Record H), *Introducing "San Antonio,"* sung by Billy Murray" (Columbia Phonograph Company, 1907), A459; *Minstrel Record G*, orchestra accompaniment (Busy Bee Record, 1907), 5414.

9. Walsh, "'Cowboy Song' Recordings," Part 3, *Hobbies*, June 1976, 126; *Discography of American Historical Recordings*, http://adp.library.ucsb.edu, s.v. "The Christy Minstrels."

10. Tinsley, *For a Cowboy*, 6; *Talking Machine World* 3, no. 6 (June 15, 1907), 62; *Edison Phonograph Monthly* 5, no. 2 (March 1907), 2.

11. Gardner, *Popular Songs*, 56–57.

Red Wing, 1907

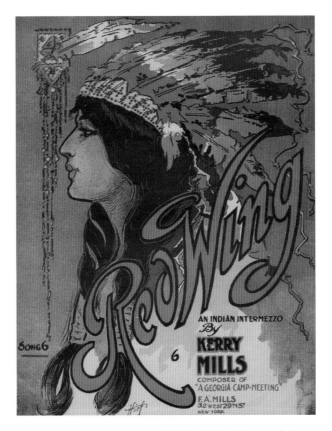

Red Wing (Indian intermezzo), by
Kerry Mills (New York: F. A. Mills,
1907). Sheet music from author's
collection.

Red Wing had everything needed for a hit. By far the most popular Indian love song ever, the melody for this 1907 hit actually got its start almost six decades earlier as "The Happy Farmer Returning from His Work" in composer Robert Schumann's *Album for the Young.*[1] *Red Wing* features a story of battle and loss, but its major key makes it light and happy. It also stays clear of references to skin color, making its message more palatable over time. The interior rhyming too is soothing: "The breeze is sighing, the night bird's crying." The full lyrics are as follows:

> There once lived an Indian maid
> A shy little prairie maid,
> Who sang a lay, a love song gay,
> As on the plain she'd while away the day;
> She loved a warrior bold,
> this shy little maid of old
> But brave and gay,
> he rode one day to battle far away.

Now, the moon shines tonight on pretty Red Wing,
The breeze is sighing, the night bird's crying,
For afar 'neath his star her brave is sleeping,
While Red Wing's weeping,
her heart away.

She watched for him day and night,
She kept all the campfires bright,
And under the sky, each night she would lie,
And dream about his coming by and by;

But when all the braves returned,
the heart of Red Wing yearned,
For far, far, away, her warrior gay,
fell bravely in the fray.

Now, the moon shines tonight on pretty Red Wing,
The breeze is sighing, the night bird's crying,
For afar 'neath his star her brave is sleeping,
While Red Wing's weeping,
her heart away.

Red Wing's composer, Frederick Allen "Kerry" Mills, was a trained violinist as well as a successful song writer and music publisher. As a child growing up in Detroit, Mills played the violin to help support his family. After training in Chicago with Florenz Ziegfeld Sr., the father of the famous showman, Mills returned to Michigan to teach music. In the early 1890s he completed his first musical piece, *Rastus on Parade*, in the form of a cakewalk, a syncopated dance music derivative of African American culture thought to be more refined than the more popular but vulgar "coon songs" of the time. Unable to get support to publish, Mills moved to New York City determined to write and produced his own kinds of songs. Once there, Kerry Mills began writing cakewalks and ragtime, hired a lyricist to add words, and then had his alter ego, "F. A." Mills, publish them. In 1899 several of his cakewalks, including *At a Georgia Camp Meeting*, became huge hits in vaudeville and among both African Americans and whites, including John Philip Sousa, who recorded them on both cylinder and disc. Mills soon published songs

by George M. Cohan and in 1904 wrote the music for *Meet Me in St. Louis, Louis. Red Wing* became another big hit in 1907, and Mills's success continued for about a decade. He later moved to California, where he died in 1948.[2]

The sheet music cover by artist Joseph Hirt is among the most beautiful created during this time—a colorful, modern advertisement for the song. With a green background, the cover features an attractive Native American woman in profile. Her long hair is braided, and she wears red lipstick and a colorful headdress of yellow, blue, white, red, and black.

This combination of music, composer, and graphics led the recording companies to *Red Wing*. In 1907, Edison made two cylinder recordings of the song including a xylophone medley that included *Red Wing* and a vocal by Frederick H. Potter and the Edison Male Quartet. The Ossman Banjo Trio recorded it for Victor, and Frank C. Stanley and Henry C. Burr made a Columbia cylinder as well. The next year, Victor produced *Red Wing* as both an instrumental medley by Arthur Pryor's Band and a duet that features S. H. Dudley and Harry Macdonough. In 1909, George Ballard sang it on cylinder for the U.S. Everlasting Record company and for Lakeside Indestructible Records. The year 1910 found three more versions recorded on cylinder, another in 1911, and still another in 1913. Such proliferation was rare and indicates nothing less than a very popular song.[3]

For such acceptance, it is somewhat surprising how little seems to have been written about the song at the time. *Edison Phonograph Monthly* for June 1907 described the Frederick H. Potter cylinder as simply "a pretty little song," and the next month's issue noted that the xylophone piece *Red Wing Medley* introduced "old friends." An ad for Columbia records and discs called the song a "captivating duet record presenting the picturesque prairie of the pretty little Indian maid and her gay warrior bold." Yet when Edison released a new version in 1910 on its new four-minute Amberol cylinders, *Edison Phonograph Monthly* wrote, "The phenomenal popularity of 'Red Wing' in the Standard List . . . induced us to respond to the general demand of the trade and public to list it as an Amberol number." Then, after describing the recording's style, the journal concluded that "Without Doubt this Record will be one of the most popular numbers in the Amberol Catalogue." Indeed, Gardner lists *Red Wing* in his top twenty from November 1907 to May 1908, peaking at number three in March 1908.[4]

NOTES

1. Kerry Mills and Thurland Chattaway, *Red Wing* (New York: F. A. Mills, 1907); Kerry Mills, *Red Wing* (intermezzo) (New York: F. A. Mills, 1907). On its Schumann roots, see Logsdon, *"Whorehouse Bells,"* 207–10.

2. Bill Edwards, "Frederick Allen 'Kerry' Mills," *RagPiano*, www. perfessorbill.com/comps/famills.shtml.

3. This information is derived from searches for *Red Wing* at *Discography of American Historical Recordings*, http://adp.library. ucsb.edu, and *UCSB Cylinder Audio Archive*, http://cylinders.library. ucsb.edu.

4. "Comments on Edison Gold Moulded Records for August," *Edison Phonograph Monthly* 5, no. 4 (June 1907), 13; "Comments on Edison Records for September," *Edison Phonograph Monthly* 5, no. 5 (July 1907), 9; "Columbia Records," *Fort Wayne (Ind.) Sentinel*, March 28, 1908, 3; "Edison Amberol Records for November, 1910," *Edison Phonograph Monthly* 8, no. 9 (September 1910), 16; Gardner, *Popular Songs*, 57–58.

Since Arrah Wanna Married Barney Carney, 1907

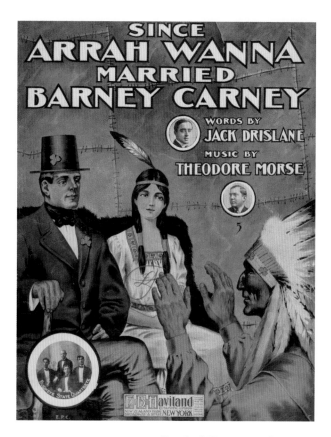

Since Arrah Wanna Married Barney Carney, words by Jack Drislane, music by Theodore Morse (New York: F. B. Haviland, 1907). Sheet music from author's collection.

Since Arrah Wanna Married Barney Carney represents the rare Indian love song sequel. The original *Arrah Wanna* recording had been so successful that its composers, Jack Drislane and Theodore Morse, repurposed the characters in a 1907 update to their Irish-Indian wedding.[1]

The lyrics to the new song hint at a one-sided, quick assimilation from Indian to Irish by not only Arrah Wanna but other members of her tribe. Suggesting that this had all been "upside down," the lyrics indicate that the Indians no longer paint their faces, all have Irish names, the wigwams are all full of Irish blarney, only green feathers are used, Irish reels have replaced Indian dances, and the tom-toms play the "Wearing of the green." The full lyrics are as follows:

> Tell me have you heard the news
> that's going all around,
> Barney Carney's back in town,
> Things have all been upside down.
> Now, no more do the Indians
> put paint upon their face,
> And each one of them has an Irish name
> On the plains and prairies gay the Shamrock now
>   is seen,
> The tom-toms play the "Wearing of the green."

Chorus

Since Arrah Wanna married Barney Carney,

The Indians don't know just what to say,

The wig-wams are all full of Irish Blarney,

They celebrate on each St. Patrick's day.

Green feathers are the only kind they're using

The Pipe of Peace is made of Irish clay.

And instead of Pow-Wow dances it's the Irish reel
   entrances

Since Arrah Wanna married Barney Carney

"Full Moon Eyes" the great big chief,

has changed his name to "Mike"

"Fighting Dog" is very tame,

Barney Carney's all to blame.

The password is "Begorra,"

and the bagpipes each one plays,

Each Red man calls his squaw sweet "Colleen"

Barney sits upon a throne as king of all the tribe,

With Arrah Wanna by him as his queen.

Repeat Chorus

Like other F. B. Haviland sheet music, the artist known only as "E.P.C." created the colorful cover artwork that illustrated the ideas of the song. Set inside a tepee adorned with shamrocks, the image shows the Irishman Barney Carney sitting next to Arrah Wanna, seemingly being blessed by an Indian chief.

Unlike the earlier score that proclaimed to be an "Irish Indian Matrimonial Venture," the sequel contains no such claim. The back cover, however, advertises the earlier song with cover images of both the *Arrah Wanna* song and the intermezzo, the first page of the instrumental score, and a paragraph praising the tune.

It asks, "Have you heard Arrah Wanna? If not, you have missed a treat," before suggesting that the song is "without doubt the greatest number ever published." It then describes both the song and instrumental arrangement before concluding that "you will be delighted with both, it is whistled, sung and played everywhere."

Despite such billing, *Since Arrah Wanna Married Barney Carney* enjoyed limited success. Period newspapers provide no references to singers performing the song in vaudeville acts or as part of an illustrated performance.[2] Likewise, Edison's decision not to record it left only a single vocal recording by Arthur C. Collins and Byron Harlan, which they made for both Victor and Zon-o-phone in 1907. The Victor recording features a strong tom-tom throughout, with the performers alternating singing solo and then as a duo. Columbia also offered the song as part of an instrumental medley by Prince's Military Band on disc the following year.[3] Perhaps because of this limited exposure, neither Gardner, era newspapers, nor the *Talking Machine World* provide any further description of the song or its success.

NOTES

1. Jack Drislane and Theodore Morse, *Since Arrah Wanna Married Barney Carney* (New York: F. B. Haviland, 1907).

2. For example, see "Eva Ray at the Grand," *Hamilton (Ohio) Journal News*, December 7, 1907, 15; or "Iris Theater ad," *Bisbee (Ariz. Terr.) Daily Review*, October 10, 1907, 4.

3. "Record Bulletins for August 1907," *Talking Machine World* 3, no. 7 (July 15, 1907), 62; *Discography of American Historical Recordings*, http://adp.library.ucsb.edu, s.vv. "Since Arrah Wanna married Barney Carney" and "Bye bye dearie medley"; Arthur C. Collins and Byron G. Harlan, *Since Arrah Wanna Married Barney Carney* (New York: Victor Talking Machine, 1907), disc # 4458B.

In the Land of the Buffalo, 1907

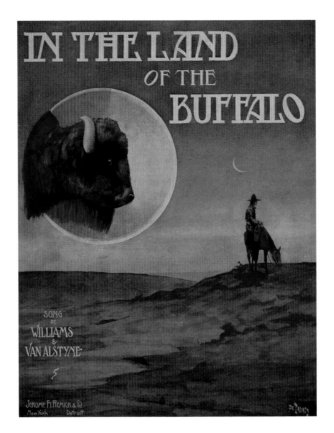

In the Land of the Buffalo, **words by
Harry Williams, music by Egbert Van
Alstyne (New York: Jerome H. Remick,
1907).** Sheet music from author's
collection.

Building on their successes *Cheyenne* and *San Antonio*, in
1907 Harry Williams and Egbert Van Alstyne published
their third cowboy song, *In the Land of the Buffalo*, with
the Jerome H. Remick company.[1] Although the song was
not a hit, the composers created a descriptive line in the
chorus that anticipated later western theme songs: "In
the land of the buffalo, where the western breezes blow,
where the goodnight kiss of sunshine, sets all the plains
aglow." Beyond that, the song is a bit hard to follow, with
a plot that tells the love story between an old rancher
and his love, Flo, and her secret love for the cattleman's
brother Lew. The full lyrics are as follows:

See that old time ranchman as he saunters from
    the train,
Oh, oh, what glad surprise,
See that hearty handshake as he greets his friend again,
Tears dim his beady eyes
"Lew them lights so sure look pretty
Long time since I've seen the city,
Where's that gal you brought back here with you."
City chap said "Never mind her
I don't ever want to find her
Cowboy tell me where's your brother Lew"
He brushed his vest, swelled his chest, pointed West

Chorus

In the land of the buffalo,
Where the Western breezes blow
Where the goodnight kiss of sunshine,
Sets all the plains aglow
It was there you discovered your Flo
In the days of long ago
But you never knew brother Lew loved her too
In the land of the Buffalo.

He's out there alone tonight and pal, he's gettin'
  grey,
You know the reasons why,
Where the howling coyotes seem to laugh at him
  and say
Oh, oh, why don't you die.
She to him was eighteen karat,
But he says he'll grin and bear it,
That perhaps the gal was meant for you,
But as long as you have "thrown" her
And you say you wouldn't own her,
Can't you find her for my brother Lew,
I'll pay her fare, on the square, way out there

Repeat Chorus

The sheet music's cover art is among the most beautiful of the era. It shows a green, treeless western plain at sunset with a crescent moon hanging above the horizon. Below that, a cowboy on a horse is silhouetted against the dusk. The song's title is in white against the darkened sky, and a large buffalo head in profile is set against a yellow-and-red circle just above the horizon. Hungarian immigrant André De Takacs painted the scene, one of many that he illustrated for Remick between 1901 and his untimely death at age thirty-nine in 1919.[2]

Although popular star Billy Murray recorded *In the Land of the Buffalo* for Edison in August and Victor in September 1907, the song had mixed reviews. *Edison Phonograph Monthly* liked both the song and the genre. It described the recording as a "fine, swinging cowboy song by the composers of the exceedingly popular 'San Antonio' . . . and sung in Mr. Murray's best style. It is certain to be very much liked. These cowboy songs strike a note of originality that is very refreshing."[3] According to Jim Walsh, however, the Victor supplement described it as a "semi-pathetic cowboy song which seems to possess all the elements of a popular success—some breezy Western humor, a touch of pathos and a pretty melody." Walsh further suggests that its complicated lyrics kept it out of most minstrel recordings or medleys, and though "mildly successful" as far as he knew, Williams and Van Alstyne did not write any more cowboy songs. Gardner does not even mention the song, and a search of digital newspapers finds only a couple of vaudeville performers featuring it, including a Miss Celia Watson who sang a "charming soubrette" of *In the Land of the Buffalo* at the Richelieu Theater in Santa Ana, California. Of course, the performance also included a "buck and wing dancer on unicycle roller skates upside down."[4]

NOTES

1. Harry Williams and Egbert Van Alstyne, *In the Land of the Buffalo* (New York: Jerome H. Remick., 1907).

2. Bill Edwards, "André De Takacs," *RagPiano*, www.perfessorbill.com/artists/detakacs.shtml.

3. "The New Edison Gold Moulded Records Advance List for October 1907," *Edison Phonograph Monthly* 5, no. 6 (August 1907), 4; *Discography of American Historical Recordings*, http://adp.library.ucsb.edu, s.v. "In the land of the buffalo."

4. Walsh, "'Cowboy Song' Records," Part 4, *Hobbies*, July 1976, 35; "Amusements," *Alton (Ill.) Evening Telegraph*, September 27, 1907, 5, reported that "Miss Gloria Dare receives many encores on her four numbers [including] in the Land of the Buffalo." See also "Richelieu Theater," *Santa Ana (Calif.) Register*, October 7, 1907, 4.

Broncho Buster, 1907

Broncho Buster, words by Edward Madden, music by Dolly Jardon (New York: Maurice Shapiro, 1907). Sheet music from author's collection.

In October 1907, Victor released *Broncho Buster* sung by Harry Tally, the performer who had ignited the Indian music craze with his version of *Navajo* in 1904. The new cowboy tune was unusual in several ways. First, with lyrics by ASCAP charter member Edward Madden and music by his wife and singer Dorothy "Dolly" Jardon, *Broncho Buster* marked the first time a woman composed the music for a recorded cowboy song and also was the first entry into the cowboy genre by the Maurice Shapiro publishing company.[1] Second, although its lyrics tell a love story between a cowgirl and a cowboy, it does so in a most unusual fashion. Rather than *The Virginian* and *Cheyenne* love story, *Broncho Buster* features a girl who first pulls a gun on her cowboy to urge him to marry her and then repeats the threat to the parson to conduct the ceremony. Perhaps because of this angle, the song plays in a minor key, giving it a moodier feel than previous cowboy songs. The full lyrics go like this:

Not many miles from Denver town,

Just as the Western sun went down;

Cowboys stole out from their corrall,

To watch their pardner woo his gal.

He was too shy his love to tell,

She seemed so bashful too;

Until the crowd set up a yell;

"Kiss her Bill, or we'll kiss her for you" Oh!

Chorus

"Broncho Buster, Why, don't you trust her"

Go on lassoo her, Somebody else will woo her,

She's no shy goose, Jump on your cayuse,

And carry her off to Denver town."

When Broncho's gal saw what he'd done

She pulled a wicked looking gun;

She yelled: " Hop on to that cayuse,

And make him gallup like the deuce."

She woke a parson out of bed,

Pointed her forty four,

"Marry us, or you'll die," she said.

Broncho heard the parson then implore. Oh!

Repeat Chorus

The sheet music cover features a Starmer illustration of a red-shirted, white-scarfed cowboy decked out in chaps and six-shooter atop a bucking horse reminiscent of and possibly intending to capitalize on Frederic Remington's famous illustration of the same name.[2] The setting is a simple blue foreground with gray hills in the distance set against a blue sky with big, puffy, white clouds that bring to mind a Maynard Dixon image. To the left of the horse is a cameo encircled by rope of a woman identified as Bonita, a vaudeville performer also known as Pauline des Landes.[3]

Although the sheet music proclaims *Broncho Buster* to be "the Terrific Western Song Success" and ads for it in *Variety* claimed it to be "the cyclonic cow-boy song hit of the plains," "the wildest, wooliest western whoop ever set

to music," and "one real rip-roaring prairie riot," Victor remained the only company to record it.[4] And although records show that Buffalo Bill's Wild West did at times feature a finale by a cowboy octet who sang *San Antonio* and *Broncho Buster*, and Victor included the song as the opening tune for its 1908 *Victor Minstrels No. 9* disc, the record received no writeups in the trade journals, Gardner does not mention it, and the song seems to have faded from the scene fairly quickly.[5]

NOTES

1. Edward Madden and Dorothy Jardon, *Broncho Buster* (New York: Maurice Shapiro, 1907); *Songwriters Hall of Fame*, www.songwritershalloffame.org/search/, s.v. "Edward Madden"; *Footlight Notes*, http://footlightnotes.tumblr.com, s.v. "Dorothy Jardon"; "Theatricals," *Out West* 3, no. 2 (February 1912), 138–40.

2. The Starmer brothers, William and Frederick, were two of the most prolific sheet music illustrators in the early twentieth century, producing about one in every four sheet music covers between 1909 and 1919, including that for *San Antonio*. See Bill Edwards, "William Starmer and Frederick Starmer," *RagPiano*, www.perfessorbill.com/artists/starmer.shtml.

   A search for "broncho buster" in 1907 on newspapers.com returned 186 hits for that year and included a *New York Times* story of broncho busters in Buffalo Bill's Wild West playing Madison Square Garden, a "lady broncho buster" that broke her shoulder in a Chicago performance, a "broncho buster" who slit the throats of his wife and two children in Kansas, "Broncho Buster" school stockings for sale in New York, a "broncho buster" who marries his cowgirl on horseback in Kansas, Frederic Remington's famous "Broncho Buster" sculpture, and a New Jersey vaudeville show called "Broncho Busters." See "Buffalo Bill's Wild West," *New York Times*, May 3, 1907, 17; "Girl Broncho Buster Hurt," *Chicago Daily Tribune*, May 8, 1907, 5; "Is Charged with Murder of Family," *Topeka Daily Capital*, February 5, 1907, 2; "The Hunter, Tuppen, Co.," *Syracuse (N.Y.) Post Standard*, March 26, 1907, 4; "Marry on Horseback," *Emporia (Kans.) Gazette*, July 9, 1907, 6; "Stuart Paintings for Art Museum," *New York Times*, April 4, 1907, 8; and "'Broncho Busters' at Trent Theater," *Trenton (N.J.) Evening Times*, May 27, 1907, 3.

3. *Travalanche*, https://travsd.wordpress.com, s.v. "Stars of Vaudeville #395: Bonita and Lew Hearn"; Frank Cullen, *Vaudeville Old and New: An Encyclopedia of Variety Performers in America*, vol. 1, s.v. "Bonita and Lew Hearn" (New York: Routledge, 2007).

4. "Broncho Buster," *Variety* 6, no. 4 (April 6, 1907), 32.

5. "Buffalo Bill's Wild West," *Variety* 6, no. 7 (April 27, 1907), 8; Walsh, "'Cowboy Songs,' Recordings, Part 4," *Hobbies*, July 1976, 117; *Victor Minstrels No. 9* (New York: Victor Talking Machine, 1908).

Broncho Bob and His Little Cheyenne, 1907

Edison finally made its version of the popular cowboy song *Cheyenne* in the autumn of 1907 with a two-minute cylinder of a vaudeville-type skit called *Broncho Bob and His Little Cheyenne.*[1] Len Spencer, a powerful baritone, wrote the act and performed it with Ada Jones, one of the most popular woman vocalists of the acoustic era. Jones had made recordings in the 1890s, but then Billy Murray supposedly rediscovered her around 1904. Spencer wrote several of these so-called vaudeville specialties, including several with western themes including *Santiago Flynn, A Cowboy Romance*, and *Little Arrow and Big Chief Greasepaint*. Jones concluded each bit singing a chorus of a popular song in hopes of capitalizing on its popularity.[2]

Available as an Edison cylinder, a Columbia disc or cylinder, and a Victor ten-inch disc, *Broncho Bob* was never reproduced as sheet music. In fact, the Columbia disc described the record as a "Vaudeville Specialty" and Victor listed it as a "descriptive specialty."[3] The recording basically tells the *Cheyenne* story: a cowboy named Broncho Bob meets his sweetheart Shy Ann and convinces her to ride off with him to get married. Along the way, Broncho Bob asks his lady to sing the song he "has been humming to her for more than a year now, sing it for me, sing *Cheyenne*." And with that, Ada Jones produces an even faster version of the *Cheyenne* chorus than Billy Murray had recorded on Victor. It was the first recording of a cowboy song by a woman. Full of sound effects, this cylinder marked Edison's only attempt to sell a version of *Cheyenne*.

The full transcript of the skit reads:

ANNOUNCER: Broncho Bob and His Little Cheyenne by Ada Jones and Len Spencer, Edison Records

[sound of a horse whinnying]

BRONCHO BOB (BB): Who is it Buck?

[sound of sheep]

BB: Where? Why you're right. It's her! Little Cheyenne, and a riding like the wind! Helloooo.

LITTLE CHEYENNE (LC): Hello! [sound of hoofbeats] Yip, yip, yip, yip, hello Bob.

BB: Ha-ha. Lean over.

[sound of smooching]

LC: See Bob, I've come after all.

BB: "After all? I was a hoping you'd only come after me.

LC: You're jealous Bob. [sing-song laugh]

BB: Got no time for teasing. The parson's waiting and now you've come and you'll go.

LC: Wrong again Bob. I've come but I can't go.

BB: Oh yes you can.

LC: I tell you I can't Bob. Look at the mare. See, Bob. Black Betsy ain't fit. She couldn't carry me another mile to save her life.

BB: Well, she won't haveta. My Buck will carry us both as easy as one. Jump Gal, up. Snuggle close, now. Hold tight for the ride of your life. We'll go as soon as the boys get here.

LC: The boys?

BB: Yes. Wait a minute. WHOOOOO

LC: Whatcha doin' that for? Have ya gone clean crazy, Bob?

BB: WHOOOOO

LC: Whatcha throwin' your hat in the air for?

[band starts playing *Cheyenne*]

BB: Well, that's the signal to the boys from the ranch. They're over in the canyon yonder with their band to hold things up at our weddin'. Hey, don't ya hear the tune they're a playin'? Why, that's the tune I been a hummin' to you for more than a year gal. Sing it for me. Sing it. Sing *Cheyenne*.

LC: [start singing to the band accompaniment]

    Shy Ann, Shy Ann, hop on my pony

    There's room here, for two dear, but after the ceremony

    We'll both ride back home dear, as one

    On my pony from old Cheyenne.

LC: C'mon boys, yip, yip.

BOYS: [cheer]

[band plays *Cheyenne* chorus, sound of hoofbeats fades in the distance, then music ends and a big cheer is heard.]

Edison Phonograph Monthly for October 1907 described *Broncho Bob and His Little Cheyenne* as a "highly original, diverting Western sketch . . . crowded with human interest and will certainly be a big seller." Then, after describing the dialogue, it suggested that "this Record is out of the common and is going to make a big hit." An advertisement for "New Edison Records" that appeared in a November 1907 Pennsylvania newspaper added that this was a "sketch picturing a western scene with a wedding as the central interest." It then noted the presence of a cowboy band and that "Miss Jones, as 'Little Cheyenne,' sings the cowboy song *Cheyenne*."[4] Despite these accolades, the recording is not mentioned in Gardner's lists.

NOTES

1. Len Spencer and Ada Jones, *Broncho Bob and His Little Cheyenne* (New York: National Phonograph Company, 1907), Edison Gold Moulded Record #9720.
2. Gracyk, *Popular Songs*, 314–19, 183–98; Walsh, "'Cowboy Song' Recordings, Part 3," *Hobbies*, June 1976, 35.
3. For the Columbia listing, see "Record Bulletins for December 1907," *Talking Machine World* 3, no. 11 (November 15, 1907), 78. For the Victor, see *Oregon Daily Journal* (Portland), December 1, 1907, 13.
4. *Edison Phonograph Monthly* 5, no. 8 (October 1907), 4; *York (Pa.) Daily*, November 26, 1907.

Rain-in-the-Face, 1907

Rain-in-the-Face, **words and music by Benjamin Hapgood Burt (New York: Jerome H. Remick, 1907).** Sheet music from author's collection.

Like *Sitting Bull* two years earlier, the comic song *Rain-in-the-Face* mocked a real Native American, a Hunkpapa Lakota leader.[1] Was it a longstanding grudge against those who fought Custer that made them the butt of these songs? Like Sitting Bull, Rain-in-the-Face fought the American cavalry, first in the 1866 Fetterman fight and then a decade later at the Little Bighorn. He received his unusual name as a boy when, during a fight with Cheyennes, blood spattered on his face. The image was reinforced years later during a fight with the Gros Ventres during a heavy rain. Some believed that Rain-in-the-Face killed Custer at Little Bighorn as revenge for imprisoning

him earlier. Henry Wadsworth Longfellow immortalized the Hunkpapa leader with the 1878 poem "The Revenge of Rain-in-the-Face." After escaping to Canada, Rain-in-the-Face returned to the Standing Rock Reservation in Dakota Territory where he lived out his life, dying in 1905 at about age seventy.[2]

Not surprisingly, the song has nothing to do with this biography or with the real Lakota man but instead ridicules the name in a stereotype that some scholars have come to call the "Ignoble Savage: The Drunk Injun." Characteristics of this trope include portraying Native Americans as "an inherently inferior race that lacks self-control, self-respect, dignity, honor, and morality." It does this by suggesting that Native Americans on the reservation are freeloading wards of the state, thus placing the blame for their plight on Indian inferiority, not conquest and forced assimilation.[3]

After first referencing other popular Indian songs *Hiawatha* and *Navajo*, the song makes a skin color reference by suggesting that this North Dakota chief could paint the town a "vermillion hue" by drinking bay rum and Irish whiskey till he was numb. It then denigrates his very name by suggesting that rain is the only thing he never drinks. The full lyrics are as follows:

> You've heard of Hiawatha, and of Navajo as well
> But out in North Dakota lived a chief who "rang
>   the bell";
> Of all the sporty Indians the nation ever knew,
> That certain man could paint the town, a dark
>   vermillion hue.
> He drank bay rum 'till he was numb, and Irish
>   whiskey too,
> Until he turned an Indian into an Irish "stew."
> The only thing he never poured into his face was
>   rain,
> So everybody wondered how he ever got his name.
> He met a chieftain's daughter, "Laughing Water"
>   was the dame,
> He liked the girl immensely, but he didn't like her
>   name,
> He said that water never handed any "laughs" to
>   him.
> In fact, he never used it on the outside or the in.
>
> *Chorus*
> Rain-in-the-face, Rain-in-the-face,
> He used to chase, all over the place
> Buy him a drink, and you were an ace;
> Rain-in-the-face, Rain-in-the-face,
> None of his race could keep up the pace,
> He had the first original "thirst";
> Poor old Rain-in-the-face.

Not much can be found on lyricist and composer Benjamin Hapgood Burt, who wrote both the music and the lyrics for this song. He was born in 1882, published his first song by age twenty, and by the early 1900s had written many songs performed on Broadway and recorded for the next three decades. Some of his bigger hits include a 1905 show *Indians on Broadway* and *The Wall Street Girl* in 1911. His 1933 comic song *The Pig Got Up and Walked Away* also lampooned alcohol, telling a temperance story of a drunk who lies down in the street to sleep it off only to have a pig come and lie down beside him. After a passing lady quips, "You can tell a man who boozes, by the company he chooses," the pig gets up and slowly walks away. Burt died in 1950.[4]

André De Takacs illustrated the cover sheet for the *Rain-in-the-Face* sheet music for the Jerome H. Remick publishing company in 1907. De Takacs had created many of the covers for Remick, including the *Arrah Wanna* intermezzo. The cover for *Rain-in-the-Face* is done in a striking two-tone of bright yellow background and a vivid red blanket surrounding a disheveled-looking Indian with missing teeth, almost-closed eyes, and two drooping feathers, tinged in red. The song's title is across the top in black letters, with the composer listed below and the publisher at the bottom left.

Billy Murray recorded *Rain-in-the-Face* for a Victor disc in December 1907, and the team of Arthur Collins and Byron G. Harlan released a two-minute cylinder for Indestructible in January 1908 and for Edison the next month. *Edison Phonograph Monthly* used the lyrics to describe the title character as a "real sporty old Indian" who had the "first original thirst." It then suggested that his "antics while in pursuit of fire-water are humorously told." The description concluded by suggesting that the song was "decidedly unique" and "certainly to be popular." The next year, the Edison Military Band recorded the *Rain-in-the-Face Medley*, which grouped it with other racist tunes that the *Monthly* described as a "merry medley" that featured two comic songs, *Rain-in-the-Face* and *I'm Afraid to Come Home in the Dark* "and the clever coon song *Much Obliged to You*." Despite an ad in Portland's *Oregon Daily Journal* that described the song as "exceptionally catchy" and warned readers "Don't Fail to Hear It," the song did not crack Gardner's charts or have much play beyond that year.[5]

NOTES

1. Benjamin Hapgood Burt, *Rain-in-the-Face* (New York: Jerome H. Remick, 1907).

2. Dan L. Thrapp, *Encyclopedia of Frontier Biography*, vol. 3 (Lincoln: University of Nebraska Press, 1991), 1188.

3. Authentic History, "The Ignoble Savage: The Drunk Injun," *Native Americans and American Popular Culture*, 2012, www. authentichistory.com/diversity/native/is2-drunk/index.html. See also Matz, "Images of Indians," 263–66.

4. "Gossip of the Stage," *Brooklyn (N.Y.) Daily Eagle*, October 24, 1905, 26; "Our Elders Sang His Songs," *Kansas City (Mo.) Times*, September 19, 1950, 7; *Discography of American Historical Recordings*, http://adp.library.ucsb.edu, s.v. "Benjamin Hapgood Burt"; *International Lyrics Playground*, http://lyricsplayground. com, s.v. "Pig Got Up and Slowly Walked Away."

5. *Discography of American Historical Recordings*, http://adp. library.ucsb.edu, s.v. "Rain-in-the-Face"; "A Word to the Wise," Indestructible Records ad, *Talking Machine World* 4, no. 1 (January 15, 1908), 76; "The New Edison Gold Moulded Advance List for February, 1908," *Edison Phonograph Monthly* 5, no. 10 (December 1907), 3; "The New Edison Gold Moulded Advance List for April, 1908," *Edison Phonograph Monthly* 6, no. 2 (February 1908), 5; "Edison Records Now on Sale," *Oregon Daily Journal* (Portland), January 29, 1908, 7.

Santiago Flynn, 1908

Santiago Flynn, **words by Edward Madden, music by Theodore Morse (New York: F. B. Haviland, 1908).** Sheet music from author's collection.

The musical comedy team of Len Spencer and Ada Jones produced their second western skit after *Broncho Bob and His Little Cheyenne* in 1908, titled *Santiago Flynn.* Theodore Morse, the composer of *Arrah Wanna,* had teamed with lyricist Edward Madden to write the song *Santiago Flynn* in the same year, and Spencer wrote his "Spanish-Irish Episode" using the song as the basis for a comedy sketch about a love story between a supposedly Mexican man and an Irish woman.[1]

Although it is not clear whether the song is set in Mexico or Texas, both places experienced long histories of Irish immigration and settlement. Mexico had invited Catholic immigrants to help settle its northern borders, and many Irish responded. They were in Texas as early as the late eighteenth century, accompanied Stephen F. Austin there in 1821. The 1850 census included more than 1,400 Irish in Texas, and ten years later that number had grown to more than 3,400. By 1950, more than a half a million Texans claimed Irish ancestry.[2]

Santiago Flynn, though, is another assertion of selective white dominance, not an accurate portrayal of Irish-Mexican relations. A comical interaction of two people considered less than white in the America of Tin Pan Alley, the skit focuses on an Irish girl and

111

the man she thinks is a Spanish don based on his being dressed like a "Spanish grandee." Refusing his favors, she calls him a "hot tamale," says that she could not "love a Mexican," and tells him she is tired of his "Spanish tunes and Spanish Moons." Once so rebuffed, Santiago replies that although he had been born "under the Mango" his father was an Irishman named Paddy Flynn. At this, the girl relents and they are joined, suggesting that an Irish/Irish coupling is more appropriate than the miscegenous threat of an Irish/Mexican one. The full song goes like this:

> Way down by the Rio Grande,
> There lived Santiago Flynn,
> He dressed like a Spanish grandee
> He rode on a pony thin
> Near by on her own plantation
> There lingered an Irish Rose
> Love songs of the dreamy nation
> He'd sing to her thro' his nose
> And she would sigh, wink her eye, giving him this
>   reply:
>
> *Chorus*
> "Santiago you're a Dago with a wicked smile,
> Faith, I like your style
> But, Macaroni, ride your pony,
> Spanish tunes and Spanish moons are making me
>   grow thin,
> Change your blarney, play Killarney Santiago
>   Flynn."
>
> She cried 'you're a hot tamale,
> I can't love a Mexican,
> Nobody can with this Molly
> No one but an Irish man."
> He jumped in a wild fandango
> He cried with an Irish grin
> "Tho' born underneath the Mango
> My father was Paddy Flynn."
> She cried "come in, Mister Flynn, I'll never say
>   agin."

The F. B. Havilland company published the *Santiago Flynn* sheet music in 1908. The cover art, drawn by the unknown artist E.P.C., features a man on horseback,

dressed as a Spanish don, playing a guitar and serenading a woman looking down on him from a small balcony. Little puns accompany the composers' names: "Music by Theodore Morse Collected from everywhere" and "Lyrics by Edward Madden Selected from here and there." These phrases are repeated on the credits on the actual score, which also includes the subtitle "A Spanish-Irish Episode."

Both Victor and Edison made versions of *Santiago Flynn* in the spring of 1908. But rather than reproduce the entire song, both companies recorded the comic skit featuring Len Spencer and Ada Jones playing Santiago and his girl.[3] A lone guitar can be heard throughout while Jones utilizes an Irish accent, narrates most of the scene, and sings a chorus of *Santiago Flynn*. Interestingly, her pronunciation of "Santiago" comes across as "San Diego" throughout the recording, and Spencer's accent seems as much stereotypical Italian as it does Mexican. Throughout the recording, the two actors mix puns and other wordplay into their conversation. The Edison version runs just over two minutes; the Victor version adds a few more jokes and runs just over three minutes. The Edison cylinder goes like this:

NORA MCCARTEY (NM): Oh the sound of the band playing in the plaza makes me think of Coney Island, oh it's a thorny time for me Nora McCartey just sitting alone in me window in this moddling Mexico. Aha! There's that Spaniard San Diego making love under me window, he's a handsome lad. What do ye want?

SANTIAGO FLYNN (SF): Oh I want Senora.

NM: Well, you can't see Nora, see? Go away with your Dago blarney.

SF: Oh, Senora, lean from thy window, place thy hand out.

NM: Well if it's a handout you're after, this is no place for beggars.

SF: Oh, My throat burns with the love I would speak.

NM: That's from the red hot tamales and chili con carne you're often eating. That's right, cool yourself, play a little music. . . . He's got the fine eyes, It's a pity he's not Irish.

SF: Oh! Senora!

NM: Me name is not Senora. it's Honorah.

SF: Well, change your name.

NM: Uh uh. I believe the Dago is proposing to me?

SF: Oh! Be my queen! Be my wife!

NM: What? Be Honorah San Diego? That's a fine name . . . for a five cent cigar.

[Nora begins to sing]

Senor, you're a hot tamale,
But I can't love a Mexican.

SF: [interrupts] What, nobody can win Honorah?

NM: No . . . No one but an Irish man!
Go away with your mad fandango.

SF: Oh please, let me explain. My Ladies are all born in Mexico . . . but my father was Paddy Flynn!

NM: Flynn? Flynn! Come in Mr. Flynn. I will never say agin.

[Nora sings the chorus to *Santiago Flynn:*]

San Diego you're a Dago with a wicked smile,
Faith I like your style.
But, Macaroni, ride your pony,
Spanish tunes and Spanish moons are making me
grow thin,
Change your blarney, play Killarney San Diego Flynn.

Edison Phonograph Monthly for April 1908, in a strange description, wrote this about the recording:

Santiago serenades Norah McCarty [*sic*] in true Spanish style. In broken Spanish he sings his love-story to the accompaniment of a mandolin. Norah has nothing for him but sneers and quips, till he tells her that, although born in Mexico, his father's name was Flynn. Then nothing in house is too good for Santiago, and the priest in due time made them possible subjects for the divorce court. Toward the close of the Record, Miss Jones sings a verse from "Santiago Flynn," of which the music is by Theodore Morse, the words by Edward Madden and the publishers are F. B. Haviland Publishing Co., New York.[4]

Later in the year when Edison re-released the skit on its four-minute Amberol cylinder, the *Monthly* changed Santiago's nationality from Spanish to Italian:

An Irish maiden is courted by an Italian wooer. He plays the mandolin beneath her bower in true Romeo fashion and asks her to be his Irish Rosie, but she is able to make very little sense out of his "dago blarney." He asks her to cast her eyes on him and she answers sweetly that she has no cast in her eye. Santiago Flynn entreats her to take the name of Signora Santiago. "A Fine name—for a five cent cigar" she exclaims. The ending is happy, however, for Santiago convinces her that his father was Paddy Flynn, a good, true Irishman. She then agrees to have him to the accompaniment of "Killarney," on the mandolin. Several clever songs are introduced by Miss Jones. Orchestra Accompaniment.[5]

Clearly there are some complex questions and ideas about race, ethnicity, and their intermingling at work here. It is strange that the Edison editor first wrote that once Norah accepted Santiago the "priest in due time made them possible subjects for the divorce court." Is this a way to say that they married? If so, then why not just say that? Someone who suggests that mutual acceptance puts someone in line for divorce certainly does not think too much of the loving couple. Is this just a more complicated way of denigrating the Irish and Mexican populations? And what about the Mexican ethnicity? How does Santiago Flynn go from being a Mexican in the first description to an Italian in the second? Does the editor not know that the pejorative word "Dago" was used to denigrate both Italians and Spaniards? Does he also confuse "Signora" with "Senora"? Did the editor read the sheet music or even listen to the song? Or is it his intention to add Italians to the list of people considered to be less than white in Jim Crow America?

Such questions remind us that this song does not represent life in Mexico or Texas but was created in the imagination of a New Yorker pondering these places. Accordingly, one place to seek answers is to look at the multiple ways in which the lyricist and performers gaze on the exotic Borderlands, symptomatic of exoticism—East Coast fascination with America's Orient on the border. In that sense, the view is dichotomous. On one hand, it is scandalous, with its concerns about miscegenation. On the other, it is titillating, for one must watch this scene of lesser peoples working through their squabble. Whatever the song suggests, it is clear that, along with other songs of the period, such interracial and interethnic love was beneath mainstream white America. Perhaps this is part of the reason that Gardner does not include *Santiago Flynn* in any top list.

NOTES

1. Theodore Morse and Edward Madden, *Santiago Flynn* (New York: F. B. Haviland, 1908).
2. Phillip L. Fry, "Irish," *Handbook of Texas Online*, June 15, 2010, www.tshaonline.org/handbook/online/articles/pii01.
3. Ada Jones and Len Spencer, *Santiago Flynn* (Orange, N.J.: National Phonograph, 1908), Edison Gold Moulded Record #9863.
4. "Advance List of New Edison Records for June, 1908," *Edison Phonograph Monthly* 6, no. 4 (April 1908), 4.
5. "First Advance List of Edison Amberol Records to Be Issued Oct. 1st, 1908," *Edison Phonograph Monthly* 6, no. 9 (September 1908), 27.

When It's Moonlight on the Prairie, 1908

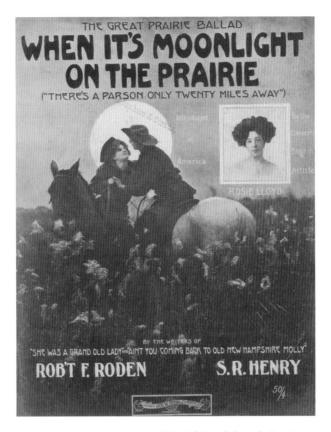

When It's Moonlight on the Prairie,
words by Rob't. F. Roden, music by
S. R. Henry (New York: Jos. W. Stern,
1908). Sheet music from author's
collection.

The cowboy song *When It's Moonlight on the Prairie*, by Robert F. Roden and S. R. Henry, was popular on stage before it became a recording thanks to "the clever English artiste" Rosie Lloyd. Lloyd's family included several popular singers in England, and Rosie had already been successful there as well as in South Africa before coming to the United States in 1908. One description noted that her "refreshingly girlish personality, her sweet and charming manner, and her lack of any fuss and frills" made her an instant hit. Describing a New York performance, the *Brooklyn Daily Eagle* wrote that Lloyd sang this "feature hit" wearing a "specially designed

cowgirl costume" and had the theater darkened with a spotlight thrown upon her, "the effect of which is striking."[1]

The Joseph W. Stern Company of New York published the sheet music.[2] Its cover is done in a bluish-purple monotone reminiscent of moonlight that looks almost like a photograph. The main scene shows a cowboy and cowgirl, both astride horses standing in a field of flowers, embracing each other as a large full moon rises in the distance. Just right of the moon, a portrait of Rosie Lloyd is shown flanked by the words "Introduced in America by the clever English Artiste." The composers' names and a testament to their popularity are included at the bottom. Across the top, a line above the title states that this is "The Great Prairie Ballad."

Written in 6/8 time, the song tells the story of a cowgirl who, against her wealthy father's wishes, promises to marry her cowboy lover when the "moon begins to shine." It also features a line reminding everyone that "there's a parson only twenty miles away." The full lyrics go like this:

> The sun slowly sets in its splendor
> Far off in the fair golden west
> The voice of a cowboy grows tender
> As he sighs to the girl he loves best
>
> You dad now is wealthy, my darling
> And vows that you ne'er will be mine
> But you said you'd wed me, Mary,
> Tonight, love, on the prairie
> Meet me when the moon begins to shine.
>
> *Chorus*
> When it's moonlight on the prairie, darling Mary
> I'll be waiting with the ponies, love for you
> There's a parson only twenty miles away, twenty
>   miles away, twenty miles away
> When the knot is tied, then side by side we'll ride
>   dear
> To a pretty little home I've built for you
> I'll be waiting, waiting waiting for you Mary
> When it's moonlight on the prairie Mary dear.
>
> 'Tis Moonlight the sweethearts are riding
> Her dad follows them o'er the plain
> But cupid, the lovers is guiding
> And the stern father rides all in vain.
>
> "Too late!" says the cowboy, "We're wedded"
> The lass sighs "Forgive us, dear dad."
> But the father cries, "You're plucky
> To win her hand you're lucky!
> That's the way I won her mother, lad.
>
> *Repeat Chorus*

Byron G. Harlan recorded the song with chorus for Edison in 1908. Like Billy Murray, Harlan was a westerner, having been born in Kansas and raised in Iowa and South Dakota. He probably was best known for his comic recordings with partner Arthur Collins, but he also sang minstrels as well as popular sentimental ballads. *Edison Phonograph Monthly* for April 1908 noted that his recording of *When It's Moonlight on the Prairie* would "gratify the oft-expressed wish of Mr. Harlan's legion of admirers that he sing something different from his usual repertoire." Similarly, an advertisement from the *Santa Cruz Evening News* called this a "breezy song of cowboy life."[3]

Victor used Harry Macdonough and the Hadyn Quarter for its version, released in June that same year. Macdonough was perhaps the most popular ballad singer of the era,[4] and he had recorded *Hiawatha*, *Anona*, and *Navajo*, so *Moonlight* may have been a chance to connect a popular Indian singer to a new cowboy song. Unfortunately, neither the Victor nor the Edison recording seems to have been as popular as Rosie Lloyd's original rendition, and neither are listed by Gardner.

NOTES

1. Johnson Briscoe, *The Actors' Birthday Book*, 2nd series (New York: Moffat, Yard, 1918), 135; "Gossip of the Stage," *Brooklyn Daily Eagle*, March 9, 1908, 22.
2. Robert F. Roden and S. R. Henry, *When It's Moonlight on the Prairie* (New York: Jos. W. Stern, 1908).
3. Gracyk, *Popular American Recording Pioneers*, 162–67; "Advance List of New Edison Records for June 1908," *Edison Phonograph Monthly* 6, no. 4 (April 1908), 3; "New Records Every Month," *Santa Cruz (Calif.) Evening News*, June 23, 1908, 4.
4. Gracyk, *Popular American Recording Pioneers*, 225–26.

Topeka, 1908

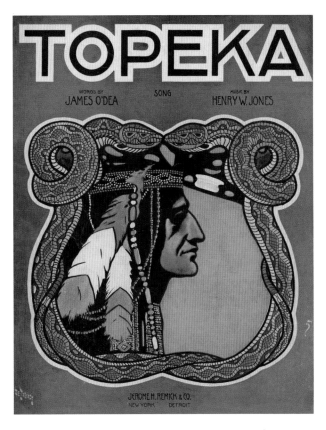

Topeka, words by James O'Dea, music by Henry W. Jones (New York: Jerome H. Remick, 1908). Sheet music courtesy Lilly Library, Indiana University, Bloomington.

Topeka (two-step intermezzo), music by Harry Jones (New York: Jerome H. Remick, 1907). Sheet music from author's collection.

It has been said that the era of Tin Pan Alley was all about finding a hit song, then figuring out why it was popular and copying the formula over and over until it wore out. This worked for both cowboy songs and Indian love songs. It also worked for songwriters. Lyricist James O'Dea had already written hit songs with *Hiawatha*, *Silver Heels*, and *Iola* when he wrote the words for another Indian love song, *Topeka*, in 1908.[1] And like *Hiawatha* and *Iola*, *Topeka* also played with the name of a Kansas town. Working with music composer Henry W. Jones, O'Dea produced another song of love between a "girlie of the golden West"

who was a "young Indian in buckskins dressed" and her "copper colored brave." The song is one of the few that contains descriptions of the West such as "where the cattle ranges are," as "barren and bare," and the place where "buffalo in days agone would roam." It contains allusions in the second verse to the Ghost Dance and the line that the warrior had "fell to the might of the paleface in the fight." Remember that the Ghost Dance movement had ended at the massacre at Wounded Knee just eighteen years before O'Dea penned his words.

Here's the full text of the song:

Westward a far, where the cattle ranges are,
Once dwelt a girlie of the golden West.
Fair as could be was this little Cherokee,
Young Indian in buckskins dressed,
Across the divide just to linger at her side,
There'd nightly come a copper colored brave,
Vowing to love her by all above her,
Singing where the corn flow'rs wave

Chorus
My own Topeka
I've come to seek her
Who'll be forever
My hope and pride
You'll be that one, dear,
My own Topeka,
My sunflow'r bride.

Repeat Chorus

Barren and bare is the prairie country where
the buffalo in days agone would roam
Gone is the brave who'd be willingly a slave
to peek around Topeka's home,
He fell to the might of the paleface in the fight,
And often in the misty shadows where
sunflow'rs a host dance
high o'er the ghost dance
Still the maiden seems to hear.

The *Topeka* song sheet music is unusual in depicting a male Indian in profile framed by a pair of intertwined rattlesnakes. Although it was unusual not to include a female, the inclusion of the snakes was quite uncommon. Drawn by André De Takacs, the image boldly uses shades of gray, white, black, and orange to make a stunning image.

In contrast, the sheet music cover for Harry Jones's two-step intermezzo version of the song, drawn by an artist named Henrich, is set in the colors of a soft autumn day with the head and shoulders of a lone Native American, whose gender is not clear, wearing a single feather while a long braid hangs down over the shoulder. Unlike the song's color scheme, in fact, this one is a muted pastel of yellows and pinks and whites.[2]

Perhaps because of its unusual illustration or lyrics, *Topeka* does not appear to have been popular. Only one recording of the song, Frederick H. Potter's 1908 two-minute Edison cylinder, is known. Potter had been one of the first vocalists to record *Red Wing*. The piece begins with a twittering flute and tom-tom, and then Potter sings the lyrics, assisted throughout by a chorus, bells, Indian yell, and orchestra.[3] *Edison Phonograph Monthly* for May 1908 described it as a "spirited song descriptive of Indian life on the plains and telling of the love of an Indian brave for his little maid Topeka."[4] Although such a description fit the bill for Indian love songs, apparently neither O'Dea's popularity as a song writer nor Potter's vocal could make *Topeka* a hit. Both the sheet music and the recording remain rare today.

NOTES

1. James O'Dea and Henry W. Jones, *Topeka* (New York: Jerome H. Remick, 1908).
2. Harry Jones, *Topeka* (New York: Jerome H. Remick, 1907).
3. Frederick H. Potter, *Topeka* (Orange, N.J.: National Phonograph Company, 1908), Edison Gold Moulded Record #9882. This is the only song in this catalogue for which I own neither original sheet music nor recording.
4. "Advance List of New Edison Records for July 1908," *Edison Phonograph Monthly* 6, no. 5 (May 1908), 4.

Big Chief Smoke, 1908

"Big Chief Smoke," *New Phonogram*
4, no. 12 (Orange, N.J.: National
Phonograph, June 1908). Ephemera
from author's collection.

Big Chief Smoke, an Indian comic song, appeared in 1908 as part of a musical comedy called *Lonesome Town* that featured the team C. William Kolb and Max M. Dill. According to period newspapers, the show featured eleven songs and chorus girls and was set in the Los Angeles suburb of Watts. Apparently, the play "conquered New York" in 1908 and then was revived the following year.[1] *Big Chief Smoke*, subtitled "Uoof, Uoof, Uoof," appeared only as part of the package of sheet music for *Lonesome Town*, and its cover did not represent Native Americans at all. Edison's trade journal, *New Phonogram*, for June 1908 depicted a line drawing of a stereotypical Indian head with large nose, war paint, and feathered headdress puffing on a pipe with the title "No. 9862 Big Chief Smoke" beneath it. Such a placement clearly suggests that *Big Chief Smoke* seemed to be the show's most popular song.[2]

The lyrics clearly exemplify a derogatory stereotype. From the opening lines, "Big Chief Smoke was an Indian joke who lived in Albuquerque," it is clear that the song not only ridicules Native American tobacco and smoking but denigrates Native Americans as well by picturing men as lazy, women as overworked "squaws," and children as uncared for "papooses." Of course, it does this through broken pidgin English. The full lyrics are as follows:

> Big Chief Smoke was an Indian joke,
> Who lived in Albuquerque.
> Had heap big squaw named Eagle Claw,
> She did all the work.
>
> In wigwam he'd lay round all day,
> And smoke, and smoke, and smoke.
> And while he'd grunt and puff away,
> She'd choke and choke and choke.
>
> Squaw heap mad starts big powwow,
> Chief talks back, starts fam'ly row.
>
> *Chorus*
> "Uoof, Uoof, Uoof," said heap big chief,
> "Uoof, Uoof, Uoof," said squaw.
> "Me no more will cook for you,
> You'll eat 'um' heap meat raw!"
> Squaw much mad grab pan of grease,
> Hit big chief's pipe a swipe;
> No more he smoke the pipe of peace,
> He smokes a piece of pipe.

> Squaw was "maw" and chief was "paw,"
> To Papoose little Puff.
> For a joke chief teach him smoke
> Said, "Makes him up to snuff."
>
> Papoose finds chief's powder can,
> "Heap new smoke," said he.
> Can did swipe put much in pipe,
> Chief sleep and he no see.
>
> Papoose powder then did light,
> Papoose quick was out of sight.
>
> *Repeat Chorus*

Billy Murray recorded *Big Chief Smoke* for Edison and Indestructible as two-minute cylinders as well as for a Victor disc in the summer of 1908. The *Edison Phonograph Monthly* description repeated the song's denigration by describing the recording as the "tale of an Indian whose chief occupation is smoking." It continued that "his fondness for the weed is objected to by his squaw" and brought on the fight featured in the lyrics. The *Monthly* concluded by suggesting that the "melody and orchestral effects are Indian like" and the "peculiar gutteral [*sic*] grunt of the Indian is well featured."[3] Despite these accolades, Gardner does not include the song in his lists.

NOTES

1. "Lonesome Town a Cheery Bit of Merriment," *New York Tribune*, January 22, 1908, 7; "News and Views of the Local Drama," *Los Angeles Herald*, June 6, 1909, 33; "Big Chief Smoke," Aschbach ad, *Allentown (Pa.) Leader*, June 8, 1908, 6.
2. C. William Kolb and J. A. Raynes, *Big Chief Smoke* (New York: M. Witmark and Sons, 1907); *New Phonogram* 4, no. 12 (June 1908).
3. "Record Bulletins for June 1908," *Talking Machine World* 4, no. 5 (May 15, 1908), 56; "Advance List of New Edison Records for June, 1908," *Edison Phonograph Monthly* 6, no. 4 (April 1908), 4.

Pride of the Prairie, 1908

Pride of the Prairie, words by Harry
Breen, music by George Botsford
(New York: Jerome H. Remick, 1907).
Sheet music from author's collection.

Historian Jim Walsh calls Harry Breen and George Botsford's *Pride of the Prairie* "one of the best of all cowboy songs." The tune, set on the "wild and wooly prairie" near Pueblo, Colorado, retells the *Cheyenne* story of a cowboy stealing his cowgirl love away by having her jump up on his horse. It also plays with western wording when it suggests "my heart's been lassoed." Lyricist Breen reported that the sheet music sold more than 300,000 copies. All three major recording companies, Victor, Columbia, and Edison, made versions of it.[1]

Breen was a New York vaudeville actor, singer, and composer most famous for his ability to create songs extemporaneously. Botsford was born and raised in South Dakota and Iowa, trained as a pianist, married a singer, and played piano for traveling shows. He moved to New York City around 1902 and published his first songs by 1906. He later became an accomplished ragtime composer.[2]

The sheet music cover illustration by André De Takacs features a badlands scene with a beautiful Gibson Girl cowgirl wearing a long gray skirt and white blouse with red vest and sitting on a mesa at center right with a cowboy hat at her feet. A saddled horse stands in the near distance, silhouetted against the colorful distant hills and a setting sun. At left, an inset photograph shows

121

three men in uniform, the popular vaudeville act of Vardon, Perry, and Wilber. Like De Takacs's work for *In the Land of the Buffalo*, this illustration uses a minimal color palette and resembles western art.[3]

The full lyrics are as follows:

Out in the wild and wooly Prairie
Not far from old Pueblo town
There lived a little girl named Mary
Blue eyes and tresses of brown.

From o'er the plains there came a cowboy
He said please name our wedding day
She bowed her head and whispered: "Now boy"
Then on their bronchos they rode away, they rode
    away one summer's day;

Chorus
Pride of the prairie, Mary my own,
Jump up beside me, ride to my home,
My heart's been lassoed, No more we'll roam
Pride of the Prairie, Mary!

When o'er the prairie day was breaking
And all was quiet on the plains
Then to his Mary he was saying
Tell me "You love me" again
He held the broncho while she mounted
And asked her "may I steal a kiss"
He stole more than she ever counted
She said, "I love you,"
He whispered this, he whispered this and stole a kiss.

Repeat Chorus

The fact that all three major companies recorded their own version of *Pride of the Prairie* contributed to the song's popularity. Victor began its 1908 *Victor Minstrels No. 9* recording with *Broncho Buster*, followed that with some jokes, then Billy Murray sang one verse and a chorus of *Pride of the Prairie*.[4] Walsh reports that Columbia offered its version on both cylinder and disc in June that year performed by its Columbia Quartet, led by Frank C. Stanley, and notes that Columbia "boldly proclaimed it to be the best cowboy song thus published."[5] Indeed, a Columbia advertisement in *Talking Machine World* stated that cowboy songs were becoming big hits on Broadway. The ad included a drawing of a

cowboy on horseback and noted that *Pride of the Prairie* and three other songs "are the *first* records of the four that have waked up Broadway. And they are as good as they are new." It then described *Pride of the Prairie* as "the best song of the Western plains that has been produced. It is full of fine, broad swing of 'cowboy' music, which is rapidly becoming the leading feature of the big music successes in New York. Sung by the Columbia Quartet, strong, tuneful, and lively."[6] A few months later, the same group recorded the song for Zon-o-phone, a Victor subsidiary that produced cheaper recordings. Its supplement called the song "a little love episode of the Western prairie, splendidly presented."[7]

The Edison cylinder of *Pride of the Prairie*, from the fall of 1908, features Billy Murray singing two verses and three choruses. *Edison Phonograph Monthly* for August 1908 summarized the song's popularity:

The past summer brought out some clever popular songs, but none to take the public fancy more than "Pride of the Prairie." It was heard in vaudeville, in illustrated songs at the moving picture shows; the bands took it up in the parks and passed it on to the orchestras on excursion boats. It is just the stripe of song that starts the gallery whistling. Billy Murray and chorus sing it with a whirlwind flourish that rivals the speed of the broncho on which Miss Mary and her cowboy lover rode away.[8]

Despite these many accolades, Gardner does not mention *Pride of the Prairie* in any of his lists.

NOTES

1. Henry J. Breen and George Botsford, *Pride of the Prairie* (New York: Jerome H. Remick, 1907); Walsh, "'Cowboy Song' Recordings, Part 5," *Hobbies*, August 1976, 35; *Variety* 13, no. 1 (December 12, 1908), 4.

2. *Internet Movie Database*, www.imdb.com, s.v. "Harry Breen"; "Popular Writers of Popular Shows," *New York Clipper*, February 15, 1913, 9; Bill Edwards, "George James Botsford," *RagPiano*, www.perfessorbill.com/artists/botsford.shtml.

3. "Vardon, Perry, and Wilber Booked in Europe," *New York Clipper*, August 14, 1909, 1; Bill Edwards, "André De Takacs," *RagPiano*, www.perfessorbill.com/artists/detakacs.shtml.

4. *Victor Minstrels No. 9* (New York: Victor Talking Machine, 1908).

5. Walsh, "'Cowboy Song' Recordings, Part 5," *Hobbies*, August 1976, 53.

6. "Columbia Records," *Talking Machine World* 4, no. 3 (March 15, 1908), 39.

7. Walsh, "'Cowboy Song' Recordings, Part 5," *Hobbies*, August 1976, 53.

8. "Advance List New Edison Records for October, 1908," *Edison Phonograph Monthly* 6, no. 8 (August 1908), 16.

I'm a Yiddish Cowboy, 1908

I'm a Yiddish Cowboy, words by Edgar Leslie, music by Al Piantadosi and Halsey K. Mohr (New York: Ted S. Barron, 1908). Sheet music courtesy Frances G. Spencer Collection of American Popular Sheet Music, Crouch Fine Arts Library, Baylor University Libraries Digital Collections, Baylor University, Waco, Texas.

"I'm a Yiddish Cowboy," *New Phonogram* 5, no. 5 (Orange, N.J.: National Phonograph, November 1908). Ephemera from author's collection.

In 1908 the Edison company issued a cowboy and Indian love song cylinder that added Jews to the list of American ethnic groups worth poking fun at with the release of *I'm a Yiddish Cowboy*. Like *Arrah Wanna*, the fact that it also brought an existing genre into the cowboy and Indian craze attests to the popularity of western music at this time. In fact, Tin Pan Alley composers had been writing comic dialect songs that perpetuated offensive stereotypes for Hebrew impersonators who performed them on stage. So many Jews worked for music publishers such as Jerome Remick, Leo Feist, and Harry Von Tilzer that one writer suggests that "Tin Pan Alley was essentially a Jewish industry," because they were so numerous, not because they had a "Jewish agenda."[1] Surviving sheet music songs include 1904's *Oi, Yoi, Yoi, Yoi* ("A Hebrew Love Song"), *When Mose with His Nose Leads the Band* (1906), and *Under the Hebrew Moon* (1909). Regular performers sung some of these so-called Jewface songs for recording companies as well. Both Edison and Victor, for example, recorded Ada Jones and Len Spencer's *Becky and Izzy* ("A Yiddish Courtship") in 1907.[2]

Jews had been in the American West in significant numbers since the California gold rush. One historian suggests that between 1850 and 1920 more than 300,000 immigrated to the region. And although many were pioneering merchants, Jews participated in all walks of life in the West, including being cowboys on the range. The connection between the urban Yiddish stage and the western frontier had begun with an 1895 play about two Jewish peddlers from New York who met in Kansas while trading with the local Indians. A dozen years later, Tin Pan Alley composers Will J. Harris and Harry I. Robinson wrote *Yonkle, the Cow Boy Jew*, and the following year Edgar Leslie, Al Piantodosi, and Halsey K. Mohr penned the story of "Tough Guy Levi" in *I'm a Yiddish Cowboy*.[3] One scholar believes the song may even have been inspired by Buffalo Bill Wild West star William Levy "Buck" Taylor, the "King of the Cowboys."[4]

All of these examples played on the stereotypical assumption that American Jews were out of place anywhere but New York, and that the power of the western frontier would make them less Jewish and transform them into true Americans. The sheet music for *I'm a Yiddish Cowboy* plays on this assumption with a photograph of a cowboy with wooly chaps, a neckerchief, and a big hat standing in profile smoking a cigarette against a western scene that includes a forest, an Indian tepee, and several wild animals on the far horizon. The lyrics, which include such western icons as the prairie, Cheyenne Indians, bronco busters, and tomahawks, tells a love story between Levi and an Indian maiden. Historian Rachel Rubenstein suggests that the song shows a "union of warring opposites—cowboy and Indian, mongrel immigrant with 'blue blood' native, the newest American with the oldest," and then summarizes historian Harley Erdman, who wrote that it was "as if in the meeting and mating of these two grotesque anomalies lay all the myriad possibilities of the nation."[5]

Its lyrics are as follows:

Way out West in the wild and woolly prairie land,
Lived a cowboy by the name of Levi,
He loved a blue blood Indian maiden,
And came to serenade her like a "tough guy."
Big Chief "Cruller Legs" was the maiden's father,
And he tried to keep Levi away,
But Levi didn't care for ev'ry ev'ning,
With his Broncho Buster, Giddyap!
Giddyap! He'd come around and say.

Chorus
Tough guy Levi, that's my name, and I'm a yiddish
     cowboy,
I don't care for Tomahawks or Cheyenne Indians,
     oi, oi,
I'm a real live "Diamond Dick" that shoots 'em till
     they die,
I'll marry squaw or start a war, for I'm a fighting
     guy.

Levi said that he'd make the maiden marry him,
And that he was sending for a Rabbi,
The maiden went and told her father,
He must not fight because she loved the "tough
     guy."
"Cruller Legs" gave the "Pipe of Peace" to Levi,
But Levi said I guess that you forget,
For I'm the kid that smokes Turkish Tobacco,
Get the Broncho Buster, Giddyap!
Giddyap! Go buy cigarettes.

Repeat Chorus

Edward Meeker, the voice-over who introduced most Edison songs at the start of each cylinder, recorded the song for Edison in 1907. Meeker was also famous for recording popular songs including *Take Me out to the Ball Game* and *Harrigan*.[6] The *Edison Phonograph Monthly* "Advance List" for its September 1908 issue described *I'm a Yiddish Cowboy* as "a dandy new cowboy song with Western effects galore. Among them, the tom-tom, cowboy chorus, cowboy and Indian yells, hoofbeats, etc.,—and all so plain and realistic that one can almost smell the alkali." It went on say that "Mr. Meeker sings this number with the spirit and fire that the unusual words and music call for—so plainly that not a word is lost, even in the yiddish dialect portion." *Edison's New Phonogram* for November 1908 featured *I'm a Yiddish Cowboy* on its cover with a cartoon illustration of a stereotypical Jewish male with protruding nose and small beard, dressed in big hat, kerchief, chaps, boots, and spurs, holding a pistol in his right hand and a lariat in the other.[7]

No other recording company, including Victor and Columbia, made this record. And although Edison writers featured it on the cover of one *Monthly*, the song was never much of a hit and one has to wonder if there was more going on.[8] Scholars today question whether Thomas Edison, like his inventor friend Henry Ford, was anti-Semitic. Although we may never know for certain, we do know that Edison capitalized on many of the popular trends in music including both the cowboy craze and the Jim Crow West, which suggests just how much such songs resonated with the American public.[9]

NOTES

1. Jonathan D. Sarna and Jonathan Golden, "The American Jewish Experience in the Twentieth Century: Antisemitism and Assimilation" *National Humanities Center*, rev. October 2000, http://nationalhumanitiescenter.org/tserve/twenty/tkeyinfo/jewishexp.htm; quotation from Jonathan Karp, "Killing Tin Pan Alley: Bob Dylan and the (Jewish) America Experience," *Guilt and Pleasure* 6 (Fall 2007), www.guiltandpleasure.com/index.php?site=rebootgp&page=gp_article&id=62.

2. Rosen, "'Cohen Owes Me Ninety-Seven Dollars,'" 9–28.

3. Edgar Leslie, Al Piantodosi, and Halsey K. Mohr, *I'm a Yiddish Cowboy* (New York: Barron Music, 1907).

4. Rubinstein, *Members of the Tribe*, 43–46.

5. Ava F. Kahn, "Looking at America from the West to the East, 1850–1920," in Kahn, *Jewish Life*, 13–14; Diner, "American West, New York Jewish," 45–46.

6. Joan Baker, *Secrets of Voice-Over Success: Top Voice-Over Actors Reveal How They Did It* (Boulder, Colo.: Sentient, 2005), 4; *UCSB Cylinder Audio Archive*, http://cylinders.library.ucsb.edu, lists seventy-two cylinders by Meeker between 1906 and 1920.

7. "Advance List," *Edison Phonograph Monthly* 6, no. 9 (September 1908), 17; *New Phonogram* 5, no. 5 (November 1908).

8. A version of the song did appear in the Columbia Pictures 1931 Krazy Kat cartoon *Rodeo Dough*, available on YouTube.com.

9. "Was Edison Anti-Semitic?" *Jweekly.com*, February 21, 1997, www.jweekly.com/article/full/5145/was-edison-anti-semitic; Neil Baldwin, *Henry Ford and the Jews: The Mass Production of Hate* (New York: PublicAffairs, 2002), 89–90.

Rainbow, 1908

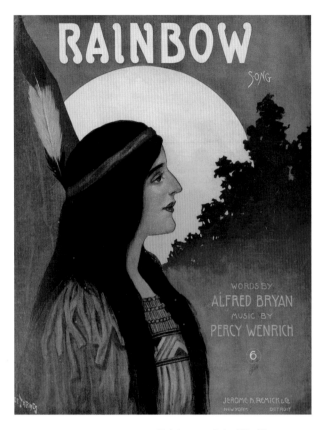

Rainbow, words by Alfred Bryan,
music by Percy Wenrich (New York:
Jerome H. Remick, 1913). Sheet music
from author's collection.

Rainbow (Indian intermezzo), music
by Percy Wenrich (New York: Jerome
H. Remick, 1908). Sheet music from
author's collection.

In late 1908, Percy Wenrich and Alfred Bryan's Indian love song *Rainbow* became a big hit.[1] Billy Murray recorded it twice that year, once with the Hadyn Quartet and again with Ada Jones, the first female to record an Indian love song. Set under a palm tree rather than the prairie, *Rainbow* tells the typical tale of a love between a chief and a "pretty maiden of a copper shade." Its full lyrics are as follows:

While the rain was softly falling in a forest glade
Beyond the prairies far away
Beneath a palm tree, so they say
There stood an Indian chief one day.

There he spied a pretty maiden of a copper shade
And as he gazed she dropped her head
To hide her cheek with blushes red
While these sweet words he said:

Come be my Rainbow, my pretty Rainbow
My heart beguile, give me a smile
Once in a while
In rain or sunshine, my Rainbow
Keep your love light a glow
I love you so, my sweet Rainbow.

Then the rainbow shone out smiling from the
    summer sky
And when she saw this sign she sighed
"Now can't you see it's fate" he cried.
Come love and be my happy bride,

Brighter than the rainbow beamed the lovelight in
    her eye,
And as they wandered home that night,
Beneath the moonbeams silv'ry light,
Oft he sang with delight:

Come be my Rainbow, my pretty Rainbow
My heart beguile, give me a smile
Once in a while
In rain or sunshine, my Rainbow
Keep your love light a glow
I love you so, my sweet Rainbow.

Rainbow marked the first hit of composer Percy Wenrich in his rise to fame. Wenrich was born in Joplin, Missouri, in 1887, was taught the organ and piano by his mother, published a couple songs, and then went to the Chicago Music College. After six months, he returned to Joplin and wrote melodies on demand for a regional music publisher and commuted to Milwaukee, where he worked as a song plugger for a department store. His biggest hit was *Peaches and Cream* in 1905. Around this time, he met and married Dolly Connolly, a beautiful and talented vaudeville singer. Wenrich wrote the *Rainbow* intermezzo in 1908,[2] and Bryan put words to the tune soon after. A Canadian newspaper, when describing Wenrich, stated that "his present success is *Rainbow*, which is sweeping the country as did only the great *Hiawatha. Rainbow* promises to outdo them all."[3] This success enabled Wenrich and Connolly to move to New York City, where he began working for the Jerome Remick

music publishing company. Over the next decade he wrote songs and dabbled in his own music publishing business while Dolly and her brother Bob made records and danced and sang in theaters to Wenrich's accompaniment.[4] A December 1910 ad for Wenrich in the *San Francisco Call* described the composer as "the man with the musical brain" and stated that he made $3,370 on his first royalty check for *Rainbow*, and "since then his musical brain has earned him from $10,000 to $15,000 per year."[5] Around the time of the Great War, Wenrich began writing Broadway musicals and continued to do so till 1930, often featuring Dolly in lead roles. The couple retired from music after that, though Wenrich published songs occasionally in retirement. The 1951 Doris Day movie *Moonlight Bay* features many of his songs. He died in 1952.[6]

Despite the lyrics suggesting a setting under a palm tree, the sheet music covers for both the intermezzo and the song depict a forest locale. The former features a green, forested glen looking down on a small lake with blue mountains rising in the distance. A rainbow arcs above the mountains, with a faint outline of a Native American woman in the sky below. For the song, a Native American woman, shown from the waist up, is cast against trees silhouetted against a large background moon.

Victor made two versions of *Rainbow* in 1908, a vocal by Billy Murray and the Hadyn Quartet, and the instrumental by the Victor Orchestra. The Peerless Quartet, which featured tenors Albert Campbell and Henry Burr, baritone Steve Porter, and bass Frank C. Stanley, recorded it along with two other songs in a record called the *Rainbow Medley* that December. The following year, Billy Murray and Ada Jones recorded *Rainbow* for Edison and Zon-o-phone. Ada Jones also recorded a duet of the song for Zon-o-phone with Len Spencer. Edison followed that in 1909 with a new version of the intermezzo performed by the New York Military Band. Not to be outdone, Columbia made cylinders that year of the song featuring the duo of Frank C. Stanley and Henry Burr as well as an instrumental of the *Rainbow Medley* by the Indestructible Concert Band. When Edison introduced its four-minute recordings in 1911, Jones and Murray re-recorded their version in the longer format and then did it again in 1913 when Edison switched to the more durable Blue Amberols.[7]

The recording by Ada Jones and Billy Murray marked the first time a female sang on an Indian love song record. According to phonograph historian Tim Gracyk, Ada Jones was the "leading female recording artist of the acoustic era, especially popular from 1905 to 1912." She sang a variety of genres including ragtime, ballads, Broadway hits, comic songs, and cowboy and Indian songs. In other words, she was very much Billy Murray's equal. Born in England in 1873, Jones began singing publicly in the 1880s and made her first records around 1893. She sang on stage with color slides projected behind her in what were called "illustrated songs." Billy Murray supposedly rediscovered Jones in 1904 and brought her to Columbia to record with him and Len Spencer. Murray and Jones made their first duet record in 1906, and *Rainbow* probably was their biggest hit, though the pair also recorded *Blue Feather*, *Silver Star*, and *Silver Bell*. After the Great War, Jones's records sold fewer copies, though she remained popular barnstorming the country doing personal appearances. She died while on the road in 1922.[8]

The many recorded versions combined with the star power of Murray and Jones made *Rainbow* a success. Gardner lists the song in the top twenty for five months, from July to November 1908.[9] *Edison Phonograph Monthly* raved about the tune. Its November 1908 issue wrote this about the Jones and Murray version: "This composition is sweeping the country and is destined to be as popular as 'Hiawatha,' which it resembles, being sung in Indian style and in much the same tempo. It is a bright and dashing two step and a fascinating ballad. It is sung by Miss Jones and Mr. Murray in the conversational style that is always so interesting."[10] And of the instrumental, the journal the next month noted that "this most popular Indian Intermezzo" by Jones and Murray "is such an attractive composition that it will bear repetition as a band number, as all who get this Record will testify." It then noted that its style was like *Hiawatha* and suggested that "its popularity ought to be none the less enduring." The song was also the only cowboy or Indian song mentioned that month in the journal's suggested list of records to include in a store "concert" meant to draw customers. Finally, when Edison issued the four-minute Amberol in 1911, the journal wrote that "everybody knows and likes Rainbow, and if the many requests we have had for it . . . be any criterion of its popularity . . . every owner . . . will want this Record"; the longer recording time allowed "greater opportunities for vocal and instrumental embellishment . . . with bells, xylo, and orchestral solos supplementing the work of the singers. . . . This Record is complete in its entertaining qualities."[11]

Talking Machine World reported similar popularity. In an ad for various record companies' new listings for January 1909, *Rainbow* was listed under the "New Double Record Zonophone Discs, 10 inch," both for the Henry Burr version and the Ada Jones and Billy Murray one. The song was also listed under the "Columbia 12-inch Double Disc Records" as being played by Prince's Military Band, and the Jones and Murray version could be found as a cylinder under the "New Edison Standard (Two-Minute) Records list.[12] In January 1909, *Talking Machine World* noted that the Indiana Phonograph Company, which sold Edison records in Indianapolis, had been "unable to keep 'Rainbow' records in stock. The selection has proved to be one of the most popular that has been presented in Indiana in many years. . . . [It] has been in demand in the rural districts as well as in the city." In July 1910, *Talking Machine World* reported that according to the Southwestern Talking Machine Owners' Association *Rainbow* and *Red Wing* were two of the four most popular records in Texas.[13]

NOTES

1. Alfred Bryan and Percy Wenrich, *Rainbow* (New York: Jerome H. Remick, 1908).

2. Percy Wenrich, *Rainbow* (New York: Jerome H. Remick, 1908).

3. "Music and Drama: Notes of Plays and Players," *Vancouver (B.C., Canada) Daily World*, December 26, 1908, 24.

4. "The Stage: The New Family Theater," *Williamsport (Pa.) Sun-Gazette*, October 6, 1908, 5, stated that the "Connolly, Wenrich, and Connolly, in their melange of mirth and music are pleasing. Wenrich is a composer, and his new Indian song-intermezzo, *Rainbow*, together with *Naughty Eyes*, is the feature of the act."

5. "The Song Shop," *San Francisco Call*, December 17, 1910, 18.

6. Bill Edwards, "Percy Wenrich," *RagPiano*, www.perfessorbill. com/comps/pwenrich.shtml; *Songwriters Hall of Fame*, www. songwritershalloffame.org/search/, s.v. "Percy Wenrich"; *The Parlor Songs Academy*, www.parlorsongs.ac, s.v. "Percy Wenrich."

7. *Discography of American Historical Recordings*, http://adp.library. ucsb.edu, s.v. "Rainbow"; *UCSB Cylinder Audio Archive*, http:// cylinders.library.ucsb.edu, s.v. "Rainbow."

8. Gracyk, *Popular American Recording Pioneer*, 183–98; Hoffman, Carty, and Riggs, *Billy Murray*, 53–54; Allen Sutton, "A Prehistory of Ada Jones, 1889–1905," American Recording Pioneers, *Mainspring Press*, www.mainspringpress.com/jones_history.html. Other Jones songs discussed in this book are *My Pony Boy, Broncho Bob and His Little Cheyenne, Rainbow, Silver Star, Silver Bell, Blue Feather,* and *Snow Deer.*

9. Gardner, *Popular Songs*, 59.

10. "Advance List of Edison Standard (Two Minute) and Edison Amberola (Four Minute) Records for January 1909," *Edison Phonograph Monthly* 6, no. 11 (November 1908), 18.

11. "Advance List of Edison Standard (Two Minute) and Edison Amberola (Four Minute) Records for February 1909," and "Selling the Goods," both in *Edison Phonograph Monthly* 6, no. 12 (December 1908), 17, 9; "Advance List of Edison Amberol and Edison Standard Records for June 1911," *Edison Phonograph Monthly* 9, no. 4 (April 1911), 15.

12. "Record Bulletins for January, 1909," *Talking Machine World* 4, no. 12 (December 15, 1908), 52. Interestingly, the ad for Zon-o-phone incorrectly listed Ada Jones and Len Spencer, not Murray. I have this recording and it is indeed Murray.

13. "Indianapolis a Busy Center," *Talking Machine World* 5, no. 1 (January 15, 1909), 34; "Four Records Popular in Texas," *Talking Machine World* 6, no. 7 (July 15, 1910), 7.

Little Arrow and Big Chief Greasepaint, 1909

Like the previous year's *Big Chief Smoke*, the Len Spencer and Ada Jones skit *Little Arrow and Big Chief Greasepaint* made Native Americans out to be stereotypical buffoons in what was described as an Indian comic song.[1] Spencer and Jones had made two previous western comedy sketch recordings, *Broncho Bob and His Little Cheyenne* and *Santiago Flynn*. Like the latter, *Little Arrow and Big Chief Greasepaint* is exceptionally racist. It tells the story of the courtship of Little Arrow, played by Jones, and Big Chief Greasepaint, played by Spencer. The skit explains that the Big Chief wears feathers to keep his "wig" "wam" [warm] and that he fights the white man twice a day at the Wild West show. Then, as in *Broncho Bob* and *Santiago Flynn*, Jones breaks into a song at its end, this time declaring Little Arrow's love for her beau. Here is the text of the full skit:

[chanting] hey aye, aye, aye [music] [chanting] hey, aye, aye, aye

BIG CHIEF GREASEPAINT (BCG): Here comes Little Arrow. Big Chief him make Little Arrow him squaw.

LITTLE ARROW (LA): Whoa whip! Big Chief Greasepaint, you wear feathers. Why?

BCG: Feathers keep Big Chief's wig wam. [grunts]

LA: Little Arrow see great Chief dance war dance. Why?

BCG: Big Chief all great warriors. Big Chief go to fight white man.

LA: Fight white man? Where? In Wild West Show, huh?

[Yells in background]

BCG: Big Chief fights heap battles every day! Two times . . . matinee and night.

LA: Big Chief heap brave.

BCG: Yes! Me take Little Arrow for squaw. Hm. Big Chief love Little Arrow. Who's Little Arrow's Father? Hmph?

LA: Little Arrow's Father Big Medicine Man. Chief Killum Quick.

BCG: MMMMM. Him take out big medicine show. Hm?

[yelling in background, horse whinnies]

LA: Yes. Will Big Chief give Father of Little Arrow ponies for Little Arrow?

BCG: Hmmm. Yes! Brandy ponies. Heap good fire water.

[yelling in background]

LA: Little Arrow Squaw's Father all great chiefs.

BCG: Big Chief Greasepaint be Little Arrow's beau? Hmph?

LA: Yes. Little Arrow be true to her beau. Never miss her mark.

BCG: No. Big Chief no mark. Big Chief wise guy. Big Chief give Little Arrow heap money.

LA: Little Arrow want chief big money. And beads. And canoes. And ponies.

BCG: [grunts several times]

LA: Why Big Chief grunt?

BCG: Little Arrow give Big Chief pain. Talk like pale face. Big Chief sick.

LA: Big Chief sick? Little Arrow get medicine man.

BCG: No. No.

LA: Little Arrow dance for Big Chief. Make Big Chief forget.

BCG: Good.

[tom-tom and music starts]

BCG: Me like! Heap good.

[music stops]

LA: Ah! Me feel good. Now Little Arrow can dance alone dance in Wild West show with Big Chief. Hm? Will Little Arrow be Big Chief's squaw? Hmph?

BCG: Me call tribe.

[lots of yelling]

BCG: Me take Little Arrow for Squaw. [yells]

BCG: [chants]

[horse whinnies]

BCG: Come Squaw, hop on pony. We go honeymoon.

LA: [sings]

> I will be your Little Arrow and you'll be my beau,
> You are Big Chief of the Indians and I love you so.
> In a tent we live together in one that's built for two.
> Little Arrow, Little Arrow, she love you.
> Little Arrow, Little Arrow, and you'll be my beau,
> You're a Big Chief of the Indians and I love you so.
> In a tent we live together one that's built for two.
> Little Arrow, Little Arrow, she love you.

Like all of the Jones and Spencer bits, there was no sheet music produced and only Edison recorded it, as a four-minute Amberol recording in early 1909. *Edison Phonograph Monthly* described it as "an original vaudeville sketch" that included an "amusing dialogue in Indian dialect." It then told the basic plot line, suggesting that "Big Chief Greasepaint represents the type of Indian seen on the stage. Upon learning that Little Arrow can dance he wastes no time in wooing her, for he sees the possibilities of her success in his Wild West Show company." It further noted that the recording was "replete with local color with its Indian grunts, yells, and music." The *Monthly* concluded by providing a verse of Jones's love song to Big Chief. No suggestions were made as to its potential popularity, and it seems the skit did not garner much attention, for Gardner does not mention the song in his book of charts. A newspaper search for the title revealed only two mentions in standard Edison song lists.[2]

NOTES

1. Ada Jones and Len Spencer, *Little Arrow and Big Chief Greasepaint* (New York: National Phonograph Company, 1909), Edison Amberol #108. This recording can be found at *UCSB Cylinder Audio Archive*, http://cylinders.library.ucsb.edu.
2. "Advance List of Edison Standard and Edison Amberol Records for April, 1909," *Edison Phonograph Monthly* 7, no. 2 (February 1909), 19; "New April Records on Sale Tomorrow," *Fitchburg (Mass.) Sentinel*, March 24, 1909, 6.

Denver Town, 1909

Denver Town, **words by Harry J. Breen, music by George Botsford (New York: Jerome H. Remick, 1908).** Sheet music from author's collection.

By late spring 1909 the cowboy song had become entrenched in American culture through recordings of *Pride of the Prairie, Broncho Buster*, and even *I'm a Yiddish Cowboy*. All of these proved that by going back to the basic cowboy love song of *Cheyenne* and setting it to a new tune one could again catch lightning in a bottle. In April 1909 singers Billy Murray, Will Oakland, John H. Bieling, and W. F. Hooley joined to form the Premier Quartet and chose for their first release a new cowboy love song titled *Denver Town*. Harry J. Breen and George Botsford, the same team that created *Pride of the Prairie*, wrote the song.[1] The plot retells the meeting tale from the novel *The Virginian* as the story of a Colorado ranchman who is out riding when he is passed by a beautiful girl who abruptly falls from her pony. He helps her up and she rides away, only to be caught by the fellow and made his bride. The full lyrics go like this:

> Out in the golden west, so goes the story,
> There lived a cattle king Alone in his glory
> Until a maiden fair rode in from Denver
> She smiled as she went flying by.

Pony fell and she went crashing down,
Quickly he is by her side
He begs of her to stay, Her cheeks grow crimson
She mounts her pony and starts to ride
"Don't go," he cried "stay be my bride."

Chorus

Now boy, Cowboy, If you want to win her,
Get your saddle and skedaddle,
Go ride her down.
Tell your pony, that your heart is lonely
He'll take you flying in to Denver town.

When evening sun's at rest, And stars grow
     brighter
Out in the golden west, Two hearts are lighter
He won the maiden fair, riding to Denver
Now there's a little cattle king.

Daddy lifts him on that pony old
Same old horse he rode that year
"Can he go fast my lad?" Just ask your mother
I rode to win her, so have no fear
I won my dear. That's why you're here.

Repeat Chorus

André De Takacs's sheet music cover for *Denver Town* is one of the most beautiful of the talking machine era with its image of a lone cowboy riding away at full gallop over a white, snow-covered landscape toward a distant setting sun. In the clouds above the sunset is the notable phrase from the song, "Tell your Pony that your Heart is lonely, He'll take you flying into Denver town."

The song became a mild hit in the summer of 1909. In fact, Breen had begun singing *Denver Town* in public in February, saying it was "the best he has written," and by April newspapers noted it as being his "latest song success." Other singers also performed it on stage by July,

with papers calling it "the very latest Western song that is a big success." An ad in a Missouri paper noted that "Miss Catherine Pulis, 'Just the Plain Little Singer,' will present for the first time in the west the great New York song hit 'Denver Town.'"[2]

At about the same time, the Premier Quartet recorded *Denver Town* for Edison. This version features no accompaniment, with the group singing four-part harmony throughout the song like a barbershop quartet. In the last chorus, hoofbeats can be heard. *Edison Phonograph Monthly* noted the new group and then simply stated, "Another cowboy song, telling how a cowboy wooed and won his bride." The Victor version called the group the "American Quartet" and includes the sound of hoofbeats at the start and orchestra accompaniment throughout. Billy Murray sings the verses and the quartet the choruses. The Victor supplement noted that the "new organization of male voice" made "its bid for popular favor with a 'cowboy' number, now quite in vogue." Still another version for Columbia named the performers the Columbia Quartet.[3] Despite these accolades, Gardner does not include *Denver Town* on any of his charts.

NOTES

1. Harry J. Breen and George Botsford, *Denver Town* (New York: Jerome H. Remick, 1908).

2. "At the Orpheum," *Allentown (Pa.) Democrat*, February 13, 1909, 3; "Bernardi Truly Is a Wonder," *Ottawa (Ontario, Canada) Journal*, April 27, 1909, 10; "Amusements," *Scranton (Pa.) Truth*, July 28, 1909, 12; "The Odeon," *Coffeeville (Kans.) Daily Journal*, July 1, 1909, 6; "The Lyric—Tonight," *Belvidere (Ill.) Daily Republican*, July 15, 1909, 6; "Amusements," *Nevada (Mo.) Daily Mail*, August 27, 1909.

3. "Advance List," *Edison Phonograph Monthly* 7, no. 4 (April 1909), 19; Premier Quartet, *Denver Town* (New York: Edison Talking Machine, 1909), Edison Standard Record #10155; American Quartet, *Denver Town* (New York: Victor Talking Machine, 1909), disc; Walsh, "'Cowboy Song' Recordings, Part 5," *Hobbies*, August 1976, 54; "Record Bulletins for June 1909," *Talking Machine World* 5, no. 5 (May 15, 1909), 44.

My Rancho Maid, 1909

My Rancho Maid, **words and music by Mabel McKinley (New York: Leo Feist, 1908).** Sheet music courtesy Historic Sheet Music Collection, University of Oregon, Eugene.

The cowgirl popularity of *Pride of the Prairie* enticed Mabel McKinley of *Anona* fame to pen a song she recorded in 1909 titled *My Rancho Maid.*[1] Like *Cheyenne*, the tune features a love story between a cowboy and his maiden. McKinley first sang the song in late December 1907 to much public approval. By the following spring, a New Jersey newspaper described the sheet music as a "new hit" and another reported that McKinley "possesses a sweet soprano voice, quite effective in popular songs and especially her own compositions."[2] The full lyrics go like this:

One Summer day, A maiden gay,
She was witty, Oh! So pretty;
Chanced to come his way,
She stopped right short, And said "what sport?"
"To have a secret meeting with The cowboy of my
    heart."
He was likewise saying
"What a happy day for me My Rancho maid to see,
Who is my fate to be."
First with agitation, Then with ease and grace,
He did sing his heart a way,
On a Summer's day.

134

Chorus

At twilights falling My Rancho Maid
Come hear this song, dear, My serenade,
I will be near thee, So whisper softly
This sweet old story I so long to hear

Then come and meet me down in the glade,
Where I will greet thee, My Rancho Maid,
We'll leap to saddle, And gladly paddle
Our own canoe, dear, Just built for two.

One Summer night, On prairie bright,
He stooped to kiss this Rancho Miss
And seal their wedding plight
He said "You'll ride Close by my side;
We a parson soon will find, Then you will be my
    bride."

She said, with a chuckle, "When the folks hear
    we've eloped, Oh!
Won't they be provoked, For them 'twill be no
    joke."
What care we my dear
Naught have we to fear
So they sang their serenade,
This cowboy and his maid.

The sheet music for *My Rancho Maid* does not include the artist's name but does feature an athletic-looking young cowgirl astride a large black horse. In the background, a small pen of horses stands on a brown plain against a background of clouds and one snowy mountain. The cowgirl is decked out in western clothes and tosses a lariat into the sky above her. She is every bit the New Woman as the figure in the *Ida-Ho* cover.

Unlike her previous songs recorded by male singers, McKinley sang *My Rancho Maid* herself in her operatic soprano voice as an Edison four-minute Amberol cylinder. *Edison Phonograph Monthly* for May 1909 described the song as "another of Miss McKinley's own compositions and as pleasing in words and melody as her others."[3] It may have been, but nothing was written of the *My Rancho Maid* recording again. Perhaps the odd line about the cowboy's canoe, "just built for two," or McKinley's soprano voice simply did not fit the cowboy genre.

NOTES

1. Mabel McKinley, *My Rancho Maid* (New York: Leo Feist, 1908).
2. "News of the Theaters: Miss McKinley and Her Injury," *Scranton (Pa.) Republican*, December 29, 1907, 6; "Barlow's Saturday Sale," ad, *Trenton (N.J.) Evening Times*, February 22, 1908, 3; "The Theaters," *Brooklyn Daily Eagle*, March 24, 1908, 12.
3. "Advance List of Edison Standard and Edison Amberol Records for July 1909," *Edison Phonograph Monthly* 7, no. 5 (May 1909), 18. Interestingly, this issue of the trade journal also featured an advertisement on pages 10–11 showing cowboys sitting around and listening to an Edison phonograph.

Blue Feather, 1909

Blue Feather, **words by Jack Mahoney,
music by Theodore Morse (New York:
Theodore Morse Music 1909).** Sheet
music from author's collection.

The Indian love song *Blue Feather* was written in 1909 by
Theodore Morse. Morse had helped write several earlier
western hits including *Arrah Wanna, Since Arrah Wanna
Married Barney Carney,* and *Santiago Flynn.* He later
became a founding member of ASCAP and was elected to
the Songwriters Hall of Fame in 1970.[1]

Blue Feather featured words by Jack Mahoney and
music by Morse. Morse published the song through
his own company in 1909.[2] Jack Mahoney, born Ruben
Kusnitt, was a popular lyricist who collaborated with
many songwriters including Percy Wenrich and Harry

Von Tilzer.[3] The lyrics feature internal rhymes such as
"Moon beams pale light the trail to the vale and the dale
away off yonder" and "Campfires gleam by the stream
where I dream, they seem to gently guide me." More love
song than Indian song, the only clear connections are
one line about an Indian maid and the André De Takacs
cover illustration. This image, with an overall blue cast,
depicts a Caucasian-looking Indian girl kneeling beside
a lake amid a pine forest and gazing at her reflection in
water. The full lyrics are as follows:

Moon beams pale light the trail to the vale and
    dale away off yonder
Come let us wander my Indian maid.
Say you will all is still on the hill beside the rill
    they're sleeping
While we go creeping down thro' the glade.

Chorus
My sweet Blue Feather
we'll be together
In stormy weather
and bright sunshine
The hours are flying,
my heart is crying,
don't leave me sighing,
Blue Feather Mine.

Campfires gleam by the stream where I dream,
    they seem to gently guide me
With you beside me life has begun
Let your heart speak its part and we'll dart and
    start to love anew, dear
To woo as two, dear, but live as one.

Repeat Chorus

Edison, Victor, Columbia Indestructible, and Zon-o-phone all issued recordings of *Blue Feather* in 1909. Ada Jones and Billy Murray recorded it as a duet for both Edison and Victor that summer, and Jones and Walter Van Brunt sang it on a Columbia Indestructible cylinder and a Zon-o-phone disc later that year.[4] Like *Rainbow*, the Edison cylinder of *Blue Feather* opens with Jones beginning the first line of the verse and Murray singing the second. The two then alternate verse lines and combine for the chorus, with a wooden block accompanying the second chorus.[5] *Edison Phonograph Monthly* for May 1909 described it as an "Indian love song on the style of Rainbow" and suggested that its publishers "expect it to be a great success . . . and predict that within a very short time it will be whistled and sung from one end of the country to the other" because it "possesses the essential qualities of attractive words and pleasing rhythm." Perhaps these characteristics contributed to the Indiana Phonograph Company's statement that the Edison version was one of the top sellers in Indianapolis that August.[6] But *Blue Feather* did not do much more than that and is not mentioned as having cracked the top twenty in Gardner's charts.

NOTES

1. *Allmusic*, www.allmusic.com, s.v. "Theodore Morse"; *Songwriters Hall of Fame*, www.songwritershalloffame.org/search/, s.v. "Theodore Morse"; *The Parlor Songs Academy*, www.parlorsongs.ac, s.v. "Theodore Morse."
2. Theodore Morse, *Blue Feather* (New York: Theodore Morse Music, 1909).
3. *The Parlor Songs Academy*, www.parlorsongs.ac, s.v. "Jack Mahoney."
4. "Record Bulletins for June 1909," *Talking Machine World* 5, no. 6 (June 15, 1909), 43–44; this column lists the Edison and Columbia Indestructible cylinders of *Blue Feather*. "Record Bulletins for August 1909," *Talking Machine World* 5, no. 7 (July 15, 1909), 68, lists the Zon-o-phon disc. "Record Bulletins for December 1909," *Talking Machine World* 5, no. 11 (November 15, 1909), 49, lists the Victor recording.
5. Ada Jones and Billy Murray, *Blue Feather* (Orange, N.J.: National Phonograph, 1909), Edison Standard Record #10162.
6. "Advance List of Edison Standard and Edison Amberol Records for July 1909," *Edison Phonograph Monthly* 7, no. 5 (May 1909), 16; "Indianapolis Happenings," *Talking Machine World* 5, no. 9 (September 1909), 18.

My Pony Boy, 1909

My Pony Boy, words by Bobbie Heath,
music by Charlie O'Donnell (New
York: Jerome H. Remick, 1909). Sheet
music from author's collection.

Probably the biggest cowboy hit to come out of the talking machine era, *My Pony Boy* adapted the love song theme of *Cheyenne* and has spanned generations through the widest variety of venues including a 1908 Ziegfeld show, a 1931 Krazy Kat cartoon, a 1950s television commercial for juice concentrate, as a character name in the 1967 S. E. Hinton novel *The Outsiders,* and even rocker Bruce Springsteen's 1992 album *Human Touch.*

Tin Pan Alley composer Charlie O'Donnell wrote the music and Bobbie Heath created the lyrics.[1] The song tells the story of a handsome western cowboy, or pony boy, named Tony, who is loved by all the girls. Then a "fluffy ruffle girl" comes to visit from New York and his "heart was lassoed"—but he refuses to follow her back east. Nevertheless, the chorus hearkens back to *Cheyenne* and *The Virginian* with its plea to "marry me, carry me, right away with you." The entire lyrics are as follows:

Way out west, in a nest from the rest, dwelt the
bestest little Broncho Boy
He could ride, he could glide o'er the prairies like
an arrow.
Every maid in the glade was afraid he would trade
his little heart away.
So each little peach made a nice little speech of
love to him.

Chorus

Pony Boy, Pony Boy, won't you be my Tony Boy?
Don't say no, Here we go off across the plains.
Marry me, carry me right away with you.
Giddy up, giddy up, giddy up, whoa! My Pony Boy.

Till one day, out that way, so they say, came to stay
a fluffy ruffle girl.
She made eyes, she surprised, and he found his
heart was lassoed.
When he thought he was caught, how he fought,
but she taught this pony boy to love.
But he balked when talked of a trip to New York, so
she sang to him.

Repeat Chorus

André De Takacs's design for the sheet music cover
incorporates an insert featuring a cowboy on a bucking
bronco framed by a beautiful cowgirl holding a long
whip whose thong spells out "Giddy Up Giddy Up Giddy
Up Whoa" beneath the song title. Below the horse, an ad
suggests "As Sung by Miss Lillian Lorraine in F. Ziegfeld
Jr.'s Latest Triumph Anna Held in 'Miss Innocence.'"
The sheet's back cover contains an advertisement for
the Columbia recording of the song performed by the
Columbia Male Quartet with orchestra accompaniment.
It reads: "A new song of the west with the spirit of the
prairies in its breezy and tuneful air. The lyrics tells of
a little pony-boy who is happy in the admiration of his
western girl friends until he meets a 'fluffy ruffles' girl
from New York. The verse is sung by the baritone, the
quartette joining in with charming effect."

As noted on the cover, Ziegfeld used *My Pony
Boy* in his 1909 play, and it became an instant hit.
Advertisements for the sheet music raved about the
song. An ad in an issue of the *Indianapolis News* priced

the music at fifteen cents and glared, "This music
number is without doubt one of the greatest cowboy
songs published. It is being sung, played, and whistled
everywhere throughout the East.... [It] has the
originality and snap which will make it one of the biggest
successes of the season. You'll like it as soon as you hear
it." Then, in true Tin Pan Alley fashion, the sheet music
ad suggested the role pluggers still played in the business
when it noted, "Come in and have it played for you."
Another ad in a Brooklyn paper a few weeks later called it
"A big cowboy Song hit."[2]

The *Harrisburg Telegraph* ran an ad under the heading
"My Pony Boy" that included four bars of the refrain's
score and illustrations of two children dressed up in
western garb and a puppy. The cowgirl on the left wears a
costume similar to the cowgirl on the sheet music score
with a big hat, and the boy at right sits astride a rocking
horse, wears chaps, and tips his hat toward the girl. In
between, a paragraph extols the song's popularity:

> You can't dodge it. My Pony Boy is in the air
> wherever you go. The most contagious song that
> ever happened. And it seems to make everybody
> more cheerful and happy. The tune just fits a
> romantic ballad of the plains. It's inspiring, full of
> "dash" and "go." Easy to play—easy to sing—hard
> to forget. Lovers of the two-step are simply wild
> over it. Fifth edition just printed.[3]

Still another ad described a sheet music sale in
Washington, D.C., that featured *My Pony Boy*. Calling
it "the song craze that's spreading like wildfire" and
showing a cowboy on a horse galloping out of the
newsprint with the same four bars of music above a
description, it read:

> If a song "goes" in New York it's a sure winner
> anywhere and everywhere. "MY PONY BOY" had
> its first hearing on Broadway and immediately
> became the musical rage of the town. Then Anna
> Held featured it in "Miss Innocence" and the
> conquest was complete. Now it's the best selling
> song in America.... MY PONY BOY is a dashing
> song of the plains, the liveliest and catchiest tune
> conceivable.[4]

A small note in an ad in the *Brooklyn Daily Eagle* in November 1909 summarized these views when it called *My Pony Boy* "the most sensational song hit in years."[5]

The talking machine companies immediately jumped on this popularity. In August 1909, the Columbia Male Quartet, featuring Albert Campbell, Henry Burr, Frank C. Stanley, and Steve Porter, recorded *My Pony Boy* as a cylinder for Columbia Indestructible Record Company and on disc for Columbia and Standard Talking Machine Company.[6] At about the same time, Ada Jones recorded it for Edison cylinders and Victor discs.[7] The three recordings are each a little different. The Indestructible cylinder is straightforward, bold, and clear, with a soloist singing the verses and the quartet doing the chorus. The Standard Talking Machine disc follows this pattern but adds whirling wind sound effects during the choruses and then whoops and hollers at the very end. Jones's version for Edison features her singing the verses and the first version of the chorus solo with hoofbeat sound effects. Then the chorus is repeated with the quartet. *Edison Phonograph Monthly* for August 1909 described the recording as a "cowboy song with all the effects characteristic of Records of this kind. The song gives Miss Jones another opportunity to display her wonderful versatility. She is quite as much at home in singing about her cowboy as she has been in songs of various dialects. The assistance given her by the chorus of male voices adds to the attractiveness of the Record."[8]

My Pony Boy proved to be just as big a hit record as it had been on the stage. In the fall of 1909, Columbia reported to *Talking Machine World* that the song was the best-selling record for August. Indeed, Gardner notes that *My Pony Boy* and *San Antonio* were the only two cowboy songs of the talking machine era to reach his number-one place on the charts, *My Pony Boy* doing so in August 1909 and staying in the top twenty between June and November that year.[9] Victor also capitalized on the song's popularity by adding it to a medley disc that same year.[10] As with *Cheyenne*, Edison never recorded *My Pony Boy* as a single song.

NOTES

1. Bobbie Heath and Charlie O'Donnell, *My Pony Boy* (New York: Jerome H. Remick, 1909).
2. "New 'My Pony Boy' 'Giddy up—Giddy up—Whoa,'" *Indianapolis News*, April 20, 1909, 16; "Sheet Music, 9¢," *Brooklyn (N.Y.) Daily Eagle*, May 16, 1909, 5.
3. "My Pony Boy," *Harrisburg (Pa.) Telegram*, August 29, 1909, 3.
4. "My Pony Boy," *Washington (D.C.) Times*, September 3, 1909, 16.
5. "Garden of Roses, a New Song," *Brooklyn (N.Y.) Daily Eagle*, November 7, 1909, 4.
6. Columbia Quartet, *My Pony Boy* (Albany, N.Y.: Indestructible Record, 1909), cylinder; Columbia Quartet, *My Pony Boy* (Chicago: Standard Talking Machine, 1909), disc. In these days of freelancing, this group was known as the Columbia Quartet and the Columbia Male Quartet while recording for Columbia and also the Peerless Quartet when making records for others. See Tim Gracyk, "Columbia Male Quartet (also Peerless Quartet)," *Tim Phonographs and Old Records*, www.gracyk.com/columbiaquartet.shtml. Porter had been heard earlier as the host of the minstrel recordings of *San Antonio*.
7. Ada Jones, *My Pony Boy* (New York: Victor Talking Machine, 1909), disc. Edison also used an instrumental version of the *My Pony Boy* chorus at the beginning of the Len Spencer and Ada Jones skit about horse racing called *A Race for a Wife*; Len Spencer and Ada Jones, *A Race for a Wife* (Albany: Indestructible Record, 1909), cylinder.
8. "Edison Amberol Records for October," *Edison Phonograph Monthly* 7, no. 8 (August 1909), 17.
9. "Indianapolis Happenings," *Talking Machine World* 5, no. 8 (September 15, 1909), 18; Gardner, *Popular Songs*, 60–61.
10. *Discography of American Historical Recordings*, http://adp.library.ucsb.edu, s.v. "Popular medley no. 1" (Arthur Pryor's Band).

Wise Old Indian, 1909

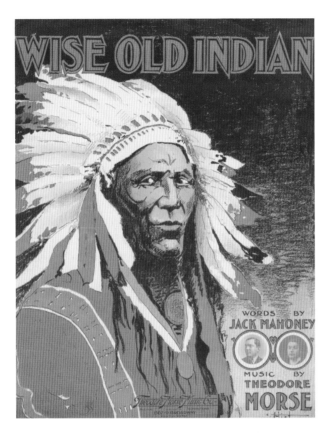

Wise Old Indian, words by Jack
Mahoney, music by Theodore Morse
(New York: Theodore Morse Music,
1909). Sheet music from author's
collection.

Big Chief Smoke and *Little Arrow and Big Chief Greasepaint* are clear representations of the stereotypical buffoon Indian; the comic song *Wise Old Indian* is less obvious.[1] Superficially touting Indian intelligence, this song by Theodore Morse and Jack Mahoney actually undercut the song's title by doing little more than poking fun at phrases that included the word Indian, thereby suggesting that Indians in fact were not wise. More subtle than other racist songs, this version of the buffoon did not rely as much on the wording, but its messages were just as potent.

Morse had written *Arrah Wanna*, *Santiago Flynn*, and *Blue Feather*, and Mahoney later wrote *Snow Deer*. *Wise Old Indian* was subtitled "A Comical Conglomeration," and its eight verses and chorus functioned much like *Tammany* to satirize American culture with references to war, politics, women's suffrage, and alcohol. Throughout all of this, the song focuses on a seemingly "wise old chief" from Indiana who is used as the foil for puns and made to look not wise but a buffoon. Probably the strangest string of lines has the wise old chief meeting a female Dutch chiropodist who he has treat his "Indian corn." The full lyrics go like this:

Way out in Indiana live an Indian long ago,

Who used to roll his war whoop down the streets
of Kokomo,

Dutch settlers came to settle and he like the girls
heap much,

But had to get up early just to beat the early Dutch.

Chorus
Wise Old Indian, wise old chief,

He met a Dutch girl and they kissed,

She was a Chiropodist,

And wise old Indian called on her each morn,

He had her kneeling at his feet to cure his Indian
corn.

He never pulled the pipe of peace but pulled a tug
of war,

He had a pull with Tammany that's what he voted
for,

He pulled a stroke with rowing clubs when time
were very dull,

And when he scalped a single man he pulled a
single scull.

Chorus
Wise Old Indian, wise old chief,

Ran ten miles on a muddy track, Met Bill Bryan
running back

And wise old Indian gave old Bill the rub,

Then bought a pair of dumbbells and he joined an
Indian club.

The old chief gave a pow-wow when he asked for
young squaw's hand,

The best man at the wedding was the worse one in
the band,

The chief heard of affinities, and thought her love
might drop,

That's why he never introduced her to a New York
Cop.

Chorus
Wise Old Indian, wise old chief,

He tried to skip his hotel bill,

Then went into vaudeville,

When wise old Indian saw the coin was real,

He went across from Dennett's and he had some
Indian meal.

His squaw believed in women's rights, she was a
suffragette,

If he had let her speak her lines she would be
suff'ring yet,

For she believed in women having ev'rything to
say,

She'd have been in the fire department if she'd
have her way.

Chorus
Wise old Indian, wise old chief,

He caught her at a fire one time

Just as she began to climb,

But wise old Indian, so the story goes,

He wouldn't let her climb because she hadn't any
hose.

He took a trip to Paris on the gay war-path to
roam,

He only went for pleasure so he left his squaw at
home,

She sued him for divorce when he came back, he
didn't care,

Some dynamite exploded and they separated
there.

Chorus
Wise old Indian, wise old chief,

He didn't even say good-by,

And she didn't stop to sigh,

But wise old Indian he was glad of course,

He looked around the place and saw 'twas good
grounds for divorce.

He stood for standing armies and he stood 'till he
was full
He stood for each pappoose, but wouldn't stand
for Sitting Bull,
He stood for almost anything, but wouldn't stand
for Hughes
And with his patent medicine shined patent
leather shoes.

Chorus
Wise old Indian, wise old chief,
He'd not eat cheese disguised as cakes,
For he'd heard of nature fakes,
And wise old Indian at a trolley balked,
Whenever he was in a hurry he got off and walked.

The old chief knew George Washington before
George Cohan's time
There came a great uprising and the Dutch began
to climb,
Then Washington implored the chief to help him
check the raid
But old chief was the playwright and refused to
give George Ade.

Chorus
Wise old Indian, wise old chief,
He let them settle there for fun,
And he settled ev'ry one,
Then wise old Indian thought he would resign,
Because on all the Yale half-backs he had the
Indian sign.

He liked his fire-water better than his only son,
And when his squaw sent him for rolls he'd come
back with a bun,
Two doctors once examined him, the day was
rather warm,
And he had such an awful thirst he drank the
chloroform.

Chorus
Wise old Indian, wise old chief,
They operated on him then,
And they sewed him up again;
When wise old Indian woke and got his breath
They'd left a sponge inside him then he drank
himself to death.

Joseph Hirt, who had created the beautiful covers
for *Red Wing* and *Reed Bird*, illustrated the cover for
Wise Old Indian in red and green, featuring a head-and-
shoulders painting of a Native American man in face
paint and a feather headdress looking sideways from the
page.

Billy Murray recorded a two-minute version of the
song for Edison and Columbia cylinders as well as for
a Victor disc, and Arthur Collins and Byron G. Harlan
made a duet for Indestructible two-minute cylinders.
Each of these contain only three full verses and
choruses because of the time constraints. The Edison
version features yells and a prominent tom-tom. *Edison
Phonograph Monthly* reminded its readers that Indian
songs remained popular and that this one "contained
all the requirements needed for success," with lyrics
"extremely funny." The *Monthly* concluded by noting that
Murray had also had great success with such songs.[2]
Despite these accolades, it appears that *Wise Old Chief*
did not sell well past the summer of 1909, and Gardner
does not include it in his lists.

NOTES

1. Jack Mahoney and Theodore Morse, *Wise Old Indian* (New York:
Theodore Morse Music, 1909).
2. "Advance List of Edison Standard and Edison Amberol Records for
August, 1909," *Edison Phonograph Monthly* 7, no. 6 (June 1909), 23. I
have not found the song in any period newspapers other than a few
sheet music and record sales lists.

Lily of the Prairie, 1909

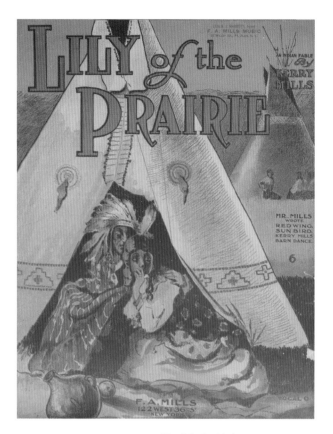

Lily of the Prairie (two-step intermezzo), music by Kerry Mills (New York: F. A. Mills, 1909). Sheet music from author's collection.

Just as cowboy songs had adopted the western plains in their titles, Indian love songs in 1909 did the same. In the summer of 1909, Kerry Mills followed his successful *Red Wing* with another "Indian fable" called *Lily of the Prairie*.[1] The song became somewhat popular as part of an illustrated song program presented in theaters.[2] Published under the pseudonym F. A. Mills, *Lily of the Prairie* is a happier love song than *Red Wing* because the warrior doesn't die in battle but marries his maiden sweetheart.

The song also hints at domestic life with "A wigwam nice and cozy / a little nest for two / Is waiting for you, Lily of the prairie." The sheet music cover, created by *Red Wing* illustrator Joseph Hirt, makes use of this theme by placing two tepees on the page. In the background, three women sit on the ground next to one lodge while an Indian man with feather headdress and wrapped in a colorful blanket comforts an Indian woman in a foreground tepee.

The full lyrics are as follows:

It was once 'pon a time in the days of old,
In a far distant clime where the braves were bold,
Lived a maiden fair as the prairie air,
but her heart was always in a whirl,
For she loved, yes, she loved, someone awful well
And he loved, yes, he loved her, but didn't tell
Until one find day when chanced to say
To this pretty little prairie girl:

Chorus
O, Lily of the prairie, the wood lark sings to you,
The breezes bring to you my love so brave and true;
A wigwam nice and cozy, a little nest for two
Is waiting for you, Lily of the prairie.

Now, she listen'd to all that he had to say,
Then with heart beating fast she ran right away
And she told her Ma, then she told her Pa
what this warrior brave and bold had said;
When she told who he was they were very glad,
They were sure she'd be happy and never sad;
Then her brave drew near, sang the song so dear
That had caused this happy pair to wed.

Repeat Chorus

Both Edison and Victor made recordings of *Lily of the Prairie* in the summer of 1909. Billy Murray sang it for Victor, but that recording is now very rare. For Edison, *Lily of the Prairie* marked the introduction of a new voice and a new cylinder for Indian love songs. The voice belonged to baritone Pete Murray, who had sung in vaudeville and in "many of the best athletic, social, and boating clubs of the East." Murray was no relation to Billy Murray, which *Edison Phonograph Monthly* made a special effort to point out, reassuring the Edison audience that Pete was a real person and not a trick perpetuated by Billy.[3] Nevertheless, *Talking Machine News* noted the "curious similarity of voices between the two men," observing that "both are baritones of about the same pitch and quality, and each has a slight lisp. It takes an expert to differentiate the two voices on records."[4]

Pete Murray's Amberol version of *Lily of the Prairie* fits the "facelift" description of many Amberol recordings whereby a two-minute cylinder was lengthened without

adding lyrics to fit the new four-minute format (see *Anona*). Murray sings the two verses and a quartet sings the chorus. For special effects, a whistling bird is heard each time the line about a wood lark is sung. After completing the two verses and two choruses, the quartet repeats the chorus another time, then Murray sings the first half of the chorus with the whistling bird before the quartet joins in for the final lines.

Edison Phonograph Monthly for July 1909 liked the new singer and tune: "an Indian song of the same style and by the same composer as 'Red Wing' (our Record Number 9622). Unlike poor 'Red Wing,' however, the Indian maid in this song finally weds her brave and is installed in a cozy wigwam. The story of this wooing is set to a very catchy air." It also noted that this was "Mr. Murray's first Record for the Edison Phonograph and we are glad to offer him our very earnest congratulations on the impression that it creates." The trade journal concluded the description by suggesting, "It looks to us like an instantaneous 'hit.'"[5] Apparently the song became somewhat successful, because Edison reissued the tune as part of the *Lily of the Prairie Medley* cylinder by the American Symphony Orchestra in December that year. For this version, the *Monthly* said that the song "will survive a long time" because of its "decided music superiority to contemporaneous selections." Unfortunately, little mention was made of the song thereafter, and Gardner does not mention it in his charts.[6]

NOTES

1. Kerry Mills, *Lily of the Prairie* (New York: F. A. Mills, 1909).
2. For example, see the ads for the "Unique Theater," *Brainerd (Minn.) Daily Dispatch*, April 8, 1909, 2; or the "Dreamland Tonight," *Seymour (Ind.) Daily Republican*, April 23, 1909, 1.
3. Pete Murray, *Lily of the Prairie* (Orange, N.J.: National Phonograph, 1909), Edison Amberol #207; "Some of the New Artists Who Are Making Edison Records," *Edison Phonograph Monthly* 7, no. 7 (July 1909), 11.
4. *Talking Machine World* 5, no. 4 (April 15, 1909), 53. In fact, Billy Murray had signed an exclusive ten-year deal with Edison and Victor in 1909 to only record cylinders for Edison and discs for Victor. See Hoffmann, Carty, and Riggs, *Billy Murray*, 68.
5. "Advance List of Edison Standard and Edison Amberol Records for August 1909," *Edison Phonograph Monthly* 7, no. 7 (July 1909), 21.
6. "Advance List of Edison Standard and Edison Amberol Records for December 1909," *Edison Phonograph Monthly* 7, no. 10 (October 1909), 19.

My Prairie Song Bird, 1909

My Prairie Song Bird, words by Jack Drislane, music by George W. Meyer (New York: F. B. Haviland, 1909). Sheet music courtesy Frances G. Spencer Collection of American Popular Sheet Music, Crouch Fine Arts Library, Baylor University Libraries Digital Collections, Baylor University, Waco, Texas.

In 1909 lyricist Jack Drislane and composer George W. Meyer produced *My Prairie Song Bird.*[1] Although both men were responsible for numerous songs, including Drislane's 1906 Indian/Irish song *Arrah Wanna* and Meyer's 1917 hit *For Me and My Gal,* there is little biographical information about either of them.[2] Drislane often worked with Theodore Morse and the F. B. Haviland Company of New York and published the sheet music for *My Prairie Song Bird.* Its cover art, drawn by a mysterious artist known only as "E. P. C.," depicts an Indian girl in front of an enormous moon. A cameo of "May Ward," presumably a singer, is in the upper right.

Despite these mysteries, *My Prairie Song Bird* fits right in with other Indian love songs through its internal rhyming, such as "Prairie Land, hand in hand, lovers stand" and "Bowed her head, nothing said, but instead," as well as its lack of anything else about Native Americans other than the cover art. Here are the full lyrics:

Prairie Land, hand in hand, lovers stand, close
together as the sun goes down,
Here him say "Come away, don't delay, you look
sweeter in a wedding gown,"
Bowed her head, nothing said, but instead, sang to
him a pretty love song sweet,
Like a bird, ev'ry word that he heard, he would ask
her to repeat.

Chorus
My Prairie Song Bird Fairy,
My little love canary
Your voice is so entrancing
It sets my heart a dancing
Your love notes seem to thrill me
With joy and gladness fill me
Sing on, my little Prairie Song Bird.

When he said, "Let us Wed," o'er his head flew the
echo of her Ha! Ha! Ha!
And he sighed as she cried "come inside, you will
have to see my Pa and Ma,"
How he danced, all entranced as he glanced at the
lovelight in her eyes aglow,
He could guess, it was "Yes" with caress, then he
whispered soft and low:

Repeat Chorus

Frank C. Stanley and Henry Burr, who had helped
popularize *Red Wing* two years earlier, recorded *My
Prairie Song Bird* for Columbia Indestructible cylinder
and Victor disc in late 1909, and Billy Murray sang it
for Zon-o-phone the following year. In the Stanley and
Burr cylinder, Stanley sings the verse and then the two
men combine for choruses, singing at different pacing
the lines "Your love notes seem to thrill me / With joy
and gladness fill me," which produces an effect similar
to a round.[3] Little publicity can be found from period
sources about the song other than one advertisement
for the F. B. Haviland Publishing Company five years
later in the *New York Tribune*. The ad features the sheet
music cover art and musical notation with chorus lyrics
for *My Prairie Song Bird* and another company song, *I'd
Rather Float through a Dreamy Old Waltz with You, You,
You*. Above these, the headline "Two Immensely Popular
Song Successes" defies the tune's written record;
little more was heard about it, and it does not make
Gardner's list.[4]

NOTES

1. Jack Drislane and George W. Meyer, *My Prairie Song Bird* (New York:
F. B. Haviland, 1909).

2. For short biographies of Drislane and Meyer, see *The Parlor Songs
Academy*, www.parlorsongs.ac, s.vv. "Jack Drislane" and "George W.
Meyer."

3. The Columbia cylinder listing is "Record Bulletins for December
1909," *Talking Machine World* 5, no. 11 (November 15, 1909), 49. The
Zon-o-phone listing can be found under "Record Bulletins for
September 1910," *Talking Machine World* 6, no. 8 (August 15, 1910), 53.
The Victor ad appears in "Record Bulletins for October 1910, *Talking
Machine World* 6, no. 9 (September 15, 1910), 57.

4. "Two Immensely Popular Song Successes," F. B. Haviland ad, *New
York Tribune*, July 5, 1914, 74.

Ogalalla, 1910

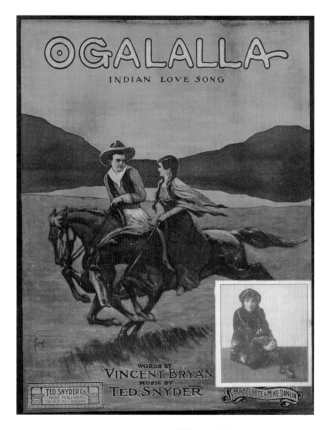

Ogalalla, words by Vincent Bryan,
music by Ted Snyder (New York:
Ted Snyder, 1909). Sheet music from
author's collection.

Vincent Bryan and Ted Snyder wrote *Ogalalla* in 1909.[1] Bryan was considered one of the best lyricists of the time, having worked with composer Harry Von Tilzer (composer of *Ida-Ho*) on an early stage version of *The Wizard of Oz* and written the classic *In My Merry Oldsmobile* in 1905. He went on to Hollywood and worked with Charlie Chaplin. Snyder had worked as a pianist for music publishers before starting his own publishing house in 1909, where he hired a young Irving Berlin as a songwriter. He later penned *The Sheik of Araby* and *Who's Sorry Now* and was a founding member of ASCAP.[2]

Ogalalla takes an uncommon angle on interracial love and threats of miscegenation by showing Indians feeling threatened by having a white man steal away an Indian girl. Of course, it does this using the racist broken English attributed to Native Americans. Set in Mexico on "the Indian reservation," the song follows a story line of a northern cowboy who rides down and steals away the "sweetest girl in all the dusky nation." He explains his love for her simply in broken English as "heap much lovee, you love me," and promises to make her "his squaw," much to the chagrin of the chief, who gets sore and makes "much war." The full lyrics are as follows:

Many moons ago, down in Mexico
Out upon the Indian reservation,
Lived a redskin queen, she was just eighteen,
Sweetest girl in all her dusky nation.
Riding from the North a cowboy came,
She met him and set his heart a flame,
Ev'ry night they'd ride, o'er the prairie wide,
While to explain his love he tried.

Chorus
Ogalalla, Ogalalla,
Heap much lovee, you love me,
Soon we ride quick my tepee
Ogalalla, Ogalalla,
Big chief get sore, and he make much war,
But we go before,
If you be my squaw
My Ogalalla, follow me.

In the starry light, of the summer night,
From the camp there steals a redskin wary
Finds these lovers two, as they bill and coo,
Soon his war cry echoes from the prairie,
Then the cowboy takes her bridle rein,
Madly gallops with her o'er the plain,
And by break of day, when they're far away,
He takes her in his arm to say.

Repeat Chorus

Illustrator John Frew created the cover art for *Ogalalla*. He had produced the cover for Bryan's earlier song *Sitting Bull* but was best known for his cover of the hit song *Alexander's Ragtime Band*. Frew often placed detailed figures in the foreground set against simple backgrounds. This is true of *Ogalalla*, which shows the cowboy and his Indian love looking into each other's eyes as they go riding across the prairie. The cowboy wears a large hat, a white neckerchief, a black vest over a red shirt, and wooly chaps. She has long braids, a fancy necklace and earrings, a long green dress, and a shawl blowing in the wind. He rides a gray horse, she a dark brown one. Although there is a little tuft of grass at their feet, the background is a tan prairie with simple dark mountains beneath a yellow sky. At lower right, the original cover includes the words "As Featured By" above an inset photo of a woman and the words "Mabel Hite and Mike Donlin" in a scroll beneath it. Hite was a vaudeville star and Donlin, her husband, a star baseball player with the New York Giants. On my copy of the sheet music, though, a larger photograph of a kneeling woman is placed over the inset of Mabel Hite, covering part of one of the horses and part of the scroll. There is no mention of her identity.[3]

Both Edison and Victor produced recordings of *Ogalalla* in 1910. The Edison version was a two-minute Standard cylinder featuring Billy Murray and chorus, despite the fact that four-minute Amberols were already in use. *Edison Phonograph Monthly* described it as an "Indian love song" that was "much superior to most compositions of its type" because of its "good, brisk air" and its many usual "Indian effects—the beating of tom-toms, warwhoops of braves, cow-boy yells, etc." It further suggested that the song reminded one of *Red Wing* and that Murray's recording should help in its promotion.[4]

Victor produced two discs, one recorded by the American Quartet (John Bieling, Billy Murray, Steve Porter, and William F. Hooley). The quartet had debuted a year earlier with the cowboy song *Denver Town*. Henry Burr and Frank C. Stanley also recorded the song as a duet in 1910 for Victor and Columbia discs and for a Columbia two-minute cylinder. This cylinder, like Murray's, is also replete with tom-toms.[5] Little was heard about the song after its release, and Gardner does not mention it.

NOTES

1. Vincent Bryan and Ted Snyder, *Ogalalla* (New York: Ted Snyder, 1909).

2. Theodore Raph, *The American Song Treasury: 100 Favorites* (New York: Dover, 1986), 361; *Internet Movie Database*, www.imdb.com, s.v. "Vincent Bryan"; *The Parlor Songs Academy*, www.parlorsongs. ac, s.v. "Harry Von Tilzer, 1872–1946"; Don Tyler, *Hit Songs 1900–1955: American Popular Music of the Pre-rock Era* (Jefferson, N.C.: McFarland, 2007), 360; *Songwriters Hall of Fame*, www. songwritershalloffame.org/search/, s.v. "Ted Snyder."

3. Bill Edwards, "John Frew," *RagPiano*, www.perfessorbill.com/ artists/frew.shtml; Bill James, *The New Bill James Historical Baseball Abstract* (New York: Free Press, 2010), 757. The original sheet music can be seen at the *Yorkspace* repository website at http://yorkspace. library.yorku.ca/xmlui/bitstream/handle/10315/25027/0001. jpg?sequence=2.

4. "Advance List of Edison Amberol and Edison Standard Records for July, 1910," *Edison Phonograph Monthly* 8, no. 5 (May 1910), 24.

5. *Discography of American Historical Recordings*, http://adp.library. ucsb.edu, s.v. "Ogalalla"; Tim Gracyk, "American Quartet with Billy Murray," *Tim's Phonographs and Old Records*, www.gracyk.com/ americanquartet.shtml; Frank C. Stanley and Henry Burr, *Ogalalla* (New York: Columbia Record, 1910), cylinder #1451.

A Cowboy Romance, 1910

Len Spencer and Ada Jones, along with Edison's Premier Quartet, recorded their final western skit, *A Cowboy Romance*, in 1910.[1] For the Edison cylinder, Spencer plays a rancher with a daughter named Ida (played by Jones) who is being courted by several cowboys but is most favored by one named Bill (played by Billy Murray), who begins serenading her. Spencer intervenes and decides to let the cowboys race for her, provided Ida can join in, outrun them all, and stay at home with "dear old Dad." After leading for most of the race on her horse Pony Maid, Ida lets Bill catch up and then he scoops her out of the saddle. Dad worries that he has lost his daughter to her beau, but Ida reassures everyone that she and Bill plan to stay on the ranch, and then the cowboys serenade everyone with a song about Pony Maid. The full text of the skit reads:

[crickets chirp]

RANCHER: Yeah, Sport!

[dog barks]

RANCHER: Where is Ida?

[dog barks]

RANCHER: Gone in huh? Watch out for your young missus, Sport. Take Good care of her, cause she's all I've got. She's got a heap of admirers but I don't think she'd leave her old daddy for any strappin' young cowpuncher, huh?

[dog barks]

RANCHER: You do, eh? Then I reckon we'll both watch, huh? Yes, good night sport.

[chorus begins singing in the background]

  I idolize Ida, the girl from Idaho

RANCHER: Hello. What this? Who's this a comin'?

[chorus continues]

  She's sweet and brighter, she tamed the wild front O
  She's sweeter than cider, and I'm her lucky beau
  There is no love like Ida, the girl from Idaho

IDA: Don't stop boys, go on.

RANCHER: Yeah, don't stop boys, go on, and keep a goin! Good night!

GROUP: Yes, good night. . . .

IDA: Yes daddy dear?

RANCHER: You close that door and go to bed.

[whistling, then Bill starts playing the banjo and serenades Ida]

BILL: Ida!
  Honey, my little gal
  Just as blue as the stars that shine
  Tell me that you love me
  And say that you'll be mine

IDA: O, is that all Bill?

BILL: It's all I know

IDA: What a pity, I think it's sweet

BILL: Sweet for the sweet Miss Ida, catch!

IDA: Oh, candy!

[the other boys begin arguing]

RANCHER: What are you boys quarreling about?

BOYS: Well we was arguing about which one would ask you first for Ida.

RANCHER: Well, no arguments, let it be a fair race, best man wins.

BILL: That's a good idea.

RANCHER: WHAT?

BILL: Why, a race for Ida.

RANCHER: Where, when, I don't understand.

BILL: Right on the prairie, the moon is up, the horses is fit.

RANCHER: Well, I kinda reckon Ida ought to have the say.

IDA: No race for me!

[the boys continue arguing]

IDA: Unless I'm in the race! Pony Maid can show her heels to anything on *this* ranch.

RANCHER: Right enough! Ha ha, good, Ida! There aint one of them that will get ya. I'll be the starter and referee. Come up three oaks and back!

[cheers and horses whinnying]

RANCHER: Now boys, fair start, go

[sound of many hoofbeats]

RANCHER: Look at em! Long, lean, with fair necks! Bill's in the rear, as they're goin' Ida on Pony Maid a way in the lead!

[dog barks]

RANCHER: She's just turnin the oaks with her hair a flyin in the wind. She's laughin at the boys. Oh, you're safe gal.

RANCHER: Uh oh, Ben and Bill have turned the oaks together. Bill's leading and closing up on Pony Maid fast. Why, Bill's most up to her and riding like the wind. Go Pony Maid, give him the spur! Ida! Well I'll be! Bill's coming along beside and grabbed Ida clean out of the saddle and if I live they're coming in together!

[cheering]

[collective whoa!]

RANCHER: Well, daughter, you've lost the race!

IDA: Yes Daddy but I'm satisfied.

[collective rumbling]

RANCHER: Now boys don't take on, remember that I've lost Ida too.

IDA: No you haven't Daddy, Bill and I will stay right here with you and the boys, hey Bill?

BILL: You bet! Now come on boys

[the chorus begins singing:]

We're here to serenade
You need not be afraid
We love you through and through
Still we do, Pony Maid
To you our hearts we gave
And off for you we crave
to be our queen alone, little Pony Maid

IDA: Thank you boys, good night!

BOYS: "Good night, Miss Ida"

According to *Edison Phonograph Monthly* for September 1910, this was

a descriptive Record reproducing with the aid of clever effects an episode of the prairie—an exciting race in the moonlight between cow-punchers for the hand of an Idaho maid. Leading up to the thrilling climax, which is made wonderfully realistic by the clatter of hoofs, the whinnying of horses and the "yipping" of the cowboys, there is a bit of comedy, some male quartet work and a serenade song (tenor) with banjo accompaniment. A novel and diverting Record which will be a good seller.[2]

Like Len Spencer's skit *Broncho Bob and His Little Cheyenne*, which appeared three years earlier, *A Cowboy Romance* harkened back to some of the earlier hits with a cowboy scooping up his sweetheart. This time around, only Edison produced the cylinder, and it was not much of a hit. Gardner does not even mention it. And to add insult to injury, Jim Walsh notes that the efforts to produce all of the sound effects and cowboy "yips" over and over to get the cylinder just right so irritated Premier Quartet singer John Bieling's throat that he was hoarse for weeks afterward and eventually gave up recording entirely in 1914 because of this one production.[3]

NOTES

1. Len Spencer and Company, *A Cowboy Romance* (New York: Edison Talking Machine, 1910), Edison Amberol #552.
2. "Advance List, Edison Amberol Records for November 1910," *Edison Phonograph Monthly* 8, no. 9 (September 1910), 17.
3. Walsh, "'Cowboy Song' Recordings, Part 4," *Hobbies*, July 1976, 35.

Silver Bell, 1910

Silver Bell, words by Edward Madden, music by Percy Wenrich (New York: Jerome H. Remick, 1910). Sheet music from author's collection.

Silver Bell (intermezzo), music by Percy Wenrich (New York: Jerome H. Remick, 1910). Sheet music from author's collection.

Percy Wenrich and Edward Madden's *Silver Bell* became one of the most popular Indian love songs before the Great War.[1] At least five different companies issued more than eleven versions of the song between 1910 and 1914, which probably accounts for its popularity. Indeed, *Silver Bell* is on Gardner's top-twenty list from October 1910 to April 1911 and reaches as high as number six in January and February 1911.[2] Wenrich had created *Rainbow* just a year earlier in 1909 and scored again with *Silver Bell*.

Silver Bell's sheet music reads like the other Indian love songs of this period. There are few references to

specific Indian items except for a "lonely little Indian maid" and "chieftain longing to woo" while "paddling his tiny canoe." The song uses a familiar internal rhyme scheme in the first line of each verse, such as "beneath the light of a bright starry night" and "as in a dream, it would seem, down the stream." Here are the full lyrics:

> Beneath the light of a bright starry night
> Sang a lonely little Indian maid
> "No lover's sweet serenade
> Has ever won me."

As in a dream, it would seem, down the stream,
Gaily paddling his tiny canoe,
A chieftain longing to woo
Sang her this song:

Chorus
Your voice is ringing, my Silver Bell.
Under it's spell
I've come to tell of the love I am bringing
O'er hill and dell
Happy we'll dwell, my Silver Bell

For many moons, many spoons, many tunes
Woke the echoes of the still Summer night
As down the stream gleaming bright
They floated dreaming.

In his canoe, only two, sat to woo,
And they listened to the sigh of the breeze,
That seemed to sing in the trees,
This sweet refrain:

Repeat Chorus

Silver Bell's sheet music is unusual for Indian love songs because it features both an Indian man and an Indian woman. It also uses the same cover for the instrumental intermezzo that it did for the vocal: the couple stands atop a rock outcrop framed by a few small pines, holding hands and looking across a vast plain cut by a river, with the moon rising against a deep blue sky.

Two of the most popular recording ensembles of the era, the Peerless Quartet for Victor and Ada Jones and Billy Murray for Edison Amberols, made the first recordings of *Silver Bell* in 1910. Over the next four years, Edison recorded an instrumental version by the American Standard Orchestra and a Standard version two-minute cylinder by Jones and Murray. Indestructible meanwhile recorded a cylinder by Frank Stanley and Henry Burr, and still another cylinder company called U.S. Everlasting made a record of the Peerless Quartette and an instrumental by the U.S. Symphony Orchestra in 1911. The following year, Edison created a better version of its Amberol cylinder, the Blue Amberol, and featured new releases of both the Jones and Murray and American Standard Orchestra versions. The Peerless Quartette

concluded the cylinder recordings with still another one for Lakeside in 1913. For Victor, both the Haydn Quartet and the "That Girl" Quartet made *Silver Bell* discs in 1910. The latter group was the first all-female barbershop quartet ever recorded.[3]

All of these recordings meant a lot of period publicity in the trade journals and no doubt explain the song's popularity. Even before its release, *Edison Phonograph Monthly* warned in an article headed "Another Special Hit" not to "fail to order liberally of this Record, which without any doubt will prove as big a seller as *Red Wing*, *Rainbow*, or any other selection of its kinds we have ever listed."[4] Then in its "Advance List," the trade journal gushed about the Ada Jones and Billy Murray Amberol:

An Indian love song which will at least equal if not surpass in popularity any song of its type yet composed. It is easily the big "hit" of the day and went on sale as a "Special" because of its immense popularity. The words are attractive, more so than usual, and the air is delightful,—a sparkling, rhythmic two-step melody which captivates on first hearing. This rendition calls for warmest praise, for both Miss Jones and Mr. Murray seem to have outdone themselves in this instance. A bell solo with violin accompaniment is introduced most appropriately between each repetition of the chorus, a novel and pleasing feature of which is Mr. Murray's singing of a few bars of "Home, Sweet Home" while Miss Jones is confining herself to the word and music of the song. This Record is expected to vie with the biggest sellers we have ever cataloged.[5]

The predictions came true. An October ad for the song's publisher, Jerome H. Remick, features a few bars of the music, a drawing of an Indian man in feather headdress holding a spear with two tepees in the distance, and a paragraph describing the song as "that wonderfully fascinating Indian melody that is sweeping the country and creating a still greater furore among music lovers than 'Hiawatha,' which we published a few years ago." *Edison Phonograph Monthly* concurred, reporting in November that *Silver Bell* "has proven to be a tremendous seller and bids fair to continue so for an indefinite time to come" and suggesting that dealers also order the instrumental version due out in January 1911. When that recording arrived, the *Monthly* reported that "many of the trade insisted upon its appearance as an instrumental Record" and that Edison did so because it was "convinced that its great popularity will continue indefinitely."[6]

The next month, a letter from the Santa Fe Watch Company appeared in the *Monthly* that helped to explain the song's success. Calling *Silver Bell* "the greatest selling Record ever put out by any company," the letter praised the "little tricks" of the Edison recording including the use of the bell and Murray's singing with the chorus. "It is something different—," the letter read, "something besides the straight, ordinary singing of the song that makes these big sellers. Frequently other companies will make the same Record your company does, using the same artists, yet it is not a large seller or does not attract special attention, merely because there is no special arrangement."[7]

Murray's "little trick" of singing *Home Sweet Home* while Ada Jones sings "Happy we'll dwell, my Silver Bell" fits into the broader theme of domesticity suggested by these Indian love songs. And the fact that the listening public directly cited this passage as one of the reasons for the song's popularity shows how this theme resonated with Americans.

Six months after releasing the Amberol version by Jones and Murray and five months after the instrumental version, Edison produced a two-minute Standard recording of *Silver Bell* and noted that "the popularity of this pretty Indian love song is unprecedented among selections of its kind." This allowed customers without the new four-minute machines called Amberolas or retrofitted two-minute phonographs to enjoy *Silver Bell* as a two-minute record, and Edison reported that half a year after its release *Silver Bell* was "in greater demand than any Record in the Amberol catalog." Finally, when Edison created the Blue Amberol in 1912, the company released still another version of the song by Jones and Murray for December that year. This time its description called the record an "Indian love song, in ragtime, which has equaled if not surpassed in popularity any song of its type yet published."[8]

NOTES

1. Edward Madden and Percy Wenrich, *Silver Bell* (New York: Jerome H. Remick, 1910).
2. Gardner, *Popular Songs*, 63–64.
3. Information gathered from the *UCSB Cylinder Audio Archive*, http://cylinders.library.ucsb.edu, and the *Discography of American Historical Recordings*, http://adp.library.ucsb.edu.
4. "Another Special 'Hit,'" *Edison Phonograph Monthly* 8, no. 10 (October 1910), 12.
5. "Edison Amberol Records for December, 1910," *Edison Phonograph Monthly* 8, no. 10 (October 1910), 16.
6. "Silver Bell," ad, *Fort Wayne (Ind.) Telegraph*, October 14, 1910, 12; "Two More Special Hits," *Edison Phonograph Monthly* 8, no. 11 (November 1910), 4, 16.
7. "For Which—Thanks," *Edison Phonograph Monthly* 8, no. 12 (December 1910), 8.
8. "Edison Standard Records for May 1911," *Edison Phonograph Monthly* 9, no. 3 (March 1911), 18; "Blue Amberol Regular List," *Edison Phonograph Monthly* 10, no. 11 (November 1912), 15.

Valley Flower, 1910

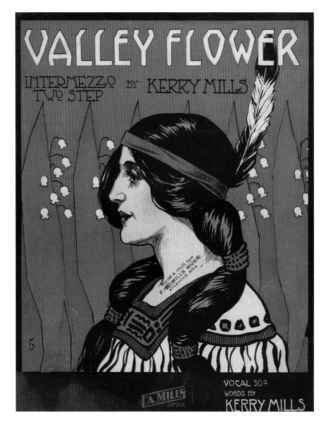

Valley Flower, **words and music by**
Kerry Mills (New York: F. A. Mills,
1912). Sheet music courtesy Lilly Library,
Indiana University, Bloomington.

About the same time that *Silver Bell* debuted, Victor and Edison issued recordings of the Indian love song *Valley Flower*, composed by Kerry Mills of *Red Wing* and *Lily of the Prairie* fame.[1] Though clearly overshadowed by *Silver Bell*, *Valley Flower*'s lyrics resonate with the themes of assimilation and domesticity as they tell the story of a young warrior who woos his sweetheart "of a reddish shade" by explaining that he has a "wigwam just right for two" and that, if she will stay at home and take care of their "papoose," he will go out and hunt for her. Just as interesting, the song begins as a sort of parable by telling the listeners that, if they are in love,

they should listen to this story. The full lyrics go like this:

> If you think that you're in love you'd better listen to
> A little story I will tell of years ago.
> All about a brave young warrior who had come to woo
> A pretty maid, of reddish shade
>
> She had loved him all the while, but never ever knew
> That he had even cared a tiny bit for her
> Till across the prairie gliding
> On his pony riding
> He came up and said to her:

Chorus

O Valley Flower

I have a wigwam just right for two

Under a great big tree

Just you and only me

You stay home and later maybe a papoose comes
too

While I "kill um" Bear "kill um" Deer for you my
little Valley Flow'r.

Years and days flew by, still he was on his hunting
ground,

But at each sunset his little wife he came

'Round the wigwam fire she and papoose could be
found

This pretty Dame, of Chiefly name.

But one day they brought the news that he'd been
borne away,

And that another tribe had taken him from her;

Many warriors came to court her,

Indians fairest daughter,

But she could only hear him say:

Repeat Chorus

The sheet music cover by André De Takacs—the illustrator for *Iola*, *Ragtime Cow Boy Joe*, *My Pony Boy*, and others—exhibits the artist's typical use of bold colors, here using green plants with small white flowers against a red background. A head-and-shoulders image of a pale Indian girl wearing a headband with single feather stands in the foreground against these colors. She wears a colorful tunic with her long hair falling in braids over her shoulders.[2] Frederick H. Potter and chorus recorded *Valley Flower* for Edison, and the American Quartet did so

for Victor. Potter, a tenor, had recorded *Red Wing* and *Topeka*. In this version, he sings the first verse and the chorus as a solo before the group joins the second chorus. Potter then sings the second verse and is followed by the group singing the chorus, an instrumental version of the chorus, and then still another group version, with the bass singing the last line of the chorus before the group repeats it again along with bird whistling, whoops, and horse trotting sounds. All in all, the three minute and forty-one second Amberol is a fine example of a two-minute song rehashed on the longer-playing cylinder.[3]

At the time, little mention was made of this song beyond the writeup in the *Edison Phonograph Monthly* just before the company released the cylinder. The journal noted composer Kerry Mills's earlier success with *Red Wing* and suggested that popularity "bids fair to be repeated in this Indian love song which possesses in a marked degree all the characteristics of a popular song of that type. The wooing of the chieftain's daughter is told in attractive verse set to an unusually 'swingy' air, and Mr. Potter sings the number most pleasingly, assisted by a well-balanced male quartet. The rendition is illuminated by clear effects."[4] Despite this praise, little more was ever said about *Valley Flower*, and it does not appear in Gardner's lists.

NOTES

1. Kerry Mills, *Valley Flower* (New York: F. A. Mills, 1910).

2. Bill Edwards, "André De Takacs," *RagPiano*, www.perfessorbill.com/artists/detakacs.shtml.

3. Frederick H. Potter, *Valley Flower* (Orange, N.J.: National Phonograph Company, 1910), Edison Amberol #562.

4. "Edison Amberol Records for December, 1910," *Edison Phonograph Monthly* 8, no. 10 (October 1910), 14.

From the Land of the Sky-Blue Water, 1911

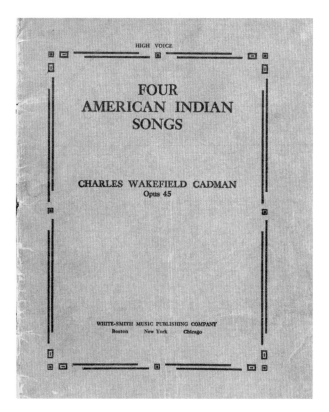

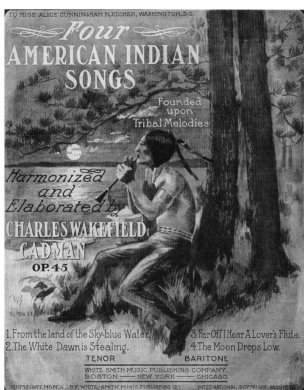

Four American Indian Songs, words by Nelle Richmond Eberhart, music by Charles Wakefield Cadman (Boston: White-Smith Music, 1909). Sheet music from author's collection.

Four American Indian Songs, music by Charles Wakefield Cadman (Boston: White-Smith Music, 1909). Sheet music inside cover illustration from author's collection.

Alice Fletcher was a pioneer American Indian ethnographer who had lived and studied among the Omaha Indians of Nebraska in 1880 and then produced the first book on Native American music, *Indian Story and Song: From North America,* twenty years later.[1] In the summer of 1909, Charles Wakefield Cadman, a music critic, conductor, and composer from Pittsburgh, followed in Fletcher's footsteps to the Omahas and Winnebagos of Nebraska, learning about Fletcher's work as well as collecting and recording tribal melodies for himself. Cadman was a follower of the Indianist movement, a group of nationalist composers who believed that to find a truly original American sound classically trained musicians should look to authentic Native American music for inspiration, doing what one scholar calls "making Indian-themes palatable to non-Indian ears."[2] After listening and recording Native American melodies, Cadman reproduced several of them, in collaboration with local poet Nelle Richmond Eberhart, in a work that he titled *Four American Indian Songs, Op. 45.*[3] Unlike Fletcher's book, Cadman's work was not an ethnographic study to preserve tribal sources but rather a set of primary sources essentialized and then commodified for the market as new sheet music.[4]

The original sheet music for *Four American Indian Songs* lists the four songs—*From the Land of the Sky-Blue Water, The White Dawn Is Stealing, Far Off I Hear a Lover's*

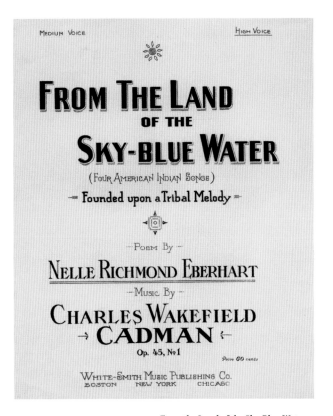

From the Land of the Sky-Blue Water,
words by Nelle Richmond Eberhart,
music by Charles Wakefield Cadman
(Boston: White-Smith Music, 1909).
Sheet music from author's collection.

Flute, and *The Moon Drops Low*—and characterizes them as founded upon tribal melodies but "harmonized and elaborated" by Cadman. Behind a basic typeset cover, the next page features a drawing by "Barton and Willard" of a Native American man playing a flute, naked to the waist and wearing leggings and moccasins. His hair is braided and contains two feathers. He sits on a tuft of grass against a pine tree overlooking a lake. There are mountains in the distance and a moon set low in the sky. Above the song title is a dedication: "Miss Alice Cunningham Fletcher, Washington, D.C." The publishers also produced a separate version of the most successful piece of this composition, *From the Land of Sky-Blue Water*, with no artwork save for small line drawings of a sun and a compass.

Although *From the Land of Sky-Blue Water* represented the appropriation and re-creation of an Indian theme by a white musician and a white poet, the sheet music is surprisingly complex, with references to ethnographer

Fletcher, Omaha tribal melodies, poet Eberhart, and composer Cadman. The music follows suit, with a reference at the beginning to a three-bar run of sixteenth notes described as "Flageolet Love Call of the Omahas"—an odd direction to play a midwestern tribal love song using an ancient English flute. The lyrics add a story of an Omaha flute player meeting a captive brought south from the land of sky-blue water, probably Minnesota.[5]

From the Land of Sky-Blue Water enjoyed great success in public performances as well as on talking machine recordings. Throughout the 1910s, Cadman toured the country with Native American singer Tsinina Redfeather Blackstone performing these Indianist songs to sold-out houses on stages decorated with Navajo rugs, baskets, and Alaskan totems. One historian wryly notes that Blackstone, of Creek and Cherokee descent, essentially "played Indian." Perhaps the popularity of these performances inspired Victor and Columbia to produce multiple discs of *From the Land of Sky-Blue Water* between 1911 and 1918. Victor created two different versions of the disc in 1911, two more in 1912, and more new versions in 1913, 1915, and 1916 during the acoustic era. Columbia also made three discs of its own in 1915, 1917, and 1918. The 1912 Victor disc features soprano Florence Hinkle in a slow, operatic style that is both beautiful and a bit screeching. It certainly is not the *Land of Sky-Blue Water* song many baby boomers remember from 1970s television commercials for Hamm's Beer.[6]

NOTES

1. Fletcher, *Indian Story and Song.*
2. Troutman, *Indian Blues*, 157.
3. Charles Wakefield Cadman, *Four American Indian Songs, Op. 45* (Boston: White-Smith Music, 1909).
4. *Naxos.com*, s.v. "Charles Wakefield Cadman," Biographies.
5. A fascinating study of captives in early American history is James F. Brooks, *Captives and Cousins: Slavery, Kinship, and Community in the Southwest Borderlands* (Chapel Hill: University of North Carolina Press, 2002).
6. Troutman, *Indian Blues*, 233–44. A search of the song's title on newspaper.com for the period 1909 to 1918 revealed 567 matches from thirty-three different states. Most of these report on local performances. Likewise, Gardner indicates that the song never cracked his top-twenty lists but did sneak into the top forty during August 1909, the same month that *My Pony Boy* topped out as number one; see Gardner, *Popular Songs*, 11, 61. The Hamm's Beer commercial song can be found on YouTube.com.

Silver Star, 1912

Silver Star, words by Wm. R. Clay,
music by Chas. L. Johnson (Kansas
City, Mo.: J. W. Jenkins and Sons, 1911).
Sheet music from author's collection.

The final Indian love song records to appear before the Great War arrived in the summer of 1912 with *Silver Star* and *Golden Deer,* and both featured earlier composers. Charles L. Johnson, the composer of 1906's *Iola,* wrote the music for *Silver Star* and William R. Clay penned the lyrics.[1] Ada Jones and Billy Murray, still popular for *Silver Bell* just two years earlier, also sang *Silver Star.* Indeed, the choice of title, lyrics, and recording artists looks like a clear attempt to capitalize on the popularity of the earlier song. Its internal rhyming schemes also fit the pattern. The full lyrics are as follows:

> There was a dusky little maid in a lonely glade,
> Sang a serenade
> Came a warrior try, every night to woo
> He would softly coo,
> I love you
> On bended knee so faithfully, he would ever be
> Pleading earnestly be my pretty bride
> O'er the prairies ride by my silver star.

Chorus

We will be dreaming by campfires gleaming, in
    lands afar,
Tell me you are, my silver star.
We'll go a creeping while squaw is sleeping, there
    will be war,
If we should tarry, my silver star.

Next morning just at break of day they were far
    away,
Looking bright and gay
Chief was feeling blue, knew not what to do
Where they journeyed to, no one knew.
One day they spied the brushing bride on the
    prairies wide,
Riding by his side then he whispered low
She is mine you know, she's my silver star.

Repeat Chorus

Published in Johnson's home town of Kansas City by
the J. W. Jenkins Sons Music Company, the sheet music
utilizes the artwork of H. G. Chilberg, a Chicago-based
artist who illustrated many covers for the Jenkins
Company.[2] Reminiscent of *Silver Bell*, the realistic sheet
music cover shows a lone Native American female with
one eagle feather in her braided hair wearing a long dress
with sash cinched around her waist. Lacking her beau
as in *Silver Bell*, this woman stands alone atop a rocky
outcrop above a fast-moving river set amid a forest.

Unlike *Silver Bell* and its many recordings, only Edison
recorded *Silver Star*. Jones and Murray recorded it as
an Edison Amberol in January 1912, and the New York
Military Band created an instrumental version of the
intermezzo that same month. Edison then released a Blue
Amberol version of the Jones and Murray record in 1913.
Edison Phonograph Monthly noted the song's resemblance
to *Silver Bell* in its January 1912 "Advance List":

Another 'Silver Bell!' Silver Bell was one of the
most catchy and popular songs ever produced on
the Phonograph and this Indian love song is sure

to make the same wide appeal. Ada Jones and Billy
Murray are old favorites and their performance
on this Record will strengthen their present grip
on the affections of Edison owners. In their usual
capable fashion, our recording experts have
interwoven tuneful bell effects between verses,
and worked up the orchestra accompaniment to
make it stand out most attractively.[3]

That same issue of the *Monthly* reported that the
instrumental version was the original form of the piece
and that the "vocal arrangement was an after-thought."
It then stated that the song was already a "great 'hit' in
the West, and it must be only a matter of weeks when
it will enjoy equal popularity the country over." In
February, a Maryland newspaper reported the song to
be the "New Indian hit of the season." Six months later,
a letter to the *Monthly* from a man in Chicago observed
that the violin and bells effects in *Silver Bell* and *Silver
Star* "cannot be equalled anywhere; it is simply great."
That writer also suggested that Jones and Murray's
popular music selections were in a "class by themselves."[4]
Nevertheless, Gardner does not include the song in his
charts, and little more was heard about *Silver Star*.

NOTES

1. Charles L. Johnson, *Silver Star* (Kansas City: J. W. Jenkins Sons
   Music, 1911).
2. There is very little information available on Chilberg. A search of
   the Charles Templeton Sheet Music Collection at the Mississippi
   State University Libraries found five covers designed by Chilberg,
   three being authored by Charles L. Johnson, though *Silver Star*
   is not among them; see http://digital.library.msstate.edu/cdm/
   landingpage/collection/SheetMusic. A search of newspapers.com
   found only an advertisement on page 13 of the December 11, 1909
   Salt Lake City Republican that mentions that the Christmas edition
   of the magazine *Goodwin's Weekly* contained a cover design that
   was "a beautiful art study in colors . . . and is the work of the great
   Chicago artist, H. G. Chilberg."
3. "Edison Amberol Records," *Edison Phonograph Monthly* 10, no. 1
   (January 1912), 17.
4. Ibid., 19; "Silver Star," *Frederick (Md.) News*, February 24, 1912, 5;
   "A. B. Coates," *Edison Phonograph Monthly* 10, no. 6 (June 1912), 2.

Golden Deer, 1912

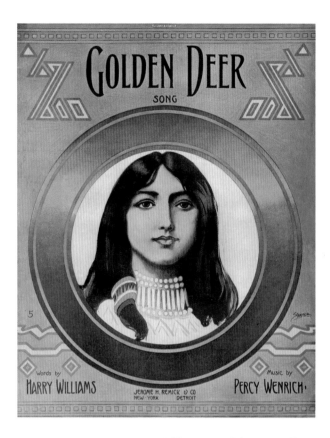

Golden Deer, **words by Harry Williams, music by Percy Wenrich (New York: Jerome H. Remick, 1911).** Sheet music from author's collection.

Golden Deer brought together several important contributors to the field of Indian love songs for a sure hit, including composer Percy Wenrich, lyricist Harry Williams, one of the Starmer brothers for the cover sheet, and music publisher Jerome H. Remick.[1] Wenrich had written the music for *Rainbow* and *Silver Bell*, and Williams had penned the lyrics to *Cheyenne*, *San Antonio*, and *Navajo*. William or Edward Starmer had created the covers for *San Antonio*, *Broncho Buster*, and *Navajo*, and Remick had published many of the era's cowboy and Indian songs. With such a pedigree, *Golden Deer* seemed destined for greatness.

The lyrics appear like other popular Indian love songs with internal rhyme patterns, and the sheet music features a head-and-shoulders image of a Native American woman wearing a necklace. She is encircled by red bands at the top and blue ones at the bottom that are then superimposed on what looks to be a stylized rug with abstract tepees on top surrounding the title and bands and diamonds at the bottom, where the composer and lyricist are named. The publisher is listed in the middle below the portrait.

Only Edison recorded *Golden Deer*, releasing it in April 1912. The Amberol cylinder features the

Metropolitan Quartet—New Yorkers Robert J. Webb, Peter J. Collins, James J. Byrne, and Richard Schumm.[2] *Edison Phonograph Monthly* called on the composer's previous successes to suggest that *Golden Deer* would also fare well: "Percy Wenrich won undying fame with his great 'Silver Bell' . . . which has never lost its hold upon the public. This new Indian love song of his is similar in style to his earlier triumph, and is easily its equal in popular favor. The mixed quartet, to whom the making of this Record was intrusted, has rendered the piece in capital style, with a most appropriately arranged orchestra arrangement."[3] Unfortunately, the song does

not break into Gardner's top twenty at any time, and none of the major cylinder repositories at the University of California, Santa Barbara, or the Library of Congress have a working copy.

NOTES

1. Harry Williams and Percy Wenrich, *Golden Deer* (New York: Jerome H. Remick, 1911).
2. *UCSB Cylinder Audio Archive*, http://cylinders.library.ucsb.edu, s.v. "Golden Deer"; *The Notorious Meddler*, http://randyspeck.blogspot.com, s.v. "Edison Files: Metropolitan Quartet."
3. "Edison Amberol Records," *Edison Phonograph Monthly* 10, no. 4 (April 1912), 16.

Ragtime Cow Boy Joe, 1912

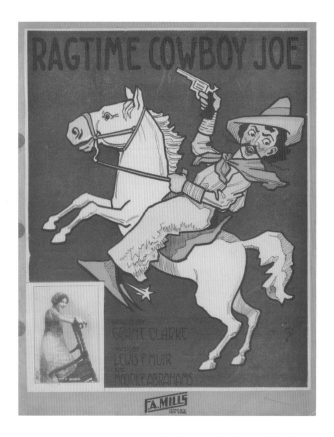

Ragtime Cow Boy Joe, **words by Grant Clarke, music by Lewis F. Muir and Maurice Abrahams (New York: F. A. Mills, 1912).** Sheet music from author's collection.

Ragtime Cow Boy Joe combined images of the frontier past with a title, lyrics, and just enough syncopated ragtime rhythm to revive the talking machine era cowboy craze in 1912.[1] Technically neither ragtime nor cowboy, the song came to be associated with each music type and, like *My Pony Boy*, has enjoyed tremendous success as a hit song for big bands, crooners, movie stars, the Chipmunks television cartoon, and country and western singers. Universities, including the University of Wyoming, have even adopted the chorus as their school fight song. The original lyrics go this way:

Out in Arizona where the bad men are,
And the only friend to guide you is an Evening
    star,
That roughest toughest man by far,
Is Ragtime Cow Boy Joe

Got his name from singing to the cows and sheep
Every night they say he sings the herd to sleep
In a basso rich and deep
Crooning soft and low

Chorus

He always sings raggy music to the cattle,

As he swings back and forward in the saddle

On a horse, that is syncopated gaited

And there's such a funny meter to the roar of his
    repeater

How they run, when they hear that fellow's gun

Because the Western folks all know

He's a high faluting, scooting, shooting son of a
    gun from Arizona

Ragtime Cow Boy Joe

Dressed up every Sunday in his Sunday clothes,

He beats it for the village where he always goes,

And every gal in town is Joes,

Cause he's a ragtime bear.

When he starts a spieling on the dance hall floor

No one but a lunatic would start a war,

Wise men know his forty four

Makes men dance for fair.

Repeat Chorus

Despite its lyrics about an Arizona badman, three Tin Pan Alley songwriters—Grant Clarke, Lewis F. Muir, and Maurice Abrahams—wrote the words and music about Abrahams's four-year-old nephew Joseph all dressed up in a cowboy costume with boots and a big hat. Apparently the introduction of the tyke as "little ragtime cow boy Joe" to the composers inspired them to write the song in 1912, drawing on the popularity of both cowboy and ragtime music.[2] The Arizona setting makes sense since it had just become a state that year, and the song's lyrics about herding cattle and sheep, gunplay, and the popularity of dance halls fit the western stereotype. Ragtime influences include Joe's ability to sing "raggy music to the cattle," his horse's strange "syncopated gaited" pace as the cowboy "swings back and forward in the saddle," and the "funny meter to the roar" of his gun. The line about being a "ragtime bear" on the dance floor refers to the Irving Berlin/George Botsford 1910 song *The Grizzly Bear*, which became a big dance hit after Fanny Brice performed it in the 1911 *Ziegfeld Follies*.[3]

André De Takacs illustrated the song's sheet music for the F. A. Mills publishing company. Like his other stylistic covers such as for *My Pony Boy*, De Takacs used a minimal color palette of green, white, black, and shades of orange. The image depicts a stylized, two-dimensional cartoon figure of a cowboy with long black hair and a long black moustache seated on a bucking bronco and pointing a six-shooter. An inset photo of Betty Bond, a stage singer who must have performed the song, is included at the bottom.[4]

Several artists recorded *Ragtime Cow Boy Joe* (sometimes spelled *Ragtime Cowboy Joe*) before the Great War. "Ragtime" Bob Roberts made discs for Victor in July 1912 and as a cylinder for the U.S. Everlasting Records Company that same year. The Victor supplement described it simply as "a new cowboy song, which looks like another 'Pony Boy.'"[5] Edward Meeker recorded a cylinder for Edison in November 1912 that *Edison Phonograph Monthly* described as "a rollicking ragtime shout breathing the free and easy spirit of the plains with all sorts of local color to assist the illusion."[6] Baritone Ed Morton also made a disc for Columbia, and Edison included an instrumental version in the 1913 *Here Comes My Daddy Now* medley played by the National Promenade Band on a four-minute Amberol cylinder.[7]

Alf Gordon, also known as "Arizona Jack," recorded a version of *Ragtime Cow Boy Joe* for the British "Cinch" record label in spring 1913. Gordon, a comedian, baritone, and prolific recorder of songs, was the British equivalent of Billy Murray. He sings without much of a British accent, though he does roll his *r*'s in "roughest," "rich," "raggedy," and "run."[8]

Despite these many recordings, *Ragtime Cow Boy Joe* was only a minor hit during the talking machine era. Although Gardner lists it in the top twenty songs between September 1912 and February 1913, he never places it above number eleven, doing so for October 1912. Jim Walsh suggests that the problem for Edison's release was that the song appeared on a regular Amberol recording the same month the company began releasing its higher-quality Blue Amberols.[9] An interesting nugget of detail comes from a 1913 *Oakland Tribune* article. On its society page under the headline "Ragtime Insists and Persists," the author wrote that "ragtime has crept into every big dance given this year . . . and has swept over conservative London and taken it by storm." Could this be Arizona Jack? The writer continued:

> In other big West End mansions rag-time is the sign for everybody to stop talking and to crowd in from the other rooms to listen to it. It is also astonishing to me to discover that so many people know the extraordinary words of some of these rag-time songs and join in the choruses. For instance, it is somewhat of a surprise to discover that prosperous and quite elderly city men can join, word-perfect in such a chorus as, "He's the high falutin,' shootin,' scootin,' son of a gun from Arizona, rag-time cowboy Joe!"[10]

NOTES

1. Grant Clarke, Lewis F. Muir, and Maurice Abraham, *Ragtime Cow Boy Joe* (New York: F. A. Mills, 1912).
2. Tinsley, *For a Cowboy*, 22–23.
3. "The Dance of the Grizzly Bear," *The Frederick Hodges Website*, www.frederickhodges.com/hellofriscolinernotes.html. Botsford also wrote the music for *Pride of the Prairie*.
4. A description of Bond's later singing abilities can be found in "Charles McCarron Presents Betty Bond," *New York Clipper*, June 6, 1917.
5. "Record Bulletins for July 1912," *Talking Machine World* 8, no. 6 (June 15, 1912), 61; Walsh, "'Cowboy Song' Recordings, Part 6," *Hobbies*, September 1976, 127.
6. "Record Bulletins for November 1912," *Talking Machine World* 8, no. 10 (October 15, 1912), 53; "New Edison Records," *Edison Phonograph Monthly* 10, no. 8 (August 1912), 18.
7. *Discography of American Historical Recordings*, http://adp.library. ucsb.edu, s.v. "Ragtime Cowboy Joe" (Ed Morton); Arizona Jack, *Ragtime Cowboy Joe* (London: Cinch Records, ca. 1913), disc; National Promenade Band, *Here Comes My Daddy Now* medley (New York: Edison Records, 1913), cylinder.
8. Arthur Badrock and Frank Andrews, *The "Cinch" Record: A History and Discography with Biographical Notes* (London: City London Phonograph and Gramophone Society, 2014), 19, 52, 54.
9. Gardner, *Popular Songs*, 67–68; Walsh, "'Cowboy Song' Recordings, Part 6," *Hobbies*, September 1976, 127.
10. "Society," *Oakland (Calif.) Tribune*, January 26, 1913, 8.

Oh That Navajo Rag, 1912

Oh That Navajo Rag, **words by Harry Williams, music by Egbert Van Alstyne (New York: Jerome H. Remick, 1911).** Sheet music from author's collection.

Just as Tin Pan Alley composers had done with *Ragtime Cow Boy Joe*, period composers jumped on the country's fervor about the syncopated rhythms of Irving Berlin's *Alexander's Ragtime Band* and appropriated the word "ragtime" or simply "rag" to all kinds of songs. Few of the hits actually contained the syncopated beats of Scott Joplin's piano music, but tunes like *The Ragtime Violin* and *Ragging My Baby to Sleep* proved popular.[1] It should come as no surprise, then, that these Tin Pan Alley masters of imitation also melded the popularity of Indian songs with the new ragtime fad to produce a hit. What is somewhat

of surprise, though, is that the composers to do this were Harry Williams and Egbert Van Alstyne, the team that had created the Indian music fervor a decade earlier with their hit *Navajo*. Future Songwriters Hall of Fame members, Williams and Van Alstyne had also created the cowboy songs *Cheyenne*, *San Antonio*, and *In the Land of the Buffalo*. Their new hit, *Oh That Navajo Rag*, brought them back to the Navajos of New Mexico.[2]

The song tells the fictional story of Navajo chief Bounding Deer after he returns from an eastern college to his reservation in New Mexico, bringing with him a ragtime dance to replace his traditional "old time prance." The song plays on the issues and language of assimilation by suggesting that Indians are lazy, have lost "their cunning," and so no longer are "in the running" and "must be the goat." It then suggests that perhaps the Indians should "massacre" some songs the white man wrote. The full lyrics are as follows:

What a celebration,
on a reservation
In New Mexico;
No more Injuns in their old time prance,
No more painting for a big war dance.
Chief is back from college,
With a lot of knowledge,
Big Chief Bounding Deer,
He bounded right into their dance one night,
And hollered, Oh see here!
You just all stand in line
And learn a dance of mine

Chorus
Oh, oh, oh, that Navajo rag (That rag, that rag, that rag)
Oh, oh, oh, that Navajo drag (That drag, that drag, that drag)
Dance me all around the old tepee,
All squaws look a like to me,
Come, come, start that tom-tom going some,
Keep it up, keep it up, keep it up,
Oh, oh, oh, that Navajo rag (That rag, that rag, that rag!)
Oh, oh, oh, that Navajo drag (That drag, that drag, that drag!)
Shake your moccasins and roll your eye,
Tear my blanket, make my feathers fly,
Whirl me, twirl me
To that Navajo Rag.

Ev'ry body's crazy,
Crazy for a lazy, good old rag time dance;
We were here before the other men,
Let's have a rag about the Indian
We have lost our cunning,
We're not in the running,
We must be "the goat,"
But pass me her
And we will massacre
Some tunes the white man wrote.
No chief from Tammany
Has anything on me.

William or Frederick Starmer created the artistic cover for *Oh That Navajo Rag*, just as they had *Navajo* eight years earlier. Because each brother signed only his last name, it is impossible today to determine which created which covers. That said, scholars of their work suggest that the two created about one-fourth of all sheet music artwork in the ragtime era. Their images usually include realistic looking people rather than caricatures, a fluid use of color, and a mixture of people and patterns.[3] *Oh That Navajo Rag* fits this description. At the top, the song's title is placed between two faces of Indian chiefs looking stoically at the viewer. Each wears a full feathered headdress, long braids, and necklaces. The one on the left is tinted in red and the one on the right in blue. Between them are patterns of lines and curves with small chevrons. Below the title, the lone figure of a dancing chief occupies most of the cover. The man's skin is clearly tinted red, and he wears a colorful long-sleeve buckskin tunic with blue breastplate, fringed leggings, and moccasins. On his head is a long feathered headdress that trails behind him almost to the ground. The songwriters' names are on the lower right above small cameo photographs of them.

The cover image clearly represents an appeal to the general public's stereotypical notion of an Indian rather than a Navajo man's clothing exhibition. The buckskin tunic, fringed leggings, moccasins, and trailer warbonnet better resemble the clothing of Northern Plains tribes like the Lakota Sioux or Crows than the Navajo's velvet shirts and cloth headbands.[4]

Before any recordings, *Oh That Navajo Rag* first rose to a certain level of popularity around the country. In Washington, D.C., an ad for a local theater in October 1911 urged people to come and "hear Johnny McGuire sing Navajo Rag—It's Great." Across the country in Oakland, California, the Berkeley Elks Club performed a blackface minstrel show that same month to positive reviews, with the local police chief's performance of it as one of the "song hits of the show." That same week, the tune became the center of turmoil for the Central High School band in Harrisburg, Pennsylvania, when it struck it up to accompany students going to chapel. The next morning, in response, the faculty ordered the band to desist playing ragtime entirely.[5]

Even stranger is an article from the *Leavenworth Times* for December 1, 1911. It seems that a convict at the federal penitentiary there wrote a farce called "Turkey Island" that was presented at the prison chapel by prisoners and featured *Oh That Navajo Rag*. The paper noted that the singer was "accompanied by four Sioux Indians" who, despite having "long since acquired the stolid decorum that age brings to the Red Man, pranced like mad men to the beating of the tom-tom by Full Bull" when the band played the song. Not to be outdone, in April 1912, Harry Tally, "the silver tenor" who had helped make *Navajo* popular almost a decade earlier, sang the song accompanied with "real Indian slides" to audiences in Monroe, Louisiana. That same month, a group of schoolchildren performed it in Atlanta, and a Mr. Leonard Chick sang the "great comic rag Indian song" to audiences at the Grand Theater in Wilmington, North Carolina, later that autumn; the local paper reported that "this song as rendered by Mr. Chick is guaranteed to dispel the blues at any time and patrons of the Grand should not miss it."[6]

Such popularity induced Edison, Victor, and Columbia to each produce a version of *Oh That Navajo Rag*. For Edison and Victor, Billy Murray sang the lead accompanied by John Bieling, Steve Porter, and William F. Hooley. These four men were known at Edison as the Premier Quartet and at Victor as the American Quartet. *Edison Phonograph Monthly* described the four-minute Amberol cylinder as a follow-up to Williams and Van

Alstyne's hit *Navajo*, saying that this was an "even bigger sensation—a timely, up-to-the-minute satirical rag." On the Victor disc, Murray really belts out the melody, and the other members of the quartet sing the tom-tom rhythms during the choruses. For Columbia, Dolly Connolly, wife of composer Percy Wenrich, recorded the song on disc in 1912. Somewhat like a later Ethel Merman recording, Connolly swoons more and more to a real drum playing the tom-tom during the choruses. Finally, in 1912, Edison coupled the song into a group of instrumental tunes played by the New York Military Band on another four-minute Amberol cylinder that it named after the publisher: *Remick's Hits—Medley Overture, No. 12*.[7] Despite these recordings, the song does not appear in Gardner's top-twenty lists.

NOTES

1. Hamm, *Irving Berlin*, 102–36; Gardner, *Popular Songs*, 64–67. Two stories on National Public Radio, one about Irving Berlin and another about *Alexander's Ragtime Band*, provide good context for the popularity of ragtime. For the Irving Berlin piece, see "Irving Berlin," *NPR Music*, 2016, www.npr.org/artists/15744000/irving-berlin, and for the song, see "Alexander's Ragtime Band," *NPR Music*, 2000, www.npr.org/2000/03/20/1071829/alexanders-ragtime-band. A search for "ragtime" at the *UCSB Cylinder Audio Archive* revealed 119 recordings.

2. Harry Williams and Egbert Van Alstyne, *Oh That Navajo Rag* (New York: Jerome H. Remick, 1911).

3. Bill Edwards, "William Starmer and Frederick Starmer," *RagPiano*, http://perfessorbill.com/artists/starmer.shtml.

4. "Navajo Culture: Clothing," *PBS, Independent Lens*, www.pbs.org/independentlens/missnavajo/clothing.html; National Museum of the American Indian, "A Life in Beads: The Stories a Plains Dress Can Tell" (Washington, D.C.: NMAI Education Office, n.d.), available at www.nmai.si.edu.

5. "At the Plaza," *Washington, D.C., Herald*, October 8, 1911, 5; "Black Face Elks Please Big House," *Oakland (Calif.) Tribune*, October 14, 1911, 3; "Want 'Alexander's Rag Time Band' Not 'Tannhauser,'" *Harrisburg (Pa.) Herald*, October 13, 1911, 11.

6. "'Turkey Island' Causes Prisoners to Forget Pen," *Leavenworth (Kans.) Times*, December 1, 1911, 10; "Theatrical," *Monroe (La.) News-Star*, April 3, 1912, 8; "Fine Entertainment Given by Fair St. School Children," *Atlanta Constitution*, April 17, 1912, 11; "Theatrical," *Wilmington (N.C.) Morning Star*, October 5, 1912, 6.

7. "Other New Edison Amberol Records," *Edison Phonograph Monthly* 9, no. 12 (December 1911), 18; Billy Murray and the American Quartet, *Oh That Navajo Rag* (New York: Victor Talking Machine, 1911), disc #17000; Dolly Connolly, *Oh That Navajo Rag* (New York: Columbia Phonograph, 1912), disc #A1102; "New Edison Records," *Edison Phonograph Monthly* 10, no. 7 (July 1912), 18.

Snow Deer, 1913

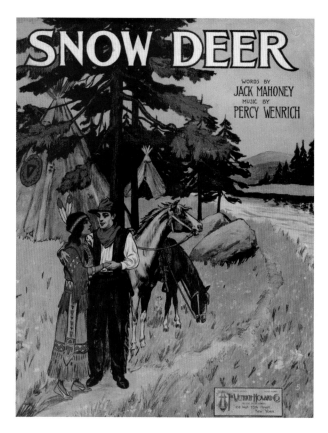

Snow Deer, **words by Jack Mahoney, music by Percy Wenrich (New York: Wenrich-Howard, 1913).** Sheet music from author's collection.

The final Indian love song before the Great War featured a love story between a white cowboy and an Indian maid. Percy Wenrich, who had written the music for Indian hits *Silver Bell* and *Rainbow* and would go on to write the cowboy song *Way Out Yonder in the Golden West*, teamed in 1913 with lyricist Jack Mahoney to produce *Snow Deer.*[1] Mahoney, the pen name for Ruben Kusnitt, was a popular songwriter who wrote several hits with Wenrich including *When You Wore a Tulip.* Like *Ogalalla*, *Snow Deer* tells the story of a cowboy who steals his Indian sweetheart away from her tribe to his ranch. Like many of the Indian love songs, *Snow Deer* relies on internal rhymes within single lines such as "Don't hesitate, it is late, ponies wait." The full lyrics are as follows:

> Sweet snow deer mine
> Moon's a-shine through the pines
> While Mohawks sleep
> Let us creep through the vale
>
> Your cowboy lover, your heart will cover
> Don't hesitate, it is late, ponies wait
> For you and me by the trees in the dale
> Hear tom-toms beating, let's hit the trail

Chorus

My pretty snow deer, say you will go, dear

From your side, I'll never part

Every trail leads to your heart

It's time to marry, no time to tarry

Let me carry you away from here

My sweet snow deer

The red men come

Bullets hum, there'll be some

Left on the trail, I can't fail, cling to me

We'll crown the story with love and glory

Now, after all must I fall, hear my call

And fly away while we may, can't you see?

Those ranch lights gleaming, safe there we'll be.

The colorful sheet music cover by one of the Starmer brothers features a cowboy in wooly chaps with his arm around his Indian maiden dressed in a buckskin tunic. Behind them, two horses graze in a forest of large pine trees beside a pair of tepees with a river running beneath distant mountains.

Although both Edison and Victor made recordings of *Snow Deer*, the song did not make much of a splash. For Edison, the old duo of Ada Jones and Billy Murray released a new Blue Amberol of the song in June 1913. But *Edison Phonograph Monthly*, which no longer carried descriptions of each of its many songs by this date, listed it only as a "tenor duet." Interestingly, phonograph historian John Walsh states that in the Diamond Disc recording of the song, Ada Jones mistakenly says "Snow Bird" instead of "Snow Deer" in one of her lines, just a hint at the difficulties of recording in the acoustic era. For Victor, Henry Burr and Albert Campbell made a disc that same year that produced little excitement.[2] Gardner does not include the song in his lists.

NOTES

1. Jack Mahoney and Percy Wenrich, *Snow Deer* (New York: Wenrich Howard, 1913).

2. Ada Jones and Billy Murray, *Snow Deer* (Orange, N.J.: National Phonograph, 1913), Edison Blue Amberol #2021; *Edison Phonograph Monthly* 11, no. 9 (September 1913), 10; Walsh quoted in Gracyk, *Popular American Recording Pioneers*, 193; *Discography of American Historical Recordings*, http://adp.library.ucsb.edu, s.v. "Snow deer."

In the Golden West, 1913

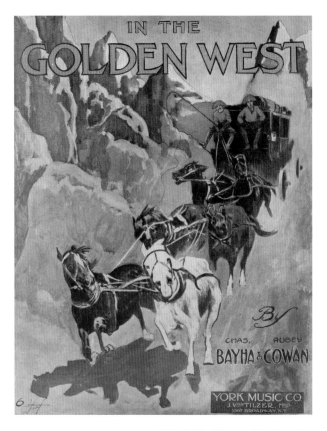

In the Golden West, **words and music by Chas. Bayha and Rubey Cowan (New York: York Music, 1913).** Sheet music from author's collection.

Charles Bayha and Rubey Cowan wrote one of the last cowboy songs of the era, *In the Golden West*, in 1913, and the York Music Company published the song that year.[1] A nostalgic piece, the song tells the story of someone dreaming of riding an old stagecoach back to his farm to see his "Pa and Marm." It includes references to other western icons including guns, a pony, and the "Texas Tommy" dance, an early swing step. Joseph Hirt, best know for his sheet music covers of Indian songs *Red Wing* and *Reed Bird*, illustrated the cover for *In the Golden West*, depicting a stage coach drawn by six horses barreling down a mountain pass.[2] The full lyrics are as follows:

I just was dreaming
I just was dreaming
I thought I saw that old stage coach a swinging
    down the mountain side;
On that bumpy thumpy rocky ride
I woke up screaming
I woke up screaming
With joy because I thought that it was bringing me
To the farm
Where my Pa and Marm
Pray that I'm safe from harm, Gosh darn!

Chorus

In the Golden West

In that eighteen caret golden West

Where every pal and friend

sticks to the end

The girls are just the kind a fellow hates to leave

    behind

Where they do that prance

that they call the "Texas Tommy" dance

Say, "Pard," just buckle your belt and gun and take

    it on the run

To the Golden West

I can't help raving,

I can't help raving,

About my pony 'way out on that ranch

I know he's waiting for me

And he's wondering where I can be

That's why I'm saving

That's why I'm saving

Each penny that I get to buy a ticket

Then I'm going some,

'Cause they wrote to come,

Out where they makes things hum, By gum!

Repeat Chorus

Victor produced two discs featuring *In the Golden West.* Newcomer baritone William Halley belted out the song in 1913 as a solo with orchestra accompaniment, and the Victor Military Band recorded it a month later as part of its *In the Golden West Medley.*[3] Rather than described as a cowboy song, the medley appeared in period advertisements as a "one step" or "trot" for dancing.[4] Neither version appeared in any document beyond a company record list thereafter.

NOTES

1. Chas. Bayha and Rubey Cowan, *In the Golden West* (New York: York Music, 1913).
2. Bill Edwards, "Joseph Hirt," *RagPiano,* www.perfessorbill.com/artists/jhirt.shtml.
3. *Discography of American Historical Recordings,* http://adp.library.ucsb.edu, s.vv. "In the golden West" and "In the golden West medley."
4. For examples of ads, see "Six New Dance Records," *News* (Frederick, Md.), May 23, 1913, 2; "Your Summer Dance Music and Your Musician," *New York Evening World,* May 26, 1913, 5; "Victor Records for Dancing," *Washington (D.C.) Post,* January 8, 1914, 7.

At That Bully Wooly Wild West Show, 1914

At That Bully Wooly Wild West Show,
**words by Edgar Leslie and Grant
Clarke, music by Maurice Abrahams
(New York: Maurice Abrahams
Music, 1913).** Sheet music from author's
collection.

Following their success with *Ragtime Cow Boy Joe*, in 1913 Maurice Abrahams and Grant Clarke, joined by Edgar Leslie, released another nostalgic cowboy song called *At That Bully Wooly Wild West Show.*[1] Played in a minor key, the song tells what a pair of visitors might see at what is presumably Buffalo Bill's Wild West show, including bronco busters, Indians, robbers, soldiers, and a burning cabin. A catalogue for its player piano recording described it as "an irresistible song, dashing in verse and winning in chorus. It has all the elements that spell success for a song, and the present arrangement is one of the most brilliant imaginable."[2] In somewhat sophisticated lines, the lyrics note that "it's make believe tonight at that wooly wild west show" and that, in the song's best rhyme, "Cowboys come and drive those red men back into their tents, We've seen it all for fifty cents." Advertisements for the sheet music explained that this was a "different sort of song from the ordinary Indian and Cowboy Number. It is treated in a unique and wonderful way, and the characteristic music reality makes the audience believe they are looking at a Wild West Show." Indeed, the bronco busters, Indian raid, and attack on the settlers' cabin are the same icons historian Louis S. Warren discusses in his biography *Buffalo Bill's America*.[3] The full song goes like this:

> Run dear, my hon dear, and put on your best, (now hurry)
> And I will make you believe you're out west (whoops)
> It will thrill you, chill you, fill your heart up with delight,
> If, you will come with me tonight; My honey,
> Don't waste a moment we'll just make that car, (hoot hoot)
> Smile and be happy, for look, here we are!
> I have got two tickets bought and we are going to go, (yelp)
> Into that wooly wild west show. My honey,
>
> *Chorus*
> At that wild west show from Idaho
> Just see those shoot 'em up, shoot 'em up broncho busters,
> See that big tepee
> Those robbers came to plunder it, red men under it
> Are shooting, now they're scooting
> Hear that gattling gun, the soldiers hon
> Have come to kill 'em all, kill 'em all, don't get nervous
> Hug, hug, hug, hug me tight
> It's make believe tonight
> At that bully wooly wild west show. My honey,
>
> Oh pet, there some yet so don't leave your chair,
> Look at that stage coach they hold up down there
> Hear those people praying, saying, please take all we've got,
> They'd rather do that than be shot; My honey,
> Just see those settlers, children, and wives,
> Their cabins burning, they run for their lives!
> Cowboys come and drive those red men back into their tents,
> We've seen it all for fifty cents. My honey,
>
> *Repeat Chorus*

Prolific sheet music artist E. H. Pfeiffer illustrated the cover scene for the music. Pfeiffer was born in 1868 in New York to German immigrant parents. He designed over 1,500 song covers for more than one hundred different publishers between 1892 and 1932. In addition to music covers, Pfeiffer also designed jewelry and illustrated newspapers and magazines. According to his granddaughter, the artist owned a horse and often raced it down New York streets. She suggests that this love for horses also made his illustrations more accurate.[4]

Pfeiffer's illustration for *At That Bully Wooly Wild West Show* does feature a raging horse at center with a young cowgirl with big hat and scarf, whip in hand, riding bareback. In the background a large tent reads "Wild West Show." In the lower left corner is a plug stating "Wm. Montgomery and Florence Moore's Big Hit in The Pleasure Seekers" with a beautiful girl below. Records show that *The Pleasure Seekers* show lasted only through a two-month run at the Winter Garden Theater in New York from November 3, 1913, to January 3, 1914.[5]

The Peerless Quartet—Henry Burr as lead singer along with Albert Campbell, Arthur Collins, and John H. Meyer—recorded the song for Victor in February 1914. The record includes sound effects, a driving tom-tom beat, cowboy and Indian yips and yells, train whistles, and gunshots.[6] Despite this energy, the recording did not prove popular. Jim Walsh notes that, in addition to Victor, only Pathé, a European recording company just beginning in the United States, recorded *At That Bully Wooly Wild West Show.* Neither Columbia nor Edison recorded it. Walsh also notes that the flip side of the Victor record contained a song by Ada Jones and the Peerless Quartet called *The Pussy Cat Rag* and that "the cat ditty was more popular than its companion."[7] Indeed, Gardner does not list it. Its only substantive mention besides record listings refers to an actual performance of the Miller Brothers and Edward Arlington's 101 Ranch Real Wild West show in Durham, North Carolina, on October 11, 1914. A writer for the town's *Morning Herald* suggested that the performance was a "bully, wooly Wild West Show" because it contained the "real rough riding, lariat throwing broncho busting girls of the plains" and Indians "of the genuine blanket variety."[8]

NOTES

1. Edgar Leslie, Grant Clarke, and Maurice Abrahams, *At That Bully Wooly Wild West Show* (New York: Maurice Abrahams Music, 1913).

2. "Abrahams, M. At That Bully Wooly Wild West Show," *New Music Rolls, October 1913* (New York: Aeolian Company, 1913), 5.

3. "Maurice Abrahams Music Company," ad, *New York Clipper*, November 29, 1913, 28; Warren, *Buffalo Bill's America*.

4. *The Parlor Songs Academy*, http://parlorsongs.com, s.v. "E. H. Pfeiffer."

5. *Internet Broadway Database*, http://ibdb.com, s.v. "Pleasure Seekers."

6. *Discography of American Historical Recordings*, http://adp.library.ucsb.edu, s.v. "At That Bully Wooly Wild West Show"; "Record Bulletins for February 1914," *Talking Machine World* 10, no. 1 (January 1914), 58.

7. Walsh, "'Cowboy Song' Recordings, Part 6," *Hobbies*, September 1976, 127.

8. "101 Ranch Real Wild West Show Here Tomorrow Free Street Parade at 10:00 A.M.," *Durham (N.C.) Morning Herald*, October 11, 1914, 3.

Navajo Indian Songs, 1914

Geoffrey O'Hara, ca. 1910–15,
Canadian American composer and
singer. Courtesy Library of Congress
Prints and Photographs Division,
Grantham Bain Collection
(LC-DIG-ggbain-12703).

Miguelito, a Navajo chanter, making
a phonograph record for O'Hara,
February 19, 1914. Library of Congress
Prints and Photographs Division.
Copyright by Geoffrey O'Hara, New York,
N.Y. (LC-USZ62–111421).

Geoffrey O'Hara's *Navajo Indian Songs* represents a complex preservationist-assimilationist view of early twentieth-century Native American history. At this time, Office of Indian Affairs (OIA) representatives had tried to eradicate traditional songs and dances because they believed this cultural history weakened their work to assimilate Native Americans into American culture. To preserve a memory of the music, in 1913 the OIA hired O'Hara, a Tin Pan Alley composer and vaudeville singer, to travel out to Indian reservations "to record the native Indian music and arrange it for use in the Indian schools." O'Hara's credentials for such a project are not clear. Born

in Canada in 1882, O'Hara had played piano and organ as a child and sang in the local Anglican church. After his father's death, he worked as a bookkeeper in a piano store and continued to sing tenor in church. In 1904 he hired on with a minstrel group that performed in blackface and toured the United States. Over the next decade he sang in vaudeville, taught some, and even recorded his first Edison cylinders as part of a quartet. He did not, however, study Native American culture.[1]

O'Hara began the project by recording a visiting group of Montana Blackfeet and then traveled to Arizona in September 1913 to record the Navajos, one of the few Native groups actually increasing in population. He spent several weeks there working with "full blooded" Navajo interpreters and "medicine men" to learn their ways before asking them to sing into his cylinder phonograph. According to one newspaper story published a year later, O'Hara explained that since there were more than 15,000 Navajo songs and each could fill a four-minute cylinder, he tried to secure "the song I knew each medicine man was most perfect in." To get them to sing, he often had to pay each man. In the end, O'Hara found the Navajos to be "extraordinary musicians, from the standpoint of range, and lovers of music."[2]

After O'Hara came back to New York City, he returned to his professional songwriting and singing work. Indeed, despite professing that he had only wanted to preserve Native music, within a year he had made his own versions of Navajo songs on both an Edison four-minute cylinder and a Victor disc. For the latter, he added the Blackfeet recordings he had made in New York on the reverse side. The Victor version, called *Navajo Indian Songs*, includes four pieces in which O'Hara introduces a song and describes its unique time signature: "A Navajo Indian War Song," "A Navajo Indian Medicine Song," "A Navajo Dance Song Used for Social Diversions," and "Dance Song Showing Various Rhythms." A period newspaper story about the record's release described O'Hara as having been "appointed by the United States government as instructor of native Indian music" then described the work as an "interesting record which explains some of the peculiar features of Navajo Indian songs."[3]

On the Edison four-minute Blue Amberol recording, O'Hara explains his understanding of each song before singing his version of it. At the record's beginning, he announces: "The Navajo Indians have thousands of songs that have been composed with care and handed down for centuries, from father to son, from teacher to pupil. They have a number of ceremonies, each one lasting from nine days and nights, each one containing more than six hundred songs." After the first song ends, O'Hara adds: "These songs are found in wonderful rhythms and melodies, many of them quite baffling and bewildering

to our ears. At first hearing, they sound as if they were simply improvisations of a savage mind. But upon investigation, the student finds that they are composed along well-established rules and are bound in poetic figures of speech. And in the performance of most of them, not the slightest error is tolerated."[4]

This last point is most important, because Navajo speakers today suggest that, although O'Hara may have used traditional music, his words were nothing more than gibberish, with perhaps a few actual Navajo words tossed in. This raises the idea, of course, that perhaps his own renditions of these songs should not be tolerated at all because they are little more than his version of playing Indian.

This complicates O'Hara's legacy. Scholars have noted that Native Americans who performed in Buffalo Bill Cody's Wild West shows, so-called show Indians, actually used the performances as a means to make money in difficult times, to assert their tribal identity publicly, and to demonstrate their virtue and skill in music. This fits O'Hara's works. His uninterpreted recordings of the Blackfeet serve as ethnographic recordings of tribal identity. And even though O'Hara clearly played Indian on the Victor and Edison recordings, at the same time he did preserve melodies without exposing what could be considered sensitive cultural materials. Though *Navajo Indian Songs* is seemingly very different from all of the other Indian songs in this book, it was released by both Victor and Edison and must therefore be considered along with the rest of the Tin Pan Alley tunes.[5]

NOTES

1. *The Virtual Gramophone, Library and Archives Canada*, www.collectionscanada.gc.ca, s.v. "Geoffrey O'Hara" (includes audio sample).
2. "Composer Cans Music of Indians, *Oakland (Calif.) Tribune*, September 6, 1914, 10.
3. Geoffrey O'Hara, *Navajo Indian Songs* (New York: Victor Talking Machine, 1914), disc #B15063; "Latest Records Are Now Ready," *Indianapolis Star*, October 29, 1914, 13.
4. Geoffrey O'Hara, *Navajo Indian Songs* (New York: National Phonograph, 1914), Edison Blue Amberol #2451.
5. Warren, *Buffalo Bill's America*, 358–90; Moses, *Wild West Shows*; Troutman, *Indian Blues*, 34–37.

Way Out Yonder in the Golden West, 1916

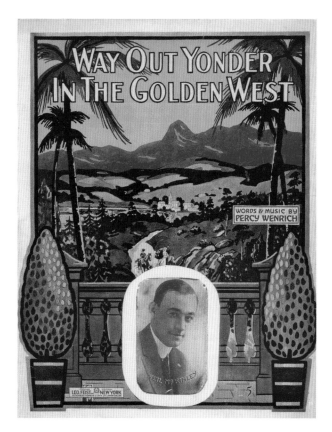

Way Out Yonder in the Golden West,
words and music by Percy Wenrich
(New York: Leo Feist, 1914). Sheet
music from author's collection.

Percy Wenrich wrote the music and score for *Way Out Yonder in the Golden West*, the final song featuring a cowboy story to appear before the United States entered the Great War in 1917.[1] Wenrich published his first song in 1897 and his last in 1946. He composed several Indian love songs including *Rainbow* in 1908, *Silver Bell* in 1910, and *Snow Deer* in 1913.[2] Harking back to *Cheyenne* and its variations, *Way Out Yonder in the Golden West* features a love story between a cowboy and cowgirl in sunny California. The brightly colored, unsigned sheet music presents a view from a verandah framed by potted junipers in the foreground and tall palm trees toward a range of blue mountains set in warm golden light. A small town can be seen in the distance with a road winding through hills, trees, and brush. A cowboy and his cowgirl ride side by side on horses in the center.

The full lyrics are as follows:

[hoofbeats and yells]
Whoa There! Pony! Whoa!

Out in the land, where the sun's ever grand,
a maiden stole my heart away
Sweet golden dreams of the hill and the stream,
Mountain made of beauty rare
Those western skies, loving sighs, and her eyes
    enraptured me one summer's day
My life would be melody, sweet to me,
Just to be there.

Chorus
Way out yonder in the Golden West
Land of the girl I love best,
Golden Sun, is shining down
On Someone with eyes of brown by the sheltering
    palm tree she waits in California
Soon I'll wander to the sunny clime
Get there in orange blossom time
Then with a simple ceremony and a honeymoon
On a pony we will stay away out yonder in the
    Golden West, in the Golden West.

The birds above, as they fly, sing of love, for each
    one knows my golden dream,
The soft winds sigh, for they know, bye and bye
    Wedding bells with joy will ring
The flowers all smile to her, and the tall Palmetto
    loves my golden girl
Our life will be melody, sweet to me,
When we two sing:

Repeat Chorus

The quartet known as the Avon Comedy Four recorded *Way Out Yonder in the Golden West* for Victor in November 1916 at the same time that Percy Wenrich's wife and vaudeville singer, Dolly Connolly, recorded it for Columbia. The Avon Comedy Four was a vaudeville comedy act that also sang harmony, and their recording features hoofbeats and cowboy yells. Newspapers announced the Victor record in October 1916. The *Leavenworth Times* noted that the song was as a "fine sample" of Victor recordings of popular songs. The following month, the Victor Military Band included a version in its recording of the *There's a Little Bit of Bad in Every Good Little Girl* medley.[3] Despite these, Gardner does not list the song.

NOTES

1. Percy Wenrich, *Way Out Yonder in the Golden West* (New York: Leo Feist, 1914).
2. Bill Edwards, "Percy Wenrich," *RagPiano*, www.perfessorbill. com/comps/pwenrich.shtml; David A. Jasen, "Percy Wenrich," in *Tin Pan Alley: An Encyclopedia of the Golden Age of American Song* (New York: Routledge, 2003), 401; *The Parlor Songs Academy*, http:// parlorsongs.com, s.v. "Percy Wenrich."
3. "Record Bulletins for November 1916," *Talking Machine World* 12, no. 10 (October 15, 1916), 112; Allen Sutton, "The Avon Comedy Four: A Short History," *Mainspring Press*, www.mainspringpress.com/ avon.html; "November Records on Sale," *Bismarck (N.Dak.) Tribune*, October 22, 1916, 2; "Christmas Classic Magnificently Sung by Caruso," *Leavenworth (Kans.) Times*, October 28, 1916, 3; The Avon Comedy Four, *Way Out Yonder in the Golden West* (New York: Victor Talking Machine, 1916), disc; "Record Bulletins for December 1916," *Talking Machine World* 12, no. 11 (November 15, 1916), 115.

Indianola, 1917

Indianola, words by Frank H. Warren, music by S. R. Henry and D. Onivas (New York: Jos. W. Stern, 1918). Sheet music from author's collection.

The Indian love song *Indianola* has an interesting history. S. R. Henry, the alias of Henry R. Stern, and D. Onivas, also known as Domenico Savino, introduced the piece as a piano solo in 1917. Stern was a music composer in Tin Pan Alley who had helped write *When It's Moonlight on the Prairie* and later became a music publishing executive. Savino was trained in Italy as a classical composer and then immigrated to the United States, where he composed music and later conducted for the Pathé music label orchestra. The partners first arranged *Indianola* as an instrumental fox-trot and then had Frank H. Warren, a writer for the *New York World*,

add lyrics. When it reemerged in 1918, *Indianola* was a big hit.[1]

Warren took the popular piece and "startled the musical world and developed it into an international hit" by capitalizing on America's growing involvement in the Great War, anti-German sentiment, and the continued popularity of Indian stereotypes of the warrior and the Big Chief as well as the Indian love song legacy.[2] From the song's very first line, *Indianola* walked a fine line of setting Native Americans apart from mainstream America while also calling upon them to come to the aid of the United States in the war.[3]

Indianola is a great example of historian Frederick Hoxie's model of assimilation that suggests that the United States saw Native Americans as not ready to be treated as equals but able, with guidance, to move toward that goal.[4] The full lyrics are as follows:

Chief Bugaboo was a Redman who,
Heard the call for War (aw, aw, aw)
Swift to the tent of his love he went,
Sighing for his little Indianola;
"Come be the bride of a chief," he cried,
"Keep me wait no more (aw, aw, aw)
Come and help me make my war paint fit,
I do my heap big bit."

Chorus
Me hear cannon roar,
Me help Yank win war,
Me much like to kill,
Scalp old Kaiser Bill;
Me go to fight in France,
Me do a big war dance,
Me love a maiden so,
Wed Chief 'fore he go.

Indianola's lover grunted twice, Huh! Huh!
Indianola think her Chief much nice, Huh Huh!
Indianola ask her dad's advice;
Chief keep pleading:
Me hear the great big cannon roar,
Me want to help Yank man win war,
Me like to fight and to heap much kill,
Got to go and tomahawk Kaiser Bill;
Me go along to fight in France
Me once again do big war dance,
Me love the Indianola maiden so,
Come and marry Bugaboo 'fore he go.

Then answered she to the Redman's plea,
"I will be your squaw (aw, aw, aw)
Chief Bugaboo I will go with you,
Riding o'er the plain to Redman's wigwam,
There I will sit and I'll knit and knit,
For my warrior bold
And when you are whooping far away,
To me you'll seem to say."

Repeat Chorus

Indianola's heart begins to yearn,
Indianola's cheeks begin to burn,
Indianola signs for his return
And his pleading:

Me hear the great big cannon roar,
Me want to help Yank man win war,
Me like to fight and to heap much kill,
Got to go and tomahawk Kaiser Bill;
Me go along to fight in France
Me once again do big war dance,
Me love the Indianola maiden so,
Come and marry Bugaboo 'fore he go.

The sheet music cover for the vocal version of *Indianola* is different from most others. As part of the war effort, the government asked sheet music publishers to shrink the size of their paper from 10 by 13.5 inches to 9 by 12 inches and to reduce the number of pages from four to two in order to save valuable paper. Publishers often also conserved by reducing the variety of colors in their palettes. This meant smaller cover art often drawn in fewer tones. The *Indianola* cover, drawn by one of the Starmer brothers, fits this description perfectly. It is noticeably smaller in size and is colored only in shades of blue. It features a navy blue border framing the image of a stern-looking Indian chief with feathered headdress, wrapped to his neck in a blanket, with dark eyes and war paint. Because of the reduced size, the score is packed into the two-page interior and a sample of another song is on the back cover.[5]

Victor recorded three versions of *Indianola* but only one vocal, a performance by Billy Murray in May 1918. Edison made a Blue Amberol cylinder of Billy Murray's version as well as a Diamond Disc version that same year. Columbia also released an instrumental version of the song by an early jazz group. Emerson, a new disc company begun in 1916, recorded its own version that featured a vocal by George Beaver, alias Irving Kaufman, another prolific vocalist. On the Victor disc, Murray belts out the song, accompanied by tom-toms and yells. As he works his way through the complicated lyrics, his energy increases and the song almost turns into a patriotic march, with Murray, accompanied by a trombone slide, accentuating the chorus lines, especially those about scalping and tomahawking Kaiser Bill.[6]

These recordings made *Indianola* an instant hit. An ad for the McDonald Music Store in Connellsville, Connecticut, described the "new and clever" music and called the song "a striking head liner, [that] throbs with the deep-voiced tom toms and drones with the war-song cadences of the dancing red skins." It continued, "As Billy Murray sings, we see the vivid war-painted figures sway about the leaping flames and hear the promise of the departing brave to 'fight for the Yank' and to 'tomahawk Ol' Kaiser Bill.'" That same day, the *Decatur Daily Review* described it as "an Indian song sung by Billy Murray with tom tom and trombone accompaniment that is very effective." The next day, the *Bismarck Tribune* called the record "the song of the Red Man preparing to 'do his bit' in the war." Two weeks later, *Talking Machine World* ran a story about a two-column ad in a Baltimore paper for the song that featured a "central drawing showing an Indian on the warpath, holding the Kaiser's hair in one hand, and ready to bounce a stone hatchet off his skull with the other." The story then related that the paper also printed the song's chorus, "and a number of record sales were directly traceable to the ad." Finally, the November 15 issue of *Talking Machine World* stated, "The popular patriotic records are still the leading features" and noted that both the Columbia and Edison versions of *Indianola* were among their "Six Best Sellers." It is no surprise that Gardner rates *Indianola* as a very popular song, first

cracking his top twenty in February 1918, peaking at number three in May, and remaining on his charts until September.[7]

NOTES

1. Frank H. Warren, S. R. Henry, and D. Onivas, *Indianola* (New York: Jos. W. Stern, 1918); *IMDb*, www.imdb.com, s.v. "Domenico Savino"; "The Musical Digest," ad, *Musical Monitor* 10, no. 1 (October, 1920), 97; "From Producer and Distributor," *Dramatic Mirror of Motion Pictures and the Stage* 78, no. 258 (January 1, 1918), 770. The last two are available at "Guide to the Henry R. Stern Papers, circa 1874–1966," Henry R. Stern papers, Ax 637, Special Collections and University Archives, University of Oregon Libraries, Eugene, Oregon.

2. "S. R. Henry's Phenomenal Record," *Music Trades* 57, no. 12 (March 22, 1919), 46. This article suggested that *Indianola*, along with three other hits made by this trio of songwriters, would sell three to four million copies, the "biggest sale on record for four compositions by the same writers, published consecutively within a period of twelve months."

3. "War Hysteria and the Persecution of German-Americans," *Authentichistory.com*, www.authentichistory.com/1914–1920/2-homefront/4-hysteria/.

4. Hoxie, *Final Promise*, 239–44.

5. Bill Edwards, "Postlude," *RagPiano*, www.perfessorbill.com/ragtime9a.shtml.

6. *Discography of American Historical Recordings*, http://adp.library.ucsb.edu, s.vv. "Indianola" (Billy Murray) and "Indianola" (Wilbur Sweatman's Original Jazz Band); Tim Gracyk, "Irving Kaufman," *Tim's Phonographs and Old Records*, www.gracyk.com/kaufman.shtml.

7. "Fifteen New Records for August," McDonald Music Company ad, *Connellsville (Pa.) Daily Courier*, August 1, 1918, 3; "August Records Now on Sale," Linn and Scruggs ad, *Decatur (Ill.) Daily Review*, August 1, 1918, 3; "Indian Songs by Princess Wahtawaso," *Bismarck (N.Dak.) Tribune*, August 2, 1918, 6; "Effective Cartoon Advertising," *Talking Machine World*, 14, no. 8 (August 15, 1918), 57; "From Our Chicago Headquarters," *Talking Machine World* 14, no. 11 (November 15, 1918), 71; Gardner, *Popular Songs*, 78–79.

Big Chief Killahun, 1918

Big Chief Killahun, **words by Alfred Bryan and Edgar Leslie, music by Maurice Abrahams (New York: Waterman, Berlin and Snyder, 1918).** Sheet music courtesy Lilly Library, Indiana University, Bloomington.

Big Chief Killahun is a typical Tin Pan Alley knockoff that traded on the World War I/Indian song popularity of *Indianola.*[1] Like so many songs discussed here, the old adage that "imitation is the greatest form of flattery" certainly rings true, though this example certainly paled in comparison. The 1918 song features music by Maurice Abrahams of *Ragtime Cow Boy Joe* fame and lyrics by future Songwriters Hall of Fame members Alfred Bryan of *Rainbow* fame and Edgar Leslie, who later composed *For Me and My Gal.*[2]

Like *Indianola*, the lyrics of *Big Chief Killahun*

combine the racist stereotypes of the Indian comic songs with words like "Big Chief," "war paint," "tomahawk," and "squaw"; the assimilation language of doing "his share" because "Uncle Sammy needs me"; and a complete denial of the relationship between Indians and the federal government with the suggestion that "Uncle Sammy feeds me." There is also the popular anti-German language with threats to "scalp the Kaiser," the title character "Killahun," and the forgettable closing rhyme, "good bye Herman, no more German." The full song goes like this:

Big Chief put his war-paint on and kissed his
squaw good bye;
Threw away his pipe of peace, and went to do or
die.
He said, "Uncle Sammy feeds me, gives me all I get,
Now that Uncle Sammy needs me, Big Chief no
forget."

Pershing wants to catch the Kaiser, take him live
or dead;
Big Chief says he's satisfied, if he can get his head.
There will be no more Budweiser, in the Kaiser's
brew,
All he's goin' to get to drink will be some Waterloo.

Chorus
Big Chief's on his way to Berlin, just to do his
share;
Big Chief's goin' to make 'em squawk,
When he hits 'em with his tomahawk.
Big Chief's goin' to scalp the Kaiser, take away his
fun;
Oh! Oh! He have heap much fun;
Good bye Herman, no more German, Big Chief
Killa Hun.

Albert Barbelle, a prolific illustrator who spent forty
years in the business and became famous for drawing
beautiful women, designed the comic image of Big Chief
Killahun.[3] Looking much like the advertisement for
Indianola discussed in a *Talking Machine World* story,[4]
the cover art features a giant Indian walking through
No Man's Land wearing a breechcloth and two feathers
in his hair and wielding a huge stone tomahawk. Tucked
under his right arm he holds three much smaller German
soldiers wearing high boots, two of them sporting
upturned moustaches and one losing his spiked helmet.

Only the upstart Emerson Records company
recorded *Big Chief Killahun*, doing so in July 1918 and
listing its performers as Collins and Harlan and its
composer as Irving Berlin. The latter is certainly a

mistake because, although *Talking Machine World*
also listed the composer as Berlin, the sheet music
clearly notes that it is Abrahams, Bryan, and Leslie. No
Berlin discography includes it. The recording includes
tom-toms, yells, war whoops, gunshots, and a few new
anti-German lines such as "good bye fritzel, no more
schnitzel" and "good bye vulture, no more culture, Big
Chief Killahun."[5]

Although Emerson listed *Big Chief Killahun* as one of
its "Six Best Sellers" in the December 1918 issue of *Talking
Machine World*, there are few references to it in the trade
journals or even period newspapers. The October 15
issue had listed the record as a new one for November,
so perhaps it was simply a matter of bad timing, coming
out about the same time as the November 11 armistice.
Nevertheless, a music shop in Wichita, Kansas,
continued to advertise the record as late as May 3, 1919,
and another in Sandusky, Ohio, advertised the song
till September 14, 1920, albeit at the bargain price of
forty-five cents, down from the usual seventy-five cent
price. This sale ad suggested that "these records have
never been played [and] are perfect in every way."[6] Unlike
Indianola, Gardner does not include *Big Chief Killahun* in
his lists.

NOTES

1. Alfred Bryan, Edgar Leslie, and Maurice Abrahams, *Big Chief Killahun* (New York: Waterson, Berlin and Snyder, 1918).
2. *The Parlor Songs Academy*, www.parlorsongs.ac, s.v. "Edgar Leslie."
3. Bill Edwards, "Albert Barbelle," *RagPiano*, www.perfessorbill.com/artists/barbelle.shtml. Interestingly, this is the only Barbelle cover included in this catalog.
4. "Effective Cartoon Advertising," *Talking Machine World*, 14, no. 8 (August 15, 1918), 57.
5. Arthur Collins and Byron G. Harlan, *Big Chief Killahun* (New York: Emerson Phonograph, 1918), disc #983.
6. "From Our Chicago Headquarters," *Talking Machine World* 14, no. 11 (November 15, 1918), 87; "Record Bulletins for November," *Talking Machine World* 14, no. 10 (October 15, 1918), 114; "What Do You Pay for Records," Emerson records ad, *Wichita (Kans.) Beacon*, May 3, 1919, 4; "Stop! Look! Listen!" Dilgart and Bittner Co. ad, *Sandusky (Ohio) Star-Journal*, September 14, 1920, 8.

Bibliography

BOOKS AND ARTICLES

Amundson, Michael A. *Passage to Wonderland: Rephotographing Joseph Stimson's Views of the Cody Road to Yellowstone National Park, 1903 and 2008.* Boulder: University Press of Colorado, 2013.

Andrews, Thomas G. *Killing for Coal: America's Deadliest Labor War.* Cambridge: Harvard University Press, 2008.

Badrock, Arthur, and Frank Andrews. *The "Cinch" Record: A History and Discography with Biographical Notes.* London: City of London Phonograph and Gramophone Society, 2014.

Basson, Lauren L. *White Enough to Be American? Race Mixing, Indigenous People, and the Boundaries of State and Nation.* Chapel Hill: University of North Carolina Press, 2008.

Benton-Cohen, Katherine. *Borderline Americans: Racial Division and Labor War in the Arizona Borderlands.* Cambridge: Harvard University Press, 2011.

Berlin, Edward A. *Ragtime: A Musical and Cultural History.* Berkeley: University of California Press, 1980.

Britten, Thomas. *American Indians in World War I: At Home and at War.* Albuquerque: University of New Mexico Press, 1997.

Chan, Sucheng, Douglas Henry Daniels, Mario T. Garcia, and Terry P. Wilson, eds. *Peoples of Color in the American West.* Lexington, Mass.: D. C. Heath, 1994.

Cohen, Ronald D., ed. *Alan Lomax: Selected Writings, 1934–1997.* New York: Routledge, 2005.

Deloria, Philip J. *Indians in Unexpected Places.* Lawrence: University of Kansas Press, 2004.

———. *Playing Indian.* New Haven: Yale University Press, 1999.

Dethlefson, Ronald. *Edison Blue Amberol Recordings, 1912–1914.* Woodland Hills, Calif.: Stationery-X Press, 1997.

Dilworth, Leah. *Imagining Indians of the Southwest: Persistent Visions of a Primitive Past.* Washington, D.C.: Smithsonian Institution Scholarly Press, 1997.

Diner, Hasia R. "American West, New York Jewish." In Ava Kahn, ed., *Jewish Life in the American West: Perspectives on Migration, Settlement, and Community,* 33–51. Berkeley, Calif.: Heyday Books, 2002.

Egan, Timothy. *Short Nights of the Shadow Catcher: The Epic Life and Immortal Photographs of Edward S. Curtis.* Boston: Mariner Books, 2013.

Emmons, David. M. *The Butte Irish: Class and Ethnicity in an American Mining Town.* Reprint ed. Champaign-Urbana: University of Illinois Press, 1989.

Fabrizio, Timothy C., and George F. Paul. *Antique Phonographs: Gadgets, Gizmos, and Gimmicks.* Atglen, Pa.: Schiffer, 1999.

Fields, Armond. *Eddie Foy: A Biography of the Early Popular Stage Comedian.* Jefferson, N.C.: McFarland, 2009.

Flamming, Douglas. *Bound for Freedom: Black Los Angeles in Jim Crow America.* Berkeley: University of California Press, 2005.

Fletcher, Alice C. *Indian Story and Song: From North America.* Boston: Small, Maynard, 1900.

Frow, George L. *Edison Cylinder Phonograph Companion.* Woodland Hills, Calif.: Stationery-X Press, 1994.

Gardner, Edward Foote. *Popular Songs of the Twentieth Century*, vol. 1: *Chart Detail and Encyclopedia, 1900–1949*. St. Paul, Minn.: Paragon Books, 2000.

Gelatt, Roland. *The Fabulous Phonograph: From Edison to Stereo*. New York: Appleton-Century, 1965.

Glenn, Susan A. *Female Spectacle: The Theatrical Roots of Modern Feminism*. Cambridge: Harvard University Press, 2000.

Goetzmann, William H., and William N. Goetzmann. *The West of the Imagination*, 2nd ed. Norman: University of Oklahoma Press, 2009.

Gordon, Linda. *The Great Arizona Orphan Abduction*. Cambridge: Harvard University Press, 2001.

Gracyk, Tim, with Frank Hoffmann. *Popular American Recording Pioneers, 1895–1925*. New York: Haworth Press, 2000.

Graulich, Melody, and Stephen Tatum, eds. *Reading "The Virginian" in the New West*. Lincoln: University of Nebraska Press, 2003.

Green, Douglas B. *Singing in the Saddle: The History of the Singing Cowboy*. Nashville: Country Music Foundation Press and Vanderbilt University Press, 2002.

Hamm, Charles. *Irving Berlin: Songs from the Melting Pot, the Formative Years, 1907–1914*. Cambridge: Oxford University Press, 1997.

Hoffmann, Frank, Dick Carty, and Quentin Riggs. *Billy Murray: The Phonograph Industry's First Great Recording Artist*. Lanham, Md.: Scarecrow Press, 1997.

Hoxie, Frederick E. *A Final Promise: The Campaign to Assimilate the Indians, 1880–1920*. Lincoln: University of Nebraska Press, 1984.

Hutchinson, Elizabeth. *The Indian Craze: Primitivism, Modernism, and Transculturation in American Art, 1890–1915*. Durham, N.C.: Duke University Press, 2009.

Iverson, Peter. *When Indians Became Cowboys: Native Peoples and Cattle Ranching in the American West*. Norman: University of Oklahoma Press, 1994.

Jasen, David A. *A Century of American Popular Music: 2000 Best-Loved and Remembered Songs*. New York: Routledge, 2002.

———. *Recorded Ragtime: 1897–1958*. Hamden, Conn.: Archon Books, 1973.

Jasen, David A., and Gene Jones. *That American Rag: The Story of Ragtime from Coast to Coast*. New York: Schirmer Books, 2000.

Jordan, Teresa. *Cowgirls: Women of the American West*. Lincoln: University of Nebraska Press, 1982.

Kahn, Ava, ed. *Jewish Life in the American West: Perspectives on Migration, Settlement, and Community*. Berkeley, Calif.: Heyday Books, 2002.

Kenney, William Howland. *Recorded Music in American Life: The Phonograph and Popular Memory, 1890–1945*. New York: Oxford University Press, 1999.

Koenigberg, Allen. *Edison Cylinder Records, 1889–1912*. New York: Stellar Productions, 1969.

Kohn, Al, and Bob Kohn. *Kohn on Music Licensing*. 4th ed. New York: Aspena, 2010.

Lavitt, Pamela Brown. "First of the Red Hot Mamas: 'Coon Shouting' and the Jewish Ziegfeld Girl." *American Jewish History* 87, no. 4 (December 1999): 253–90.

Lears, T. Jackson. *No Place of Grace: Antimodernism and the Transformation of American Culture, 1880–1920*. Chicago: University of Chicago Press, 1994.

Lee, J. J., and Marion R. Casey, eds. *Making the Irish American: History and Heritage of the Irish in the United States*. New York: New York University Press, 2006.

Logsdon, Guy. *"The Whorehouse Bells Were Ringing" and Other Songs Cowboys Sing*. Urbana-Champaign: University of Illinois Press, 1995.

Lomax, John A., and Alan Lomax. *Cowboy Songs and Other Frontier Ballads*. 18th ed. New York: MacMillan, 1969.

Lott, Eric. *Love and Theft: Blackface Minstrelsy and the American Working Class*. New York: Oxford University Press, 1993.

MacCannell, Dean. *The Tourist: A New Theory of the Leisure Class*. Berkeley: University of California Press, 1999.

Magowan, Fiona, and Karl Neuenfeldt. *Landscape of Indigenous Performance: Music, Song, and Dance of the Torres Strait and Arnhem Land*. Canberra, Australia: Aboriginal Studies Press, 2005.

Maken, Neil. *Hand-Cranked Phonographs: It All Started with Edison*. Huntington Beach, Calif.: Promar, 1994.

Malone, Bill C. *Singing Cowboys and Musical Mountaineers: Southern Culture and the Roots of Country Music*. Athens: University of Georgia Press, 1993.

Matz, Duane A. "Images of Indians in American Popular Culture since 1865." Ph.D. dissertation, Department of History, Illinois State University, 1988.

Meeks, Eric V. *Border Citizens: The Making of Indians, Mexicans, and Anglos in Arizona*. Austin: University of Texas Press, 2007.

Millard, Andre. *America on Record: A History of Recorded Sound*. New York: Cambridge University Press, 1995.

Milner, Greg. *Perfecting Sound Forever: An Aural History of Recorded Music*. London: Faber and Faber, 2010.

Molony, Mick. "Irish-American Popular Music." In J. J. Lee and Marion R. Casey, eds., *Making the Irish American: History and Heritage of the Irish in the United States*. New York: New York University Press, 2006.

Morris, Edmund. *The Rise of Theodore Roosevelt*. New York: Random House, 2001.

Moses, L. G. *Wild West Shows and the Images of Indians*. Albuquerque: University of New Mexico Press, 1999.

Nakata, Martin, and Karl Neuenfeldt. "From 'Navajo' to 'Taba Naba': Unravelling the Travels and Metamorphosis of a Popular Torres Strait Islander Song." In Fiona Magowan and Karl Neuenfeldt, eds., *Landscapes of Indigenous Performance: Music, Song, and Dance of the Torres Strait and Arnhem Land*. Canberra, Australia: Aboriginal Studies Press, 2005.

Parman, Donald L. *Indians and the American West in the Twentieth Century*. Bloomington: Indiana University Press, 1994.

Payne, Darwin. *Owen Wister: Chronicler of the West, Gentleman of the East*. Lincoln: University of Nebraska Press, 1985.

Peterson, Richard A. *Creating Country Music: Fabricating Authenticity*. Chicago: University of Chicago Press, 1997.

Pisani, Michael V. *Imagining Native America in Music*. New Haven: Yale University Press, 2005.

Porterfield, Nolan. *Last Cavalier: The Life and Times of John A. Lomax, 1867–1948*. Urbana-Champaign: University of Illinois Press, 1996.

Raph, Theodore. *The American Song Treasury: 100 Favorites*. New York: Dover, 1986.

Read, Oliver, and Walter L. Welch. *From Tin Foil to Stereo: Evolution of the Phonograph*. Indianapolis: Howard W. Sams, 1976.

Reiss, Eric L. *The Compleat Talking Machine*. 5th ed. Chandler, Ariz.: Sonoran, 2007.

Rice, Edward Le Roy. *Monarchs to Minstrelsy, from "Daddy" Rice to Date*. New York: Kenney, 1911.

Rochlin, Harriet, and Fred Rochlin. *Pioneer Jews: A New Life in the Far West*. Boston: Houghton Mifflin, 2000.

Rollins, Philip Ashton. *The Cowboy: An Unconventional History of Civilization on the Old-Time Cattle Range*. Revised ed. Norman: University of Oklahoma Press, 1997.

Rosen, Jody. "'Cohen Owes Me Ninety-Seven Dollars:' Images of Jews from the Jewish Sheet Music Trade." In Bruce Zuckerman, Josh Kun, and Lisa Ansell, eds., *The Song Is Not the Same: Jews and American Popular Music*, 9–28. West Lafayette, Ind.: Purdue University Press, 2011.

Rothel, David. *The Singing Cowboys*. New York: A. S. Barnes, 1978.

Rothman, Hal K. *Devil's Bargains: Tourism in the Twentieth-Century West*. Lawrence: University Press of Kansas, 2000.

Rubinstein, Rachel. *Members of the Tribe: Native America in the Jewish Imagination*. Detroit: Wayne State University Press, 2010.

Ruhlmann, William. *Breaking Records: 100 Years of Hits*. New York: Routledge, 2004.

Rydell, Robert, and Robert Kroes. *Buffalo Bill in Bologna: The Americanization of the World*. Chicago: University of Chicago Press, 2005.

Schlereth, Thomas J. *Victorian America: Changes in Everyday Life, 1876–1915*. New York: Harper Perennial, 1992.

Schroeder, Patricia R. "Passing for Black: Coon Songs and the Performance of Race." *Journal of American Culture* 33, no. 2 (June 2010): 139–53.

Schwartzman, Arnold. *Phono Graphics: The Visual Paraphernalia of the Talking Machine.* San Francisco: Chronicle Books, 1993.

Sherman, Michael W. *Collector's Guide to Victor Records.* 2nd ed. Tustin, Calif.: Monarch Record Enterprises, 2010.

Smith, Sherry L. *Reimagining Indians: Native Americans through Anglo Eyes, 1880–1940.* New York: Oxford University Press, 2000.

Stanfield, Peter. *Horse Opera: The Strange History of the 1930s Singing Cowboy.* Urbana-Champaign: University of Illinois Press, 2002.

Swartz, Mark Evan. *Oz before the Rainbow: L. Frank Baum's* The Wonderful Wizard of Oz *on Stage and Screen to 1939.* Baltimore: Johns Hopkins University Press, 2000.

Tatum, Stephen. "Pictures (Facing) Words." In Melody Graulich and Stephen Tatum, eds., *Reading "The Virginian" in the New West,* 1–38. Lincoln: University of Nebraska Press, 2003.

Thrapp, Dan L. *Encyclopedia of Frontier Biography,* vol. 3: *P–Z.* Lincoln: University of Nebraska Press, 1991.

Tinsley, Jim Bob. *For a Cowboy Has to Sing.* Orlando: University of Central Florida Press, 1991.

Toll, Robert C. *Blacking Up: The Minstrel Show in Nineteenth-Century America.* London: Oxford University Press, 1974.

Troutman, John W. *Indian Blues: American Indians and the Politics of Music, 1879–1934.* Norman: University of Oklahoma Press, 2009.

Tyler, Don. *Hit Songs 1900–1955: American Popular Music of the Pre-rock Era.* Jefferson, N.C.: McFarland, 2007.

Utley, Robert M. *The Lance and the Shield: The Life and Times of Sitting Bull.* New York: Random House, 1994.

"Visions of the Song of Hiawatha." *Longfellow House Bulletin* 5, no. 1 (June 2001): 5, 8.

Walsh, Jim. "The Coney Island Crowd." *Hobbies: The Magazine for Collectors,* May 1942, 15.

———. "'Cowboy Song' Recordings," Parts 1–6. *Hobbies: The Magazine for Collectors,* April–September 1976.

———. "Indian Songs on Edison Cylinders," Parts 1–3. *Hobbies: The Magazine for Collectors,* April–June 1977.

Warren, Louis S. *Buffalo Bill's America: William F. Cody and the Wild West Show.* New York: Vintage, 2006.

Welch, Walter L. *From Tin Foil to Stereo: Evolution of the Phonograph.* Indianapolis: Howard W. Sams, 1976.

White, Richard. *"It's Your Misfortune and None of My Own": A History of the American West.* Norman: University of Oklahoma Press, 1991.

Wilentz, Sean. *360 Sound: The Columbia Records Story.* San Francisco: Chronicle Books, 2012.

Williams, William H. A. *'Twas Only an Irishman's Dream.* Bloomington: Indiana University Press, 1996.

Winchester, Juti A. "All the West's a Stage: Buffalo Bill, Cody, Wyoming, and Western Heritage Presentation, 1846–1997." Ph.D. dissertation, Northern Arizona University, 1999.

Wister, Fanny Kemble, ed. *Owen Wister out West: His Journals and Letters.* Chicago: University of Chicago Press, 1958.

Wister, Owen. *The Virginian: A Horseman of the Plains.* New York: MacMillan, 1902.

Woodward, C. Vann. *The Strange Career of Jim Crow,* 2nd ed. London: Oxford University Press, 1969.

Wrobel, David. M. *The End of American Exceptionalism: Frontier Anxiety from the Old West to the New Deal.* Lawrence: University Press of Kansas, 1993.

Young, Elliott. "Red Men, Princess Pocahontas, and George Washington: Harmonizing Race Relations in Laredo at the Turn of the Century." *Western Historical Quarterly* 29 (Spring 1998): 48–85.

Zuckerman, Bruce, Josh Kun, and Lisa Ansell. *The Song Is Not the Same: Jews and American Popular Music.* West Lafayette, Ind.: Purdue University Press, 2011.

PERIODICALS

Aberdeen (S.Dak.) Saturday Pioneer, 1890–1891

Abilene (Tex.) Daily Reporter, 1907

Albuquerque Evening Herald, 1913

Allentown (Pa.) Democrat, 1909

Allentown (Pa.) Leader, 1908

Alton (Iowa) Democrat, 1938

Arkansas City (Kans.) Daily Traveler, 1907

Atlanta Constitution, 1895, 1912

Belvidere (Ill.) Daily Republican, 1909

Bisbee (Ariz. Terr.) Daily Review, 1907

Bismarck (N.Dak) Tribune, 1918

Boston Globe, 1905

Brooklyn Daily Eagle, 1903, 1905, 1906, 1908, 1909, 1913

Chicago Daily Tribune, 1903, 1913

Chicago Inter-Ocean, 1906

Cincinnati Enquirer, 1904

Coffeyville (Kans.) Daily Journal, 1909

Connellsville (Pa.) Daily Courier, 1918

Decatur (Ill.) Daily Review, 1918

Durham (N.C.) Morning Herald, 1913–1914

Edison Phonograph Monthly 4–14, 1906–1916

Fitchburg (Mass.) Sentinel, 1909

Fort Wayne (Ind.) Daily News, 1907

Fort Wayne (Ind.) Journal Gazette, 1904

Fort Wayne (Ind.) News, 1904

Fort Wayne (Ind.) Telegraph, 1910

Frederick (Md.) News, 1913

Daily Arizona Silver Belt (Globe, Ariz. Terr.), 1907

The Guardian, 2014

Hamilton (Ohio) Journal News, 1907

Harrisburg (Pa.) Evening News, 1932, 1945

Harrisburg (Pa.) Herald, 1911

Harrisburg (Pa.) Telegram, 1909

Harrisburg (Pa.) Telegraph, 1906, 1908, 1913

Humboldt (Kans.) Union, 1903

Indianapolis News, 1904, 1909

Indianapolis Star, 1914

Kansas City (Mo.) Star, 1907

Kansas City (Mo.) Times, 1950

Leavenworth (Kans.) Times, 1907, 1911

Los Angeles Herald, 1909

Maysville (Ky.) Evening Bulletin, 1903

Minneapolis Journal, 1904, 1905

Monroe (La.) News-Star, 1912

Muskogee (Okla.) Times-Democrat, 1913

The Native American (Phoenix Indian School), 1905

Nevada (Mo.) Daily Mail, 1909

The New Phonogram, 1908

New Castle (Pa.) News, 1906

New York Clipper, 1909, 1913

New York Dramatic Mirror, 1898

New York Evening World, 1903, 1913

New York Times, 1905

New York Tribune, 1908, 1914

Newark (Ohio) Advocate, 1883

Oakland (Calif.) Tribune, 1911, 1913–1914

Oregon Daily Journal (Portland), 1907–1908

Ottawa Journal (Ontario, Canada), 1909 *Phoenix Republican*, 1903

Plymouth (N.C.) Roanoke-Beacon, 1913

Salt Lake City Republican, 1909

San Francisco Call, 1896, 1910

Sandusky (Ohio) Star-Journal, 1920

Santa Ana (Calif.) Register, 1907

Santa Cruz (Calif.) Evening News, 1908

Santa Cruz (Calif.) Sentinel, 1905

Scranton (Pa.) Republican, 1906–1907, 1913

Scranton (Pa.) Truth, 1909

Sedalia (Mo.) Democrat, 1905

Seymour (Ind.) Daily Republican, 1909

Spokane Spokesman-Review, 1907

St. Louis Republic, 1903

Talking Machine World, 1906–1918

Trenton Evening Times, 1908

Vancouver (Canada) Daily World, 1908

Variety, 1907

Victor Records Catalog, November 1913

Washington (D.C.) Evening Star, 1906

Washington (D.C.) Herald, 1911, 1913

Washington (D.C.) Post, 1905, 1906, 1914

Washington (D.C.) Times, 1909

Wichita (Kans.) Beacon, 1904, 1919

Williamsport (Pa.) Sun-Gazette, 1908

Wilmington (N.C.) Morning Star, 1912

Wilmington (Ohio) New Journal, 1903

Winnipeg (Canada) Tribune, 1907, 1913.

York (Pa.) Daily, 1907

Index